THE CENTRAL SELF

A STUDY IN ROMANTIC AND
VICTORIAN IMAGINATION

The Central Self

A Study in Romantic and Victorian Imagination

by

PATRICIA M. BALL

UNIVERSITY OF LONDON
THE ATHLONE PRESS
1968

Published by
THE ATHLONE PRESS
UNIVERSITY OF LONDON
at 2 Gower Street, London WC1

Distributed by Constable & Co. Ltd
10 *Orange Street, London* WC2

U.S.A.
Oxford University Press Inc
New York

Canada
Oxford University Press
Toronto

© *Patricia M. Ball, 1968*

485 11102 0

Printed in Great Britain by
WESTERN PRINTING SERVICES LIMITED
BRISTOL

TO THE MEMORY
OF MY MOTHER AND FATHER
CECILIA AND REGINALD BALL

ACKNOWLEDGEMENTS

I should like to thank the many past and present members of Royal Holloway College, staff and student, who have played a part in the development of this book through their helpful discussion of nineteenth-century poetry and other topics less obviously relevant but equally valuable for the themes I have tried to handle. In particular I am indebted to Professor Barbara Hardy for her generous critical guidance, advice and encouragement. I am also grateful for the typing feats of Mrs L. Williams and Mrs P. Barry.

I have incorporated into Chapters V and VI some material previously published in articles contributed to *The Modern Language Review* and *Victorian Poetry*.

Royal Holloway College   P.M.B.
November 1967

CONTENTS

KEY TO EDITIONS USED
AND ABBREVIATED IN NOTES
(Place of publication London unless otherwise stated)

Coburn *The Notebooks of S. T. Coleridge*, ed. K. Coburn, 2 vols., 1957–

Ingpen *Letters of P. B. Shelley*, ed. R. Ingpen, 2 vols., 1909

LJ *Letters and Journals of Lord Byron*, ed. R. E. Prothero, 6 vols., 1898–1901

PB *Poetry of Lord Byron*, ed. E. H. Coleridge, 7 vols., 1898–1904

PK *Complete Works of John Keats*, ed. H. Buxton Forman, 5 vols., Glasgow, 1901

PS *Complete Poetical Works of P. B. Shelley*, ed. T. Hutchinson, Oxford, 1940

Rollins *Letters of Keats*, ed. H. E. Rollins, 2 vols., Cambridge, 1958

Shawcross S. T. Coleridge, *Biographia Literaria*, ed. J. Shawcross, 2 vols., Oxford, 1907

INTRODUCTION

REAPPRAISAL of nineteenth-century poetry is now well advanced, especially from the point of view of the continuity from Romantic to modern literature. In some ways, this book aims to contribute to research of this kind, since it deals with aspects of Romantic and Victorian poetry which remain active elements and determining principles in the contemporary imagination. But my central concern is first, the character of Romantic imagination and second, the role of Victorian poets as its inheritors and as the channels through which it flows to the present century. Less attention has so far been paid to this Victorian situation, and it is commonly assumed that the mid-century poets in some way failed to shoulder their responsibilities and that the element of revolt in modern poetry springs from rejection of this Victorian inadequacy. In the many studies of Victorian poets, the bias is still towards what the poets did not do, why they went wrong, or where they fell short; there is a failure to recognize their essentially positive function, both in their attitude to Romanticism as it came down to them and in their shaping of that Romanticism into a form acceptable to their own poetic descendants and ready for them, in their turn, to use creatively.

There is a maturity in the Victorian poets which is not always matched by Victorian critics, and this discrepancy has led to confusion. The prejudice against 'Romanticism' earlier in the twentieth century, and the assumed weaknesses of Victorian poets can both be traced back to the influence of an oversimplified theory. This state of affairs is most strikingly apparent in the concept of 'sincerity' when it comes to be regarded as a criterion of poetic quality, and I therefore include an outline of its history as a standard, especially in its Victorian prime.

In my discussion of the nature of the Romantic imagination, my starting point is the same as that of Robert Langbaum in his book *The Poetry of Experience* (1957),[1] a work which I gratefully acknowledge as an invaluable stimulus. As the basis for his argument on the evolution of the dramatic monologue during and since the nineteenth century, Langbaum claims that 'the romantic quality of mind grows out of a total crisis of personality'. The eighteenth century left the 'individual isolated within himself', and hence poetry's role becomes a 'process of self-realization', its doctrine that of 'experience'. The individual seeks his values and his poems in scrutinizing his own sensations and reactions, all the phenomena which make up his living and, more crucially, his awareness of living.

My intention is to extend the implications of these ideas by showing that the Romantic sense of the self as an experiencing agent habitually seeks two kinds of imaginative expression. There is, as Langbaum demonstrates, the impulse to the dramatized utterance, and coexistent with it, the more directly personal voice. Keats distinguishes these two creative modes with his contrasting terms of 'egotistical sublime' and 'chameleon' poets, and he is not alone in his awareness of them, as I try to show in my first chapter on aspects of Romantic critical theory. The association of the two modes within the creative imagination of each poet is, however, the central matter. This relationship is fundamental to the structure of that imagination, and is consistently displayed; each Romantic poet is at once Miltonic and Shakespearean, capable of egotistical and chameleon creative effort. To call these modes the two poles of the Romantic imagination is helpful, because it suggests the necessary intimacy of the relationship, the underlying unity in the kind of power being exerted, and at the same time indicates the various patterns and tensions which are set up by the distinctive operation of the two forces.

In his book *The Romantic Survival* (1957),[2] John Bayley notes this feature of polarity in the Romantic imagination, but remarks that the egotistical character, 'the self-conscious Imagination' is 'by far the more influential'. This I do not accept; rather, I suggest that Bayley's view of the nature of the two poles is misleading when he implies that the chameleon mode is

[1] See Introduction, especially pp. 14–28.
[2] See Chapter I, and p. 8 for statement quoted.

2

not self-aware. On the contrary, the Romantic poet is exerting 'the self-conscious Imagination' whether he adopts the egotistical or the chameleon approach; and furthermore, both modes continue to appear in Victorian and twentieth-century poets. Whether they write dramatically or directly of themselves, what is sought by all these poets is their own identity, the realization of which will provide a basis for their ultimately evaluative purposes.

In this context the question of the nineteenth-century poets' interest in drama arises, and my chapter on the plays and dramatic aims of the Romantic poets attempts to show how central these are to their work, although so often critics dismiss them as marginal, or damn them as mere closet-dramas. There is failure in these plays, but it is a bold and creative failure, closely related to their authors' imaginative successes in other forms such as the monologue, the lyrical ballad, or the conversational poem.

In tracing a principle of imagination which I find active in Wordsworth, Coleridge, Byron, Shelley and Keats, and in maintaining its continued relevance in the work of the major Victorians, I do not intend to reduce all these poets to a state of uniformity, nor to exalt a common feature at the expense of poetic independence and variety. Each poet in fact becomes most distinctly himself by the nature of his response to the challenges of the self-rooted imagination and its dual modes of activity. As Coleridge says, 'the rules of the Imagination are themselves the very powers of growth and production',[1] and the poets support his point by achieving a development wholly individual while operating from the same imaginative principle.

One further point. Whether this book is critical in the sense that it tests poetic quality is a question worth considering. My primary aim is to investigate the nineteenth-century imagination from a specific point of view and to show Victorian participation in the Romantic enterprise. In the course of this study, major poems are grouped with others less satisfying and more tentative; for example a minor lyrical ballad may for my purpose seem as significant as *The Ancient Mariner*. I do not think this detrimental, for other critical approaches may easily redress

[1] *Biographia Literaria*, ed. J. Shawcross, ii, p. 65.

3

the balance. There is the wider issue: am I arguing that the Victorian poets stand equal with their Romantic forebears because they react to the same law of imagination? This would obviously leave too much out of account, and again, other critics could offer a more valid answer. But, with these reservations made, I think that some fundamental assessment is offered here. I consider the explorations made by the nineteenth-century imagination to be vitally important, both for what they achieve and what they symbolize. Moreover, in arguing the essential courage of the Victorian poets I am urging that their work be regarded at least with the same attentive sympathy as that afforded to Keats or Wordsworth, and for some of the same reasons. Both ages of poets stretch out living hands to us, and a greater understanding of their imaginative strength will help us to increase our own.

4

I

THE POETICAL CHARACTER:
ASPECTS OF THE ROMANTIC
VIEW

... the Feeling is deep and steady—and this I call *I*, identifying the percipient and the perceived.

Coleridge, *Notebooks*

THE ROMANTIC concern with personal identity emerges in
theoretical comment; in particular the poets are very ready to
observe the phenomenon of the creating self. They do so in the
course of propagandist essays, philosophic notes, journal entries
and letters intense and relaxed, and they suggest in their various
ways that the relationship of poet to poem holds for them a
distinctive place in the whole issue of self and non-self. The
creator and his experience which together yield the created
work present a psychological situation with a unique mirroring
intimacy—and hence a mutual illumination—of subject and
object. Only Coleridge pursues the philosophical implications of
this, but each of the poets has his own kind of perception of it,
and his own reaction to it. These reactions themselves can
become creative stimuli; Romantic theory and poetic practice
are unified in their fundamental preoccupation with creativity
as an aspect of self-discovery.

Recognition of the variant possibilities of creative power, its
different modes of operation, is integral to the Romantic concept of the poetical character, as I intend to show in the following selection of comment and opinion.

2

Coleridge's readiness for abstract thinking is only matched by
his appetite for factual information, as any page of his Notebooks
will illustrate. But he has none of the instincts of the magpie: his
capacity for observation, ubiquitous interest and annotation is

5

directed by his belief in the universe as a cohesive structure, with his own mind as a microcosm of this, so that the relation of his perceptions one to another is crucial. His two worlds of idea and fact cannot be sustained separately; the idea, or subjective emanation, and the fact, or symbol of objective reality, are essentially interdependent, and their coalescing releases the spark of consciousness. Without this collision, the idea remains formless, the fact is dead. Subject and object only take on meaning from each other; each is distinct, yet neither survives in isolation.

In his life-long meditations on these issues, Coleridge's starting-point, and also his goal, is his mind in its consciousness of itself. He provides himself simultaneously with a first-hand example of the thinking and perceiving subject and with the most incontrovertible fact of his experience; this conjunction and all its implications is the incentive to his close psychological study of himself. But as always for Coleridge such empirical thinking —rooted in eighteenth-century philosophy—takes on larger metaphysical connotations. Regarding the cosmos as an ascending stair from opaque matter to pure spirit, he places man on his appropriate step by defining the 'human soul' as the 'first and lowest' of

that class of Being . . . which is endued with a reflex consciousness of its own continuousness, and the great end and purpose of all its energies and sufferings is the growth of that reflex consciousness...[1]

God is considered to be 'the supreme Self-consciousness',[2] and clearly Coleridge prizes the individual's awareness of himself for two reasons. First, because it offers an experimental basis for speculation on the universe as a whole, and secondly, because he holds this awareness to be the key to man's ascent to a more spiritualized identity: the more self-conscious he grows, the more self-possessed he becomes in the fullest sense. Knowing himself, man inherits his most profound nature. From the above quotation, it is also apparent that to Coleridge, as to Keats after him, all the experience of the individual, his 'energies and

[1] Letter to Clarkson, 1806; quoted R. H. Fogle, *The Idea of Coleridge's Criticism* (Berkeley, 1962), p. 26.
[2] Fogle, p. 27.

6

sufferings', feed and contribute to this recognition of self, the steady refining of the consciousness until it beholds itself *in esse*. Here therefore in its most philosophically developed form is the Romantic ideal of self-realization by way of the data of experience. In this sense their poetry is egotistical. How this purpose embraces also the chameleon mode is indicated by J. H. Muirhead. In his study *Coleridge as Philosopher* (1930), Muirhead expounds Coleridge's views on 'self-conscious personality' and the attainment of it, saying that Coleridge sees personality as 'a circumference continually expanding through sympathy and understanding, rather than as an exclusive centre of self-feeling, and consequently . . . the meaning of individuality and uniqueness as something to be won'.[1] And in a further passage: 'in human life the seat of individuality, now become self-conscious personality is . . . to be sought for not in any centre of isolated and isolating feeling, but in the degree to which a man passes beyond the limits temporal and spiritual within which mere feeling confines him, and identifies himself, in thought, feeling, and action, with the larger life about him while remaining a self-integrating member of it . . .'[2]

Such ideas of self as involving the extension of personal boundaries are the context for Coleridge's observations on the Miltonic and Shakespearean forms of genius in Chapter XV of *Biographia Literaria*. In the contrast he there suggests, the two creative modes with their common integrity stand clear. He rejoices in the twin 'glory-smitten summits of the poetic mountain', and characterizes them in this way:

While [Shakespeare] darts himself forth, and passes into all the forms of human character and passion, the one Proteus of the fire and the flood; the other attracts all forms and things to himself, into the unity of his own ideal. All things and modes of action shape themselves anew in the being of Milton; while Shakespeare becomes all things, yet forever remaining himself.[3]

In both poets, Coleridge hails the union of subject and object and is excited at this creative, quickening contact of self and non-self, with its results of a deeper self-experience, whether the method is that of the assimilating, magnetic power of Milton, or

[1] p. 229. [2] p. 264. [3] Shawcross, ii, p. 20.

the 'darting forth' of Shakespeare, who remains none the less 'forever himself'.

3

Awareness of the different possibilities of creative power, and the self as it is manifested in exercising them recurs in Romantic theorizing. Comparisons of Shakespeare and Milton on the lines of Coleridge's distinctions are not uncommon. The Romantics here are in some respects taking up eighteenth-century ideas on the 'sympathetic imagination', which were connected with the debate on the existence and nature of an intuitive moral sense,[1] but despite this link and debt it is important not to impose the wrong kind of moralistic overtones on the nineteenth-century interest in egotistical and chameleon. Hazlitt's tone and phrasing in his Shakespeare-Milton comparisons might seem to invite a moral interpretation when he apparently condemns Milton because 'he saw all objects from his own point of view' and praises Shakespeare because 'he was the least of an egotist that it was possible to be'.[2] But even when preference like this is shown, the issue is not the ethical one of the 'self-less' opposed to the 'self-centred': as the level of Coleridge's thinking shows, the morality involved reaches a more profound kind of perception. To the Romantic mind, all creativity is concerned with self, the protean equally with the Miltonic: self is sought and discovered by the process of darting forth as much as by the opposite, drawing-in activity, and both modes may be approved and welcomed. Selfishness is not in question.

Keats confirms the level of interest, for like Coleridge he plumbs the deeper layers of significance in the Romantic response to the creating self. The terminology I have adopted for the two poles of the poetical character—egotistical and chameleon—is coined by Keats in his letters, and though he speaks of them from a partisan position rather than with the impartial appreciation shown by Coleridge, he gives each positive honour. Writing to Woodhouse in October 1818, he

[1] For discussion of the links between eighteenth-century and Romantic thought, see W. J. Bate, 'The Sympathetic Imagination in Eighteenth-Century English Criticism', *English Literary History*, xii (1945), pp. 144–64.
[2] *Complete Works of Hazlitt*, ed. P. P. Howe (1930), v, pp. 230, 47.

discourses on his own lack of identity and offers his classification of poets. He acknowledges the 'Wordsworthian or egotistical sublime' with a reverence that sets it apart from himself—it is 'a thing *per se* and stands alone', while the 'camelion Poet' is described from his inner knowledge of such a condition, which 'lives in gusto be it foul or fair':

it is not itself—it has no self—it is everything and nothing—It has no character . . . A Poet is the most unpoetical of any thing in existence; because he has no Identity—he is continually [informing] and filling some other Body. . . .[1]

Shakespeare delighting in his Iago equally with his Imogen belongs to this category, in which Keats then places himself. His familiarity with this creative temperament animates what he has taken over from Hazlitt[2] and the generally current theorizing on the topic, and all his comments on the chameleon state are vividly personal.

Other people, he says, 'press upon him', leaving him no sense of himself:

not one word I ever utter can be taken for granted as an opinion growing out of my identical nature—how can it, when I have no nature? . . . the identity of everyone in the room begins [so] to press upon me that I am in a very little time annihilated. . . .[3]

He is so imaginatively impregnated with the illness of Tom that he is 'obliged' to go out or to write, 'to ease' himself of 'his countenance his voice and feebleness', and living in such a 'continual fever' he feels must be 'poisonous to life'.[4] His friends recognized the chameleon quality in him as a letter from Woodhouse to Taylor commenting on the 'poetical character' letter shows.[5] Woodhouse offers a small illustration of the range of the poet's sensibility when he observes: 'he can conceive a billiard ball to be soothed . . . and feel pleasure from a consciousness of its own smoothness—and the rapidity of its motion'.[6] If Keats could pass into the world of a billiard ball and become its

[1] *Letters of Keats*, ed. H. E. Rollins, i, p. 387.
[2] See K. Muir, 'Keats and Hazlitt' in *John Keats: a Reassessment* (Liverpool, 1958).
[3] Rollins, i, p. 387.   [4] Dilke, 21 September 1818; Rollins, i, p. 369.
[5] Rollins, i, pp. 388–90. This ready ability to discuss the concept illustrates further its congenial and familiar presence in the literary thinking of the age.
[6] Rollins, i, p. 389 n. 4.

consciousness, it is not at all surprising that he reacts similarly to a living creature: 'if a sparrow come before my window I take part in its existence and pick about the gravel'.[1]

Chameleon versatility and its insatiable, even painful, appetite are well suggested in these varied examples, which show also its power over Keats. But if we assume that this dominance of the protean spirit simply means that he is not a poet of the 'reflex consciousness' concerned with the process of self-evolution, we miss much of what is involved in the Romantic chameleon character. Unlike his model Shakespeare, Keats is not content merely to be a chameleon: he is fascinated by the fact of so being, and his art is rooted in this consciousness, which is, paradoxically, a strong self-consciousness.

In the moment of living as something or someone else, it may seem to the poet that such experience is its own end and fulfilment. But Keats, the poet without identity, perceiving so acutely what his condition is and pondering it so intensively, betrays that this very issue of identity is central to him. The effort towards self-creation draws all his energies together. He may reject the egotistical mode, but the whole nature of his avowedly chameleon attitude testifies to the strong egotistical drive working within him. His very consciousness of the pressure of others upon him is a symptom of a peculiarly sensitive response to the phenomenon of self and the idea of an 'identical nature'. Throughout his letters this is borne out by the predominant theme of formative struggle, the continual urge towards discovery, consolidation, realization, that converting of experience into consciousness which alone can create the fully self-realizing individual. To become such a being is Keats's ambition, carrying him on through letters and poems alike: 'Give me this credit— Do you not think I strive—to know myself?'[2]

In the Journal-letter of February–April 1819, this is his text, the central effort to which all else, meditative thought or light gossip, is related. 'Nothing ever becomes real till it is experienced,'[3] he insists here, and as the letter goes on to generate his theory of 'soul-making', it becomes clear that he finds this most essentially true of self-definition. Individual identity, recognized and

---

[1] Bailey, 22 November 1817; Rollins, i, p. 186.
[2] George Keatses, 19 March 1819; Rollins, ii, p. 81.   [3] ibid.

possessed as such, is the fruit of the interaction between heart and mind, the result of experience assimilated into consciousness. Starting off equipped with a mind or 'intelligence', a man is able to become a 'soul'—that is, 'an intelligence destined to possess the sense of Identity'. To attempt such a development is to travel a difficult road. Or, to use the cliché Keats himself transforms, it is to learn in a hard school:

I will put it in the most homely form possible—I will call the *world* a School instituted for the purpose of teaching little children to read—I will call the *human heart* the *horn Book* used in that School, and I will call the *Child able to read, the Soul* made from that *School* and its *hornbook*. Do you not see how necessary a World of Pains and troubles is to school an Intelligence and make it a Soul? A Place where the heart must feel and suffer in a thousand diverse ways! Not merely is the Heart a Hornbook, It is the Minds Bible, it is the Minds experience, it is the teat from which the Mind or intelligence sucks its identity. As various as the Lives of Men are—so various become their Souls, and thus does God make individual beings . . .[1]

The creating of an 'individual being' is an invitation to chameleon adventure as well as to direct self-study, for the final richness of the identity possessed will be enhanced by the range of experience going into the crucible. A deep acceptance of all experience and a full entry into it will lead to the climax of egocentric realization.

Here again are Coleridge's views on the 'self-conscious personality'; Muirhead's account of the philosopher's theory of self as 'a circumference continually expanding through sympathy and understanding', with individuality and 'self-feeling' as the reward of this process, applies to Keats's vision also. The younger poet, in the eager informality of his intuitive thinking corroborates the researches of a speculative mind. Both Keats and Coleridge affirm that the nub of Romantic creative life is the relationship between the 'larger life' and the crucial entity of the experiencing self, as it labours to reach the full measuring of its 'individuality and uniqueness'. The polar tension, egotistical and chameleon, of which they are both vitally aware, work together to the single end, the achieved identity.

---

[1] Rollins, ii, pp. 102–3.

4

Wordsworth is set squarely by Keats in the camp of those who draw everything into 'the unity of their own ideal', impressing all their materials with the stamp of themselves. He is named as the living epitome of the 'egotistical sublime'. His Preface to *Lyrical Ballads* gives support to this classification, but it also shows that even such an apparently extremist temperament can be drawn by the opposite chameleon pole. Wordsworth as critic demonstrates an important Romantic characteristic, the tension of the dual response.

In his analytical study of the two versions of the Preface, the additions and changes made in 1802 to the 1800 text, W. J. B. Owen[1] has shown that the motivation for the changes is Wordsworth's move from a mimetic to an expressive theory of poetic activity. But 1802 does not see a complete withdrawal from the earlier view of the poet as imitator of passions and language; this remains even while the rival theory of the poet as creator from his own mind is developed by means of autobiographical scrutiny of the processes involved. The contradiction seems only partly apparent to Wordsworth, but he offers some attempt to reconcile the theories, or rather to explain their coexistence in his argument, and in his attempt the two modes make their appearance, helping to salvage his logic.

The mimetic activity, he has implied, allows no scope for subtle operations within the creative mind; it is a 'mechanical' business. Yet the creative mind, he is also arguing, is an instrument capable of most subtle and self-aware operations. One way out of the confusion is to distinguish as he does between the poet writing dramatically and 'in his own person and character'. The poet is an imitator, 'confounding and identifying his own feelings' with others in the 'dramatic parts of composition' where he 'speaks through the mouths of his characters';[2] elsewhere, in his personal work, the expressive theory holds good. In this distinction, the mimetic activity takes on a more positive character than the description 'mechanical' would seem to

[1] Introduction, *Wordsworth's Preface to Lyrical Ballads* (*Anglistica*, Copenhagen, 1957).
[2] ibid., pp. 122–5.

allow, and it shows some sense of the energy of the chameleon mode. It also hints that poets can experience two kinds of creative power, and in further comment, Wordsworth admits the chameleon kind to full status, as an integral part of the mind's self-conscious power. The poet he claims possesses 'an ability of conjuring up in himself passions'.[1] That is, the playing of a part is at root an egotistical feat, an aspect of lyric display and performance, and so the dramatic gift becomes a means of enlarging the poet's 'own person and character',[2] of realizing an extended range of his own voice, not of descending to some lower plane of parrot-utterance.

Thus Wordsworth succeeds in admitting the mimetic as an equally valid mode of creation, not independently, but as a part of the egotistical resources. His refusal merely to abandon it in favour of the expressive, or better, the self-researching, view is indicative of his instinctive recognition of its value for a poet. In the Preface of 1802, the survival of the mimetic theory of art and the sophistication of its character within the credo of the egotistical sublime is a suggestive pointer first, to the Romantic experience of a creative duality, and secondly, to the poets' complex and ambivalent attitude to dramatic composition.

5

The Romantic goals of bringing experience alive into consciousness and of realizing the self as a fusion of action and reaction are acknowledged by Shelley too in his prefaces and prose essays. In his *Speculations on Metaphysics* he speaks of the arduous and thwarted effort of thinking to wind back on itself in those 'intricate chambers' it inhabits, the 'caverns of the mind'. He goes on:

if it were possible to be where we have been vitally and indeed—if, at the moment of our presence there, we could define the results of our experience—if the passage from sensation to reflection—from a state of passive perception to voluntary contemplation, were not so dizzying and so tumultuous . . .[3]

then, 'a faithful history' of our being might be achieved.

[1] ibid., p. 121. [2] ibid., p. 125.
[3] *Shelley's Literary and Philosophical Criticism*, ed. J. Shawcross (1909), pp. 68–9.

Romantic poetry strives to bring about such a union of sensation and reflection and to show the import of experience
'vitally and indeed'. To do so it employs its dual resources,
sympathetic excursion from self and unsparing egotistical
incursion, and Shelley displays his version of both categories in
A Defence of Poetry. We can discover also here more about the
Romantic attitude to drama.

The emotion of the *Defence of Poetry* burns as a single flame,
but the argument feeding it involves two distinct theories, rather
as Wordsworth's does. The Romantic commitment to a double
view of imagination is again suggested in Shelley's contrasting
ideas, which do not conflict, but operate equally in proving the
value of poetic activity. He writes from a conviction of underlying unity, from his own response to polarity, not as a man
straining logic, though from the purely analytical view, he may
seem to do so. The two aspects of the *Defence of Poetry* I want to
discuss may be described as the dramatic argument and the neo-
Platonic view.

Some of the most forthright, and most lucid, sections of the
Defence are those where Shelley asserts the moral importance of
poetry. The concept of the dramatic imagination is at the heart
of his case:

The great secret of morals is love; or a going out of our own nature,
and an identification of ourselves with the beautiful which exists in
thought, action or person, not our own. A man, to be greatly good,
must imagine intensely and comprehensively; he must put himself in
the place of another and of many others; the pains and pleasures of
his species must become his own. The great instrument of moral good
is the imagination . . .[1]

and 'Poetry and the principle of Self . . . are the God and
Mammon of the world'.[2] This is near to the 'sympathetic'
eighteenth-century moralists, but Shelley has made great capital out of their initial deposit. He attributes chameleon powers
to the poetic mind, not with Keats's delight in the process as
such, but laying emphasis on the consequences, and he extends
the effects of enlarged awareness to the recipient of imaginative
work, making this extension the primary weapon in the battle

[1] ibid., p. 131.   [2] ibid., p. 152.

for moral enlightenment. We are all to 'imagine that which we know'.[1] He cautions the poet against impeding the full exercise of the sympathetic faculty by seeking to impose 'his own conceptions of right and wrong' onto his 'poetical creations',[2] and such a warning underlines the argument that the poet must lose his personal identity in order to fulfil his mission. A more profound self-discovery therefore can only be approached through this persistent journeying 'out of his own nature' into others, and the imagination is, it seems, defined by its capacity for self-submergence.

But not exclusively. The *Defence of Poetry* is also nourished by Shelley's neo-Platonism, and when the poetic mind is presented from this angle, its attributes and its role appear somewhat different. 'A poet participates in the eternal, the infinite and the one',[3] he claims; and 'a poem is the very image of life expressed in its eternal truth'. This is not mere rhetoric, but an argument rooted in Shelley's favourite philosophy. He regards the imagination as an 'imperial faculty', penetrating the veils of the world, showing forth reality. Dwelling in the ideal light, removed from the accidents of time, its creative power lies in its ability to illuminate all it touches with the same light:

a poem . . . is the creation of actions according to the unchangeable forms of human nature, as existing in the mind of the Creator, which is itself the image of all other minds.[4]

Poetry may deal in 'impersonations', but all is 'clothed in its Elysian light'.[5] Whether we can accept these statements as being philosophically valid or not, there is implicit within them at the least an idea of poetic activity which suggests a relationship between mind and material different from the dramatic or chameleon contact envisaged in other sections of the *Defence*. Here Shelley in his choice of imagery is taking up a position much nearer to the 'egotistical' pole, as he depicts the imagination operating on its materials, affecting them by its own nature, not entering into imitative union with them. The world and its experiences are transfigured by their entry into the orbit of the

[1] ibid., p. 151.   [2] ibid., pp. 131–2.   [3] ibid., p. 124.
[4] ibid., p. 128.   [5] ibid., p. 131.

imagination. It throws its distinctive light round them, they in their inner nature are responsive to this power.

We need not debate here the validity or otherwise of such neo-Platonic argument; what matters is the copresence of such a conception of the mind with the theory of its sympathetic propensities. Shelley's neo-Platonism leads him to postulate a transcendent egotistical sublimity, the unifying of all variables in the light of the One mind, and to see each poet's creativity as a participation in this process. The imagination may be a chameleon, but it is also to Shelley's view capable of exerting the power which Coleridge calls 'the unity of its own ideal'.

Both arguments assist Shelley to substantiate his claims for the high prestige of poetry, and to demonstrate how indispensable it is in the development of human values and self-awareness. His excited allegiance to both illustrates how much each rouses the Romantic mind, and his essay, like Wordsworth's, suggests also the creative tension which exists between these two powerful, counter-attractive forces.

6

I have so far traced the theme of the poetical character in the reflections of Keats and Coleridge, both obsessed with the problems of identity and being, and in the polar thinking of Wordsworth and Shelley. Byron was not given to intellectual commentary, either on himself as poet or on the nature of poetic composition; but his whole character, the various enigmas of his behaviour, can be seen to involve the same elements as the others display in their discussions of the creative personality.

He is himself dramatic, in his readiness to settle into any kind of society, to live as nobleman, ascetic, debauchee, sportsman, poet, pirate or liberating soldier, and in his ability to run through every mood from Timon-misanthrope to the most poised social sophisticate. He admired in Burns the 'antithetical mind',[1] and he possessed it himself; any list of his traits reads like an exercise in antonyms. A theory of the chameleon temperament is almost forced into existence to explain this 'plura-

[1] Journal, 13 December 1813; *Letters and Journals of Lord Byron*, ed. R. E. Prothero, ii, p. 376.

lity'[1] of Byron's: and, indeed, many of his Boswells and bio-
graphers have noted his vulnerability to the impression of the
moment as a way of explaining the shifts and contrasts, from
hour to hour, in his behaviour and conversation. Moore,
amazed by his 'exuberance of faculties', writes of his 'natural
tendency' to 'change with every passing impulse',[2] and Stan-
hope observes '. . . the innumerable modifications under which
his character was daily presenting itself'.[3] Lady Blessington in
her *Conversations* concludes that he is wholly governed by 'the
feeling of the moment' and is a 'perfect chameleon'.[4] In *Lord
Byron: Christian Virtues*, G. Wilson Knight sums up the mass of
evidence on this Byronic instability, and makes a positive
reading of it, when he describes him as 'compact of opposites',
with a dramatic capacity for balancing opposing forces. To
Professor Knight, Byron encompasses a 'Shakespearian variety'.[5]

But the more pertinent point, and one which comes a step
nearer to the distinctive Romantic position, is Byron's own
recognition of this chameleon cast of temperament. He talked to
Lady Blessington about 'being everything by turns and nothing
long',[6] and in *Don Juan*, he defines the condition and christens it
'mobility'. Juan doubts how much of Lady Adeline is 'real':

> So well she acted all and every part
> By turns—with that vivacious versatility,
> Which many people take for want of heart.
> They err—'t is merely what is called mobility,
> A thing of temperament and not of art,
> Though seeming so, from its supposed facility;
> And false—though true; for surely, they're sincerest
> Who are strongly acted on by what is nearest.
>
> (xvi, xcvii)

Byron's explanatory note to this stanza shows both his interest
in this phenomenon of temperament and his personal familiarity
with it:

[1] The word is Moore's. *Life, Letters and Journals* (1901), p. 643.
[2] ibid., p. 646.   [3] *Greece in 1823 and 1824* (1825), p. 528.
[4] *Conversations of Lord Byron with the Countess of Blessington* (new ed. 1893), pp. 311,
95.
[5] *Lord Byron: Christian Virtues* (1952), pp. 187, 44–5, and see index A, section IV,
'Balances opposites', p. 292.
[6] *Conversations*, p. 352.

In French 'mobilité'. I am not sure that mobility is English, but it is expressive of a quality which rather belongs to other climates, though it is sometimes seen to a great extent in our own. It may be defined as an excessive susceptibility of immediate impressions—at the same time without *losing* the past: and is, though sometimes apparently useful to the possessor, a most painful and unhappy attribute.

Such a comment is a salutary check if we are inclined to over-simplify this protean agility of response and deny it tension, or if we would reduce it to an evasive strategy which avoids the responsibilities of a fixed orientation of mind. Byron and Keats stand opposed and out of sympathy with each other superficially; but they share a deep understanding of the pressures and strains that 'mobility' brings with it. Moreover, the couplet to the stanza on Lady Adeline throws out a general moral challenge which is central to literary theory and practice throughout the century; its wording could only tease Victorian readers, asser-tive as they were in their ideas on poetic sincerity, as I shall amplify in Chapter V.

Byron is thoroughly alert to the implications of the tempera-ment he lives with. Tasting the variety of sensation has the ulterior aim of proving 'that we exist',[1] he perceives: to feel is to find reassurance and a tangible conviction of identity. Here is the driving force of the Romantic chameleon; excursions into other natures and objects, the indulgence of contrasting moods, are circular activities, leading back to the sharpened conscious-ness of a fundamental self. 'He is always himself', Coleridge stated of Shakespeare, and this is an observation as crucial for Byron as for his fellow poets.

It points also, more directly, to the other side of his tempera-ment. Often as Byron's mobility has been remarked on, his egocentricity is a theme which rivals it. Moore, in discussing this, shows his own Romantic bias when he says: 'it is, indeed, in the very nature and essence of genius to be for ever occupied intensely with self, as the great centre and source of its strength'.[2] Opinion from 1812 onwards has maintained that Byron's heroes share a single character, his own. Contrasting him with Shakespeare's 'freedom from egotism', Jeffrey in the *Edinburgh Review* asserts: 'he cannot draw the changes of many coloured

---

[1] Miss Milbanke, 6 September 1813; *LJ*, iii, p. 400.   [2] op. cit., p. 268.

life, nor transport himself into the condition of . . . infinitely diversified characters . . . the very intensity of his feelings . . . the pride of his nature . . . withhold him from this identification; so that in personating the heroes of the scene, he does little but repeat himself'.[1]

Listing the heroes of his works from Harold to Cain, Jeffrey says that they are 'all one individual'. John Wain in 1963 sees his purpose in composition 'from first to last . . . to present the character of the poet'.[2] Most critics agree with the implication of Wain's verb 'to present': only the naïve have assumed Byron innocent of stage-managing the character so revealed. If he 'projected an image of himself', as Wain puts it, this image was 'assumed, edited, deliberately posed'. His egocentricity, in other words, is subject to manipulation, and so the complex nature of his self-consciousness is again hinted.

A further complication is the violence with which he at times repudiated the charge of continual self-duplication. Aware of his mobility, acknowledging it, he is not ready to admit his critics' version of the mirror element in his work. What seems to irritate him is any falsely simple notion of the relationship between poet and poem; he regards the activity of creation as a distinctive sphere of being, wherein self is not mirrored but uniquely exercised. Thus in the *Blackwood's* Defence he declares

who have made me thus egotistical in my own defence if not they, who, by perversely persisting in referring fiction to truth, and tracing poetry to life, and regarding characters of imagination as creatures of existence, have made me personally responsible for almost every poetical delineation which fancy and a particular bias of thought may have tended to produce.[3]

Elsewhere he turns off the egotistical notion with a chameleon explanation: 'like all imaginative men, I, of course, embody myself with the character while I *draw* it, but not a moment after the pen is from off the paper'.[4] And to Moore in November

---

[1] February 1822. *Jeffrey's Literary Criticism*, ed. D. Nichol Smith (1910), pp. 164–165.
[2] 'Byron: the Search for Identity', reprinted in *Byron. A Collection of Critical Essays*, ed. P. West (1963), pp. 158–9.
[3] *LJ*, iv, Appendix ix, p. 477.
[4] Moore, 4 March 1822; *LJ*, vi, p. 32.

1821, he goes to extremes in separating the ordinary personal self from the creative experience:

A man's poetry is a distinct faculty or soul, and has no more to do with the everyday individual than the Inspiration with the Pythoness when removed from her tripod.[1]

Who, then, is the Byronic hero? Who, more widely, speaks in a poem by Byron and who is portrayed? The remarks quoted above are one swing of the pendulum, where he is moved to establish his poetic explorations in their own right as free enterprises, reducing his personal presence in them to a 'bias of thought'. The instinct for 'mobility' prompts him here. But clearly, the egotistical element felt by readers is not a total illusion, and Byron is indeed aware of it, knowing that his work is fed by it, often to a degree which torments him. His Alpine journal of 1816 confirms his sense of the inescapable presence of self:

neither the music of the shepherd, the crashing of the Avalanche, nor the torrent, the mountain, the Glacier, the Forest, nor the Cloud, have . . . enabled me to lose my own wretched identity in the majesty and the power, and the Glory, around, above, and beneath me.[2]

What G. Wilson Knight has called 'his life-long horror of egotism'[3] shows itself here. But Byron's very sensitivity to the 'wretched identity' asserts its power within him; the patterns of compulsion and repulsion around this pole of his imagination are intricate. The passionate tensions of his situation can be gauged by the exclamation in his Journal for 27 November 1813: 'To withdraw *myself* from *myself* (oh that cursed selfishness!) has ever been my sole, my entire, my sincere motive in scribbling at all.'[4] This is acute self-consciousness, and although he may endeavour to shatter it, it is at the same time his goad and his goal. The 'past', or the continuity of awareness, is not to be lost, nor does he wish that it should be: the true egotistical explorer must struggle free from a constricting selfishness, but centred upon himself he must remain. Byron's life exemplifies this.

Teresa Guiccioli's claim for him may be appropriated to the

[1] *LJ*, v, p. 479.
[3] *Lord Byron: Christian Virtues*, p. 273.
[2] *LJ*, iii, p. 364.
[4] *LJ*, ii, p. 351.

present context: '. . . when one has a mind eager for emotion, variable, with width and depth capable of discovering simultaneously the for and against of everything, and thus being necessarily exposed to perplexity of choice, it is surely marvellous if a mind so constituted be also constant.'[1]

Constant in values, she meant: but he is first of all constant to himself, in that 'the thought runs through',[2] the identity persists to be manipulated, confronted and realized, though yielding itself to the immediate colouring and the behests of 'what is nearest'.

The chameleon never fixed for a moment, yet always seeking to feel himself existing, the egotistical consciousness at once dominant and trying to revoke its power: the complexity of Byron epitomizes the Romantic poetical character—its chief properties, and the intricacies which follow from their polar relationship.

We may now study the 'self-conscious personality' operating as a creative force.

[1] Quoted *Lord Byron: Christian Virtues*, p. 44.
[2] Journal, 17 November 1813; *LJ*, ii, p. 323.

II

THE ROMANTICS AS DRAMATISTS

Royal Zapolya! name me Andreas!
Zapolya

THE INTEREST of the Romantic poets in drama has rarely been regarded as central to their character. Each of them wrote at least one play and each gave his views on drama and the theatre, but these facts may well seem incidental beside the quality and quantity of their other work. We have seen, however, that a response to the dramatic is closely related to one pole of the Romantic poetical character, and this invites a revised estimate of the place of drama in their creative lives. It might seem that I could now propose a straightforward division: the chameleon instinct finding its outlet in the poets' attempt at play-writing, the egotistical element accounting for all the rest of the work. But from the evidence in Chapter I, this would be too simple. Within the temperament of each poet, there is a complex inter-play between the two alternatives for creative expression, and underlying both is the search for values by the empirical method of learning through the experience of the individual self.

Given this temperamental complexity, it is reasonable to suppose that both the plays and the poetry of the Romantics will be marked by it; and this is so. In each branch of their work, chameleon activity coexists with egotistical. First, in the plays, where orthodox chameleon creativity is inherent in the form, the expected 'Shakespearean' qualities—sympathetic character delineation and the submergence of the dramatist's own per-sonality—are crossed with the egotistical tendency and with the peculiarly Romantic significance of the chameleon itself. If we study the plays, therefore, the Romantic creative temperament is illuminated for us; and furthermore, they emerge as central efforts of the Romantic imagination, not peripheral mistakes.

22

2

A brief guide to the plays will be helpful. Wordsworth wrote his one play, *The Borderers*, in 1796–7,[1] at the same time as Coleridge was engaged on *Osorio*, a work later revised and produced at Drury Lane in 1813 as *Remorse*. At Byron's invitation, Coleridge contributed another play called *Zapolya* to the Lane in 1816, but it was not performed. Byron himself is the most prolific Romantic dramatist: *Manfred* appeared in 1817, *Cain* in 1821, and at the same period as the latter, a group of historical plays, *Marino Faliero*, *The Two Foscari* and *Sardanapalus*. There are also *Werner* (1821–22), the dramatic poem *Heaven and Earth* (1821), and the unfinished *Deformed Transformed*. Shelley's contribution provides contrast if not bulk, with *Prometheus Unbound* (1819), *The Cenci* (1819), *Hellas* (1821) and the satirical skit, *Swellfoot the Tyrant* (1819); a few scenes exist of a play on Charles I. English history was also attracting Keats towards the end of his life: after the joint effort with Brown, *Otho the Great*, in August 1819, he chose as his first independent venture *King Stephen*, of which part of the first act was completed.

Romantic drama as a collective term encompasses mythical soul-operas such as *Manfred* and *Prometheus Unbound*, semi-Gothic pieces in *The Borderers* and *Remorse*, Shakespearean imitation in *The Cenci* and *Otho the Great*, and Byron's attempts to form a 'regular' English drama in his historical trio.[2] This variety speaks for the vigour of the poets' interest in drama: they were experimental as well as traditional, and ready to employ the popular apparatus of the contemporary theatre for their own ends. The blanket term 'closet-drama', overworked as it is in connection with these plays, makes no concession to the variety any more than it allows the poets a theatrical sense. In fact their letters and comments as well as the plays themselves provide plenty of evidence that they were equipped with a real conception of practical stage requirements, even if they did not envisage their plays in terms of the London theatre of their day, as Byron at least did not. I do not deny that they can write

[1] For controversy over this date, see J. W. Macgillivray, *Modern Language Notes*, xlix (1934), pp. 104–10, 'The Date of Composition of *The Borderers*'.
[2] See below, p. 41.

scenes which betray inadequate technical control and which are
theatrically gauche or bathetic. But the attempt at dramatic
communication is authentic, just as the *Lyrical Ballads* transcend
their blunders and exist as a positive effort to push back imaginative frontiers.

The poets chose drama, and their own kind of drama, because
they were drawn to this method of expression; the attraction
sprang from their poetic needs, not from any less urgent external
cause. Their serious motives are more readily acceptable in the
works just grouped as 'mythical', Byron's *Manfred, Cain* and *Heaven
and Earth*, Shelley's *Prometheus Unbound*, these being obviously
homogeneous with the poets' non-dramatic writing, embodying
their familiar imaginative concerns. In *Manfred* and *Cain*, Byron
uses the dramatic form to prosecute the conflict of forces within
a single mind. The plays are wholly conditioned by this central
consciousness: and in *Prometheus Unbound*, setting, changes of
scene, 'choruses of spirits' as well as the named personages all
speak for the mind of Shelley, illuminating its thought. The
mountains, caves, and forests of the action are the same mental
landscape which is to be found in his poetry from *Alastor* onwards. The mind of the poet impregnates every part of these
works. This mythological category of Romantic drama may
therefore be described as the egotistical sublime of their dramatic work, and it begins to be apparent how the compulsion to
drama, and to a varied drama, is rooted in the duality of their
temperament and the needs which spring from it.

The pattern is confirmed by a survey of the other kinds of
play written by Byron and Shelley, and those of Coleridge,
Wordsworth and Keats. Despite the range already indicated,
these works have a common denominator: all are psychological
dramas, involving moral conflicts. They present an individual
in either personal or social relationships, confronted with
demands and decisions which involve him always in suffering
and often in guilt, and in the deeper recognition of his own
nature. And however divergent they are otherwise, from *The
Borderers*, exploring its hero's satanic experiences, to *Marino
Faliero*, with its dilemma of the Doge's opposed loyalties, the
plays seek to explore human character by means of an act of the
sympathetic imagination. All of them are indebted to Shake-

spearean drama in this sense; they posit a group of people embarked on a certain action, and the dramatist surrenders himself to this situation so that it shall become revelatory. They are chameleon plays.

If we read or see them in the light of this expectation, however, and with the Shakespearean freedom in mind, we shall probably be disappointed by them. But if the Romantics had been capable of writing straightforward chameleon drama, abandoning themselves to its protean energies, they would not be the poets they are: very little of their work would exist as we have it—neither *The Prelude*, nor *Childe Harold*, nor the Odes of Keats. And in these plays the creating self is not abdicating its consciousness of itself in the chameleon act, however genuinely engaged in this it may be. The Romantics are not latter-day Shakespeares merely exercising the gift of self-annihilation; they are poets aware of their power as a means to an end, and the end is self-knowledge. Hence creating protean drama is only a partial activity to them: it is completed by the poet's awareness of the relevance to himself of what he is doing. That is, in these plays, the sympathetic delineation of persons, passions and actions is effected by dramatists who see this activity as a process of subjective revelation. They are plays in leading-strings, deliberately introspective as well as outward-going works of character and action. Once we recognize this, it helps us to explain more exactly why they seem to fail, and it also suggests that they may achieve their own kind of success. At least they can be tested by more suitable criteria.

The movement of their action is towards self-revelation on two levels: for the hero and possibly other characters, and also for the poet himself. He experiences the drama as a parable of his mental journeying even though he chooses to suppress his own voice in favour of his characters. He knows himself because he becomes other than himself. The plays are expressions of this self-awareness, a method of exploring experience, and they are thus drawing back again towards the egotistical pole as a direct consequence of their response to the pull of the dramatic creative powers. The result is a distinctive body of drama, and in its common element of self-exploration, it is crucial to the Romantic quest as a whole.

I now want to look at some of the plays individually to show how they bear out these ideas.

3

Wordsworth began *The Borderers* in the autumn of 1796, a period of his life of great interest to his commentators; most of them allude to this sole venture of his into fully dramatic composition and make use of it as an indication of the trend of his thinking at this time. But while it is accepted as a 'document for Wordsworth's biography',[1] its five acts are none the less condemned as tedious and 'irksome',[2] wellnigh 'unreadable',[3] and its plot is written off for its 'morbid tortuosity'[4]—'all but unintelligible'.[5]

Most criticism centres on the part played by William Godwin in the genesis and character of the work, and clearly it is relevant to an understanding of *The Borderers* that Wordsworth was moved to write it at his time of moral and philosophical crisis. What is most interesting, however, and yet has been on the whole overlooked, is his choice of the dramatic form in which initially to set down a disturbed state of mind. Later of course with the full strength of sublime egotism, he sets it down again in *The Prelude*, notably in Book XI. But the whole bias of the poem is towards recovery from the crisis, the flowing of the tide after 'the soul's last and lowest ebb'.[6] Unlike the play it was composed in the afterlight of tranquillity when he was assured of peace and of potential salvation from the threat of human evil. Aiding the more blunted impact of the despair itself is the cumulative emphasis of all the preceding sanguine books as well as the immediate sequel, Book XII, with its title 'Imagination and Taste, how Impaired and Restored'. There is no place in *The Prelude* for the naked force of the crisis to reveal itself: the work where this is experienced is *The Borderers*.[7] He chooses

[1] E. de Selincourt, *Oxford Lectures on Poetry* (Oxford, 1934), p. 159.

[2] G. W. Meyer, *Wordsworth's Formative Years* (Ann Arbor, 1943), p. 214.

[3] M. Moorman, *Wordsworth's Early Years* (Oxford, 1957), p. 302.

[4] H. W. Garrod, *Wordsworth: Lectures and Essays* (Oxford, 1927), p. 91.

[5] Meyer, op. cit., p. 153. Two exceptions to these hostile verdicts may be acknowledged here: Lascelles Abercrombie, *The Art of Wordsworth* (Oxford, 1952), pp. 68–74, and G. Wilson Knight, *The Starlit Dome* (1941 and 1959), pp. 24–35.

[6] *The Prelude* (1850), Book XI, line 307.

[7] And also, in a rather different and retrospective way, *The Excursion*; see below, pp. 72–5.

drama as a way of facing his desperation and his discovery of evil as a reality growing like nightshade even in the best and most gifted of persons. *The Prelude* can afford to narrate retrospectively what his confusions were; *The Borderers* is written in response to the more urgent need to enact the state of mind he was either still enduring or, at the most, only just emerging from. In Wordsworth's work, the play stands out for its lack of retrospective vision. It is the work of a mind grappling, and being thrown.

In the prose essay which he prefixed to the play when it was finally published in 1842 he says:

the study human of nature suggests . . . as . . . sin and crime are apt to start from their very opposite qualities, so are there no limits to the hardening of the heart and the perversion of the understanding to which they may carry their slaves. . . During my long residence in France . . . I had frequent opportunities of being an eye-witness of this process. . . .[1]

And his hope is that the reader of the play 'might be moved, and to a degree instructed, by lights penetrating somewhat into the depths of our nature'.[2] In the play itself this determination to research into a frightening darkness is expressed in a soliloquy by Oswald:

> We dissect
> The senseless body, and why not the mind?—
> These are strange sights—the mind of man, upturned,
> Is in all natures a strange spectacle;
> In some a hideous one. . .
>
> (III, 1166–70)

The 'hideous' then, is what he is primarily trying to cope with in the mid-1790s, and the way he tries to do it is by enactment. He seeks to clear his own mind, to learn what human nature is capable of, by the usual Romantic method of testing in terms of direct experience. Because he is in a state of shock, not sure of his position or his reactions, he chooses the chameleon method at its dramatic extreme, so that one state can be challenged by

---

[1] *Poetical Works*, ed. E. de Selincourt (Oxford, 1940), i, p. 342. Wordsworth still considered the work important in 1842, saying in the same preface that there were 'impressions' on his mind which made its destruction inimical to him.
[2] ibid.

another, one emotional attitude can be realized by means of an opposed condition. In order to find out his true experience in these years, he must examine evil by submitting to it, by creating it in its own image. He must know its power both as willing participant and as victim, exulting in its strength and recoiling desperately from its grip. This I suggest is why he writes *The Borderers*, and why it is a drama centred on the two persons of Oswald and Marmaduke with everything else proportionately less vivid.

The play is set in Gilpin border country and it employs some of the properties of tales of mystery and terror: a wronged baron with a beautiful daughter, a band of outlaws, an enigmatic stranger associating with the leader of this band, scenes which include ruined chapels, caverns, wild moors, raging torrents, and violent storms. Oswald is the influential stranger, Marmaduke the outlaw chief, betrothed to Idonea whose days have been spent wandering with the blind and aged Herbert, denied his rightful baronial status. Such an outline suggests melodrama, but these are merely supports for the crucial situation which is the relationship between Marmaduke, initially noble and innocent, and the satanic Oswald. Wordsworth depicts the gradual corruption of Marmaduke as Oswald, Iago-like, lures him on to the point of murdering Herbert. Reasons are given to Marmaduke to convince him intellectually of the necessity of this act; and after the deed, the revelation that in fact the old man was entirely guiltless is intended by Oswald as the final liberating stroke for Marmaduke. He is to surmount feelings of remorse, just as he previously overcame the instincts of pity and respect for helpless life. Then, according to Oswald, he will have 'cast off the chains that fettered [his] nobility of mind' (v, 2248–9), and be saved from 'the blank Of living without knowledge' that he lives (iv, 1870–1). Such a 'blank' is indeed abhorred by the Romantics, and what Oswald argues is a dark version of their creative psychology.

He and Marmaduke are teacher and pupil. But the relationship is a closer one; Oswald has narcissus motives. He sees in the boy 'a mirror of [his] youthful self' (iv, 1865) and he intends to produce in Marmaduke a replica of his own experience. In Act IV he narrates with a vividness recalling the

Ancient Mariner[1] his own act of murder which was also based on a mistaken assurance of his victim's guilt. The sequel, his repudiation of remorse, brought him moral independence: a belief in the sheer irrelevance of guilt and an allegiance solely to his own intellect and the 'immediate law From the clear light of circumstances'. (III, 1494–5). Oswald's confidence in his emancipation is to be enhanced by noting its occurrence in someone else. In Marmaduke he aims to see his own psychological processes played back to him, and so to double the proof that his course expresses human potential—a freedom beyond the normal concepts of morality. Wordsworth, in giving Oswald a plan of self-duplication, is trying out a dual investigation of this particular condition of mind, showing it at different stages so that it is understood simultaneously as a developing and a completed experience. The young and the mature Oswald— mature in evil that is—are both explored by the poet.

Although Wordsworth shows Marmaduke undergoing 'the hardening of the heart', he does not confine his hero to a slavish conformity with Oswald's design. Marmaduke's ultimate state is one of remorse; he finally knows himself as one committed to expiation, an ostracized sinner, 'by pain and thought compelled to live Yet loathing life'. (v, 2319–20). He is a shocked victim of evil, but he discovers some energy of resistance to it; he can be seen as the bewildered yet resistant Wordsworth, forced to suffer in his realization of propensities within himself and all mankind, but not forced to embrace them. The play therefore opposes to the remorseless power of evil other emotional reactions which challenge its supremacy. It concedes that tendencies to evil can dominate human life, but denies that they must do so. The poet boldly explores in Oswald the curious passionless freedom across the furthest moral boundaries, and follows in Marmaduke the same journey to its different destination, a painful awareness of personal responsibility.

Of such complexities was Wordsworth's moral crisis composed. *The Borderers* gives him the opportunity to articulate them all, and only a chameleon creative act could have done so. He is identified with each aspect of his warring views on 'the depths of

[1] That his tale has affinities with Coleridge's poem was pointed out in a note by H. F. Watson in *The Times Literary Supplement* for 28 December 1935, p. 899.

our nature'. In both Oswald and Marmaduke, he displays the Romantic bid to 'learn that one lives'—and how one lives—by means of the self-conscious realization of experience.

As a result, the interest of the drama is focused sharply on the persons of Oswald and Marmaduke, leaving the other persons dim. Judged by the standards of Shakespearean, or fully protean drama, this is where *The Borderers* fails. In the pale, unconvincing characterization of Herbert and Idonea in particular, Wordsworth's dramatic gifts are shown up in their paucity. Yet given the Romantic motive of this play—that is, its requisitioning of the sympathetic imagination for a subjective purpose—the feebleness of these characters is inevitable: in the world which Wordsworth has recently entered, the innocent and virtuous are feeble and their role is passive. Herbert is inevitably a victim and he is adequately realized for the purposes of this drama in being old, weak, blind, and at the mercy of others. Similarly, Idonea cannot be realized as an individual: she is merely young, trusting in love, innocent, and therefore helpless. This is her dramatic function; untouched inwardly by evil, she is not a fully developed Romantic 'identity', and has no opportunity, unlike Marmaduke, to achieve self-awareness. Wordsworth's visual rather than his dramatic imagination is moved by this pair of undeserving sufferers: he frequently sets them within a landscape, as in the scene where Herbert is 'seated on a stone' in 'a desolate moor':

Herb. For mercy's sake, is nobody in sight?
        No traveller, peasant, herdsman?
Marm.   Not a soul:
        Here is a tree, ragged, and bent, and bare,
        That turns its goat's-beard flakes of pea-green moss
        From the stern breathing of the rough sea-wind;
        This have we, but no other company. . .

                                        (III, 1292–97)

Struggling within such impressions is Wordsworth's sense of 'visionary dreariness', that healing power of his egotistical imagination which *The Prelude* conveys so positively; but here the menace is too immediate for the operation of this retrospective faculty. The discrepancy of effect between the dramatic force of evil in *The Borderers* and the more descriptively distanced, non-chameleon, portrayal of the other main characters is indicative not of Wordsworth's failure as a playwright but of the state of mind from which the work springs.

From this, we can see that *The Borderers* offers some clues to Romantic chameleon drama in general. Judged as work limping after the Elizabethans, this drama can only remain unconvincing, as critics suggest. But if we are not assuming it to be merely an attempt to copy a worn-out form, its more experimental qualities can and do emerge. The Romantic work is groping—albeit primitively—towards new possibilities and new purposes in dramatic expression, feeling its way to a drama neither realistically and autonomously protean in all its parts, nor yet formalized to an entirely symbolic presentation of action and persons. Wordsworth writes from a genuine chameleon impulse, but he does so in order to explore regions of himself he could not otherwise reach. Only by creating Oswald and Marmaduke, venturing into minds 'shaken till the dregs float on the surface' (III, 1163), is he able to penetrate the darkness which overwhelmed him. Moral self-assessment is his goal, and the key to his concept of drama.

4

The French Revolution played a large part in precipitating Wordsworth into drama, and its upheavals had a similar effect on Coleridge, for his first effort at play-writing was *The Fall of Robespierre*, which he wrote in collaboration with Southey in 1794. Only the first act is his, but in a dedicatory note he shows his active response to events in France, saying that he has tried 'to detail, in an interesting form the fall of a man, whose great bad actions have cast a disastrous lustre on his name'. His aim has been 'to develope the characters of the chief actors on a vast stage of horrors'.

'Great bad actions', even before Napoleon, were exercising the English poetic imagination. A paradox is implied in Coleridge's phrase, as in his 'disastrous lustre', and this mysterious stature which evil can attain to is what the poets seek to understand by creating an Oswald and dramatizing Robespierre's history. In fact Coleridge too creates his own figure of

31

destructive power in his first full-length play, called *Osorio* originally in 1797, but later revised and produced as *Remorse*.

Although the *Lyrical Ballads* are the most eloquent record of the time of mutual inspiration enjoyed by Wordsworth and Coleridge, it is a fact worthy of more attention than it has received that they saw each other as dramatists at the beginning of their association. *The Borderers* and *Osorio* were written during the Racedown period of excited friendship, and this excitement is partly expressed in their admiration for each other's tragedies:

Wordsworth admires my Tragedy—which gives me great hopes. Wordsworth has written a Tragedy himself. I speak with heartfelt sincerity and (I think) unblinded judgement, when I tell you, that I feel myself a *little man by his* side; and yet do not think myself the less man, than I formerly thought myself.—His Drama is absolutely wonderful . . .—There are in the piece those *profound* touches of the human heart, which I find three or four times in 'The Robbers' of Schiller, and often in Shakespeare . . .[1]

This at least suggests that they were able to recognize a kinship of imaginative outlook in these two works. To segregate the plays therefore is to impose a false division which the poets themselves would not allow. They hailed each other in their dramatic as in their poetic enterprises, and the Romantic chameleon need is acknowledged in their enthusiasm.

Coleridge's method of probing 'the depths of our nature' in *Remorse* is that of *The Borderers*. In both plays the darker characters are the most prominent: Coleridge is less totally committed to them, for his play ends more cheerfully than *The Borderers*, but by his own statement, the focal personage and dynamo of the whole drama is the guilty Ordonio. Writing to Southey about the play, at the time of its London production, Coleridge says that its 'best quality' is 'the presence of one all-pervading, all-combining Principle', that is, the particular emotional condition known as 'remorse': 'the anguish and disquietude arising from the self-contradiction introduced into the soul by guilt'. The character of Ordonio is this principle incarnate: 'as

---

[1] Cottle, 8 June 1797; *Collected Letters of S. T. Coleridge*, ed. E. L. Griggs (Oxford, 1956), i, p. 325.

from a circumference to a centre, every ray in the tragedy converges to Ordonio'.[1]

The relationship with Wordsworth's Oswald is close: Ordonio seems to be an Oswald at an earlier stage, the criminal who is in the grip of torment for actions he admits to be evil, and yet still does not repudiate his chosen course. Where Oswald's next step was to overthrow such torments, Ordonio's pride and independence are intimately connected with the burden he carries. There is a strain of Milton's Satan in this version of a mind strong through its knowledge of sin and the pangs of guilt, as there is also in the more passionless intellectual criminality of Oswald. But to both characters their creators allow the full licence of their natures: they are not part of a cosmic vision, active in a design held in the eye of a Miltonic God, but beings who must be known in their own universe before any evaluation of the powers called 'good' and 'evil' can be made.

Remorse is a less complex drama than *The Borderers*. Wordsworth is fighting his way out of moral confusion and he needs the two figures of Oswald and Marmaduke to enact his situation, whereas Coleridge is conducting a more personally detached experiment, investigating a given psychology rather than seeking an answer to an urgent problem of living.[2] He writes with the energy of a mind devoted to the study of the human organism, intent to observe, record, and deduce. This play is the offspring of his total concern with behaviour, from its principles to its results. In a comment written on a manuscript version of *Osorio* he analyses his intentions:

In the character of Osorio I wished to represent a Man who from his childhood had mistaken constitutional abstinence from vice for

[1] 8 February 1813; *Letters*, ed. E. H. Coleridge (1895), ii, p. 608.

[2] In connection with entry no. 2928 (*Notebooks*, ed. K. Coburn, ii), the editor does, however, suggest that in the original drama of *Osorio*, the central figure is associated with Southey and Coleridge may have seen himself in Osorio's brother Albert, the hero of the play, later in *Remorse* called Alvar. Dr Coburn also notes (entry no. 2869) that 'remorse is a word frequently used by Coleridge', and it is therefore probable that he was spurred on to make his dramatic investigation by personal incentives as well as his more scientific enthusiasm. As a further illustration of the drama's being an integral part of Coleridge's thinking, Dr Coburn's note to entry no. 210 (Coburn, i), on a source for *Osorio*, may be quoted: 'Coleridge's choice of tragic themes, involving as they seem to do, unprovoked injury, a child-parent relation or its substitute, sympathy, conflict, remorse and premature death, shows a recurrent pattern.'

strength of character—thro' his pride duped into guilt—and the endeavouring to shield himself from the reproaches of his own mind by misanthropy.[1]

The incentive of psychological curiosity is active in this summary; the play is a means of satisfying it. Wordsworth too, as is shown by his essay accompanying *The Borderers*, had his 'mental abstract' of his central characters, and this is a mark of the Romantic chameleon effort, resulting in a drama distinct from the Elizabethan, but not for this reason inferior to it.[2] This is self-conscious drama, the extension of the creator's being in response to the desire to grasp more of human nature in all its myriad variants, and it is close to the central energies of Romanticism.[3]

The action of *Remorse* must be understood in the light of its 'all-combining principle', and Coleridge stresses this in the first scene, when he acquaints the audience with the situation. The theme imposes on the plot the role of a demonstration; and the movement of the action is the fulfilment of a statement proffered at the outset, and to be regarded not as a philosophic aside but as the engine of the whole drama. Alvar's mission in returning disguised to his homeland is Coleridge's mission in writing the play: to test his brother Ordonio, to discover his true nature. Ordonio is guilty, this scene discloses, of fratricidal intent, for he thinks Alvar was murdered at his command. One of his motives was love of Teresa, his brother's wife, and it is Alvar's reluctant half-belief that she, assuming her husband dead, has been successfully wooed by Ordonio. Now Alvar, disguised as a Moorish chieftain, returns not in revenge but in charity to learn if his wife is constant, and to read his brother's heart. He speaks with his Moresco companion:

---

[1] Coburn, ii, note to entry no. 2928.

[2] As implied by Allardyce Nicoll, *XIX Century Drama* (Cambridge 1930), i, p. 156: 'A Romantic poet only too often started from a theory, attempting to discover and devise a plot which should illustrate his mental abstract, in this providing a sufficient contrast to the methods of the Elizabethan dramatists whose prime interest was in the human personality and in the story, thought of in the first place as a stirring or amusing theme.'

[3] Also in the work of Joanna Baillie, the 'Plays on the Passions', the clash of an old method with a new, self-conscious dramatic ambition is apparent: she fails, but the Romantic potential is recognizable in her theory.

Alvar. Remember, Zulimez! I am his brother,
        Injured indeed! O deeply injured! yet
        Ordonio's brother.
Zul.   Nobly-minded Alvar!
        This sure but gives his guilt a blacker dye.
Alvar. The more behoves it I should rouse within him
        Remorse! that I should save him from himself.
Zul.   Remorse is as the heart in which it grows:
        If that be gentle, it drops balmy dews
        Of true repentance; but if proud and gloomy,
        It is a poison-tree, that pierced to the inmost
        Weeps only tears of poison!
Alvar.   And of a brother
        Dare I hold this, unproved?

                                        (I, i, 14–25)

This is the Romantic poet's question, asked of himself as much
as of his brother: and his proof is found by becoming Ordonio
while he does not cease to be the scrutinizing consciousness of
Alvar. Such is the mechanism of Romantic drama, purpose-
fully chameleon.

Ordonio's 'sickness of the heart' and 'gusts of the soul' (II, i,
127, 134) which arise from remorseful but not repentant guilt
are realized in the action and settings of the drama, not merely
in descriptive speeches. Coleridge ensures a complete submergence in Ordonio's experience by scenes as well as words of
nightmare. In *The Borderers* too there is scenic coordination with
the inner action: Marmaduke's first attempt to murder the old
man involved a descent into a cave on a wild and desolate night,
so that the active step into Oswald's satanic world was physically a movement into thicker darkness with a sense of separa-
tion from the ordinary world. Similarly in *Remorse*, there are
scenes in 'a cavern, dark, except where a gleam of moonlight is
seen' (IV, i), and later in a 'burial vault' (V, i) of a dungeon. In
both these scenes, the character of Ordonio's mind is communicated by place, situation, and the reactions of the other characters, who are subjected to the experience as to a waking dream
of evil. They are in these scenes either fatally or temporarily at
the mercy of the powers which rule Ordonio permanently. His
mind is both cavern and dungeon, and Coleridge, his audience,

and these other persons engaged in the drama must all dwell there for the play's purpose to be achieved.

But, again as in *The Borderers*, the poet's effort to become an Ordonio is only a part of the Romantic chameleon operation. Self-awareness remains, and the creator controls as well as submits to his experiment. In *Remorse*, this is almost diagrammatically apparent because Coleridge gives Alvar a Prospero role, showing him testing Ordonio, not merely entering into that zone of experience. Act III, scene 1, presents Alvar 'in a sorcerer's robe', challenging Ordonio, the 'self-created god' (105) and confronting him with his guilt by means of a ritual involving a picture of the assumed assassination, strange fires, incense, and mysterious music. Such apparatus could well be ludicrous, but it is explicitly a psychological manoeuvre. Alvar notes his brother's reactions to increase his own understanding, and this is the poet's incentive, devising scenes to enlarge emotional and moral comprehension. Whatever conventions of the contemporary spectacular theatre he may use, the Romantic dramatist is at once detached sorcerer and participant, analysing the behaviour he sees even as he takes on its colouring.

Zapolya, Coleridge's second play, exhibits further the motives, interests and methods of Romantic drama, although it is a play of many contrasts with its predecessor. The action of *Zapolya* seems to possess a more directly symbolic appeal for Coleridge: there is no compelling psychological centre as in *Remorse* and no one character is explored in depth. Yet the heart of the drama is concerned with human consciousness and its effort to reach a knowledge of itself. This theme is simply expressed by the dramatization of a search for identity.

The play shows a marked kinship with Shakespeare's late work: families separated, reunion after many years of parent and child, the revelation of a royal destiny after a pastoral childhood with peasant foster parents—all these ingredients familiar from *Pericles*, *The Winter's Tale* and *Cymbeline* are present in *Zapolya*. It is a play of discovery and reclamation, with the emphasis on those characters engaged in this process, not on those whose intrigue seeks to prevent it; Emerick the usurper is no Ordonio. But Andreas, the royal child finding his kingdom and his mother, does not replace Ordonio as the governing principle of the drama. His story is central but its significance is realized through the working out of events, the impact of the settings and the prevailing tone, and not through the penetration of his mind or the probing of his nature. *Zapolya* enacts the process of self-discovery itself, demonstrating what the struggle for identity is like. The borderline of the egotistical approach is close here, for the action and characters are conceived more as vehicles for the theme than as a semi-autonomous world into which the poet is venturing beyond himself. *Zapolya* is almost a myth of the Romantic consciousness in its quest for full awareness, the apotheosis of self. Egotistical energy goes into it, but at the same time the play is the result of Coleridge's entering into the situation of Andreas, and if the latter is not an Ordonio, neither is he a Manfred or a Prometheus. The work shows well how the chameleon instinct is conditioned by the pull of the opposite pole, a story becoming a symbol of the obsessions of the creating consciousness.

The play is in two parts, a prelude showing the flight of Queen Zapolya and the baby heir from the palace, and the main action twenty years later, the purpose of which is to bring Andreas to a knowledge of his mother and his real status so that he can come into possession of his kingdom. The sensation of Andreas throwing off a dream-life and emerging into his proper world is vivid and central, from the first scene of Part II. Here Andreas, living the life of a forester's adopted son, is first made aware of the possibility of learning how he arrived there, and who he is. The urgency of emotion in this scene all springs from his passionate desire for such revelation. 'Who is my father?' and 'give me a father' he entreats Sarolta (309, 314), a lady from the court who hints she has knowledge of him. 'Restore to me A name in the world' he prays (318–19), and the straining instinct for this vital illumination is suggested by his simile:

> Blest spirits of my parents,
> Ye hover o'er me now! Ye shine upon me!
> And like a flower that coils forth from a ruin,
> I feel and seek the light I can not see!
>
> (321–4)

The play is dominated by this reaching for the light, the quest of a man for the reality of himself. As he hears of his fate as an abandoned baby, left in the forest by his apparently dying mother, he begins the painful and difficult process of discarding confused dreams and false assumptions for full awareness, and Sarolta's comment on his emotion at hearing of a mother 'left to perish' (374) points beyond the immediate cause of suffering. Here is the struggle and the movement of the whole action, expressed in phrasing that shows well Coleridge's unique powers of imaginative psychology:

> It is the ground-swell of a teeming instinct:
> Let it but lift itself to air and sunshine,
> And it will find a mirror in the waters
> It now makes boil above it.
>
> (375–8)

'Check him not!' she adds, and the play obeys this command. It attempts to lift the 'teeming instinct' of the sense of self into the sun and air of consciousness, so that it can be contemplated and possessed like an inherited kingdom, and the play culminates in a triumphant feeling of fulfilment which marks the achievement of this goal. Defeating his enemies, clearing the way to his throne, Andreas finally breaks out of his dim forest world and exultantly demonstrates his belief in his personal sovereignty:

> Royal Zapolya! name me Andreas!
> Nor blame thy son if being a king, he yet
> Hath made his own arm minister of his justice.
> So do the gods who launch the thunderbolt!
>
> (IV, i, 174–7)

Coleridge's evocation of a nightmare world in *Remorse* was a device for exploring the mind gripped by the horror of the evil it served: the direction of movement in that drama was predominantly downwards, to the darkest chasms of this condition. In *Zapolya*, he still employs dream-sensation to suggest the menacing presence of evil, but the direction is upwards to other powers of light and the vigour of an innocent consciousness in full control of itself. There is even a move to a more externalized impression of evil, in the military notes of the play, the briskness of 'horns and clarions' (IV, i, 58), the 'summoning drum and horseman's clatter' (Prelude, 9–10). This is clearcut opposition, localized, unsinister, and hence controllable. But first the forest setting stimulates understanding of the state of mysterious, confused danger in which Andreas finds himself living as he leaves childhood. It is primitive place only partly known, where fugitives have wandered, strange events occur, and where monsters may lurk:

> I dreamt
> That the war-wolf had gored him as he hunted
> In the haunted forest.

(I, i, 226–8)

But to the question 'must I, hag-ridden pant as in a dream?' (Prelude, 88), the answer is no. Andreas is to emerge from the 'haunted forest' and enter his castle, 'royally attired'. Throughout the action, the experiences of *Remorse* are reversed. Teresa, Alvar and other characters were forced to enter the darkness of cavern and dungeon which expressed the consciousness of Ordonio: here, innocence is never subdued to nightmare, it is always on the offensive, defying the shadows, potentially victorious. This is the active power in the drama, allied with the basic quest for self-recognition.

In his two plays, therefore, Coleridge demonstrates the chameleon at its exploratory work and, in the second of them, the play of apotheosis, reveals its distinctive goals, mythologizing the intuitions of the Romantic imagination as it senses the freedom which comes with self-possession in its fullest meaning. Both plays have their weaknesses, but neither can be left out of any attempt to understand the English Romantic mind. They and *The Borderers* show not the tired aping of Elizabethan drama, but the experimental zest of Wordsworth and Coleridge, operating as boldly as in the *Lyrical Ballads* themselves.

5

So far it has only been possible to show the polarity of the Romantic imagination in its quest for self-revelation in a partial way because Wordsworth and Coleridge confine themselves to chameleon drama. Both egotistical and chameleon plays are to be found in Byron, however, and we shall now therefore be able to see something more of the creative duality which is the distinctive state of this imagination. Byron's first play was the egotistical *Manfred*, a close relation of Canto III of *Childe Harold*. When he turned to drama again three years later, in 1820, he produced very rapidly a series of historical plays, quite distinct from that first attempt: *Marino Faliero*, *The Two Foscari*, and *Sardanapalus*. But immediately after this group, he wrote *Cain*, finishing it by early September 1821, and the affinities of this work are with *Manfred*, as he himself said. So he swings from one pole to the other and back again.

Byron's idea of drama deviated sharply from what passed for it on the contemporary stage; indeed his reaction against the sickly or ludicrous fare usually offered, and its robust reception by audiences, led him to his most extreme position: he announced that his plays were primarily conceived for a 'mental theatre'. Considered in the context of the Romantic imagination itself, this is a most interesting decision. Such a concept of 'theatre in the mind' is most obviously applicable to *Manfred* and *Cain*, the works in his 'gay metaphysical style'[1] as he called it, but he coined the actual phrase 'mental theatre' in discussing the other group of plays, and this is therefore one feature unifying Byron's whole dramatic programme.

Most of his allusions to *Manfred* in letters to Murray and others indicate his awareness of its eccentricities as a drama, and within the self-mockery, its distinctive and serious nature is made clear. He informs Moore of its existence in this way:

I wrote a sort of mad Drama. . . Almost all the *dram. pers.* are spirits, ghosts, or magicians, and the scene is in the Alps and the other world, so you may suppose what a Bedlam tragedy it must be. . . [2]

Clearly, the presence of spirits and ghosts, the action in the 'other world', all demand the stage in the mind for their realization, and suggest more fundamentally a particular kind of creative effort. The poet has felt the need for different voices and settings because he is making an attempt to enact fully and precisely a state of mind, the world of Manfred's inner experience. *Cain* repeats this, using an established myth instead of an

[1] Murray, 12 September 1821; *LJ*, v, p. 361.
[2] 25 March 1817; *LJ*, iv, p. 80.

invented apparatus, but using it once more to reach the inner reality of a single personage. This is mental theatre in every sense, in its visionary conceptions, its ranging spheres of action, and in its appeal to the reader who must re-enact it within himself.

When, however, Byron explains what he is trying to do in the historical plays, he insists on the very different virtues of discipline, clarity and simplicity. 'Wildness' is displaced in favour of Greek method: 'my dramatic simplicity is *studiously* Greek'. Eschewing Shakespeare and 'the old English dramatists' as models, he declares to Murray:

I want to make a *regular* English drama, no matter whether for the stage or not, which is not my object—but a *mental theatre*.[1]

He was aiming, not to revive the Greeks, nor to follow the modern French drama, but to reach a dramatic form of his own at once 'simple and severe',[2] with a clarity like that of a 'clear spring bubbling in the sun'.[3] Rather as Matthew Arnold saw the danger in poets copying Shakespeare's verbal richness to the exclusion of the qualities of structure, Byron regards the former as incompatible with his austere design; alluding to *Sardanapalus* and *The Two Foscari*, he says that he has 'broken down the *poetry* as near as I could to common language'.[4] The *Lyrical Ballads* manifesto is recalled in these views on his formal and linguistic innovations. But as with those poems, the experiment goes deeper, and its real importance lies beneath the apparent preoccupation with aspects of technique. Creating a 'regular' drama does not automatically lead to a demand for a mental theatre in which it is to be played; as we have seen, the highly irregular kind of drama Byron had already practised invites such an arena much more obviously. The fact that Byron did all the same link his severe style with mental performance provides the clue to the deeper motivations, and the whole trend of drama and dramatic purpose in the Romantic imagination. Without disputing that he was in the first place protecting himself from the probable failure of any production in the current

[1] 23 August 1821; *LJ*, v, p. 347.
[2] Murray, 16 February 1821; *LJ*, v, pp. 243–4.
[3] Murray, 4 January 1821; *LJ*, v, pp. 217–18.
[4] Murray, 14 July 1821; *LJ*, v, p. 323.

English theatre, we may reasonably pursue further the question of what he was doing, when he stressed clarity and discipline and offered such a simplified dramatic line specifically to the mind of a reader.

His material for this regular drama is historical: *Marino Faliero* and *The Two Foscari* are stories from the records of Venice, its Doges and government; *Sardanapalus* is based on the account of that Assyrian monarch by Diodorus Siculus. Each play centres on some irony or paradox in the situation of the prince who is its hero: the Doge Foscari is presiding at the trial of his son for treason to the state, Doge Faliero joins in a plebeian conspiracy to bring down the Senate of which he is in theory the overlord, and *Sardanapalus*, the 'woman-king', prefers to wield power by means of the olive rather than the sword. They are plays on public themes, problems of authority and its relation to private values, explorations of such concepts as honour and loyalty, power and leadership. In them Byron clarifies the conflicts of Manfred and Cain and transfers them from the individual to the political and social scene. The search is still for a convincing ethic, and these self-aware historical heroes are closely related to the two 'metaphysical' figures. Here too we have genuine Romantic plays, conceived in the empirical imagination. Entering into the world of ancient Assyria and its untypical king, or into the politics of fourteenth-century Venice and its tormented Doge is to Byron an opportunity to examine the always pertinent issue of sovereignty, with its implications that extend far beyond the administration of law. Because the plays are born from an idea of drama as an exploratory activity, a way of sounding new areas of the psyche, Byron's stage is indeed the 'mental theatre'. If his plays are not events of the inner experience, they are nothing. Of course drama in a theatre is an event in the mind too. But it is in keeping with the tenets of Romanticism that Byron should see this mental, or psychological, impact as the chief object of dramatic as of lyric composition.

So far in my discussion of the unity of dramatic ideal in Byron's plays, their conformity to the two modes of egocentric and protean writing has only been briefly pointed. We may now look at this more explicitly.

6

Manfred and *Cain* are examples of 'the egotistical sublime' in drama in two ways. They are both expeditions into Byron's imaginative universe, dealing directly with issues that move him in all his writing; they provide him with a means of exploring himself, a dramatic mirror. And in both the real scene of action is the inner world of the hero; Manfred and Cain alone possess autonomous life in the drama, everything else takes its colour from them, and is in fact part of them, just as they in their turn are expressions of Byronic—and Romantic—preoccupations.

Manfred, like *Zapolya*, affords evidence of the Romantic imagination's instinct for mythologizing itself. This Faustian drama of a man alone in the universe presents the spectacle of the individual at once exultant and dismayed by his solitude and his dependence on his own resources to furnish his life with meaning or wreck it with remorse. The fundamental challenge which brings the nineteenth-century 'poetry of experience' into being is here the whole impulse of the drama; it sets out to realize and to test the human condition. Manfred is a Romantic Everyman, cherishing 'the mind, the spirit, the Promethean spark', the 'lightning' of his being (i, i, 154–5) and aware of what threatens it:

> How beautiful is all this visible world!
> How glorious in its action and itself!
> But we, who name ourselves its sovereigns, we,
> Half dust, half deity, alike unfit
> To sink or soar, with our mix'd essence make
> A conflict of its elements, and breathe
> The breath of degradation and of pride,
> Contending with low wants and lofty will,
> Till our mortality predominates. . .
>
> (i, ii, 37–45)

In all the scenes of the play Manfred continues to define his own nature, to establish his responsibility for himself, and to exercise the powers of his 'most bright intelligence' (ii, ii, 96). He reaches also the more bitter self-realization which is the interior sense of evil. Refusing to bow before Arimanes, abstract 'Principle of

43

Evil' and destruction in the universe, he sets up the Romantic standard, the empirical, self-attested knowledge of sin:

> I have known
> The fulness of humiliation, for
> I sunk before my vain despair, and knelt
> To my own desolation.
>
> (II, iv, 39–42)

And as he rejects externally-imposed concepts of evil, so he asserts to the Abbot his independence of orthodox religion, on the same grounds of the sovereignty of inner experience. His self-confrontation affords the most intensive judgment possible, the only full realization of right or wrong:

> Old man! there is no power in holy men,
> Nor charm in prayer, nor purifying form
> Of penitence, nor outward look, nor fast,
> Nor agony . . .
> . . . can exorcise
> From out the unbounded spirit the quick sense
> Of its own sins, wrongs, sufferance, and revenge
> Upon itself; there is no future pang
> Can deal that justice on the self-condemn'd
> He deals on his own soul.
>
> (III, i, 66–78)

'The lion is alone, and so am I' (II, i, 123) is Manfred's text. He dissociates himself from the hunter who prevents him leaping from the mountain—'I am not of thine order' (II, i, 38); he opposes Arimanes and Abbot alike, and at his death, this absolute fidelity to his own being and its self-generated values is reiterated in his further refusal of religion and, finally, in his defiant rout of the 'demons':

> I knew, and know my hour is come, but not
> To render up my soul to such as thee:
> Away! I'll die as I have lived—alone.
>
> (III, iv, 88–90)

When he claims that 'the mind which is immortal makes itself Requital for its good or evil thoughts' (129–30), the argument is close to Keats's 'that which is creative must create itself'. Neither good nor evil are being denied—the Romantic con-

sciousness is strenuously ethical—but the validity of such concepts must be sought within, their nature being proved on the
pulses and learnt as a part of the individual identity.

In *Manfred*, Byron finds a means of expressing this central
intuition by dramatizing the mind itself as it makes its universe
and grows to perceive the significance of its situation. By his
apparatus of nature-spirit emanations showing the capacity of
human intelligence, the range of scene from the Alps to the halls
of the dark spirits, and the functional figures of the hunter and
the priest, Byron gives form to the inner movements, enacting
that initial self-discovery on which the rest of Romantic poetry,
including his own, depends.

Cain continues this vein of expository drama, the mind in its
own nature displayed for the reader to experience. In this second
egotistical and 'metaphysical' play, the restlessness, ambition
and frustrations of the human mind are focused more sharply,
though not more passionately, than in *Manfred* because of the
greater opportunities of the given material. Byron finds in the
biblical story of Cain elements which suggest the dawning of a
basic awareness of self. Humanity is new, and death is only a
haunting idea; but suddenly it becomes a part of human
experience at the hand of Cain, as his blow changes the theory
of mortality into the shock of the first lifeless body. To this
fundamental action, charged with significance to a Romantic
imagination prizing the fruits of personal experience, Byron
adds a visionary superstructure, endowing Cain with Manfred's
aspiration and ferment. Stretching his mind with Lucifer, ranging the cosmos, agonized by the idea of ultimate destruction,
Cain too knows himself 'half dust, half deity':

> I look
> Around a world where I seem nothing, with
> Thoughts which arise within me, as if they
> Could master all things . . .
>
> (I, i, 175–8)

His debates with Lucifer are the arguments of the vigorous
soliloquizing intellect presented as dialogue; his journeys
through space, beyond time and his own 'little world' (II, ii,
448) dramatize all imaginative and visionary freedom; and his

45

return to earth to murder his brother is the first step towards a more immediate grappling with the contradictions of living. As the cry goes up 'death is in the world', Cain realizes the change from the shadow of death as it seemed, to the fact it now is, branding him emotionally:

Zillah. Death is in the world!
Cain.   And who hath brought him there?—I—
                    who abhor
        The name of Death so deeply, that the thought
        Empoisoned all my life . . .
        I am awake at last . . .

                                        (III, i, 370–3, 378)

His passionate request to Lucifer, 'Let me but Be taught the mystery of my being' (I, i, 321–2) takes on a grim fulfilment: his own experience brings home to him the realities of life and death. He learns more by this action and its effect on him than by any speculative flights or intellectual arguments, integral though these are to his nature. This makes Cain a Romantic hero.

Again the sovereignty of self, the need to learn and follow 'inward feeling' is explicitly propounded in the drama's speeches just as it is exhibited in the whole action. Lucifer exhorts Cain not to be 'over-swayed'

        By tyrannous threats to force you into faith
        'Gainst all external sense and inward feeling:
        Think and endure,—and form an inner world
        In your own bosom—where the outward fails;
        So shall you nearer be the spiritual
        Nature, and war triumphant with your own.
                                        (II, ii, 460–6)

The argument is Romantic rather than Satanic; *Cain* is not really a work to be regarded theologically at all. Like *Manfred*, it dramatizes the conscious movement inwards of the poetic imagination, the declaration of faith in the value of individual feeling and thought.

7

In the three historical works with their princes in paradoxical situations, Byron dramatizes the stories of specific rulers caught in the dilemmas of their place and time. History, that is, is utilized: instead of freeing his heroes from all bonds of actual circumstance as he does in the metaphysical works, he demands that the problem be seen from the point of view of medieval Venice, or the Assyrian empire. Manfred exists within *his* world, his own and his creator's mental territory and so essentially does Cain. In these other plays, however, the creative act is one of metamorphosis, the opposite impulse from the self-mirroring *Cain* and *Manfred*. In order to extend understanding of man and his obligations as a public figure, Byron imagines his way into the worlds of Faliero, Foscari and Sardanapalus, never relinquishing his keen grasp of the implications of their stories, but realizing them in their own milieu with chameleon sensitivity.

Marino Faliero turns on issues of loyalty, especially to the state, and the responsibilities of the head of that state. Faliero is Doge, yet power rests with the Venetian Senate, the 'Forty'. A crisis is precipitated by an insult to Faliero's wife, which he feels as a wound both to his personal honour and to that of his office; in his bitterness he agrees to join with a group of conspirators to overthrow the despotic Forty, by murder. The play explores the conflicts set up in him by this alliance, the intensity of devotion a ruler may expend on his state, and further, the opposition of personal and public feelings which may arise in plotting of this kind. The mixed passions of conspiracy are faced, including the darker elements.

An intricate web of argument is already hinted at here. Byron uses drama to convey his awareness of the multiple issues raised by such a situation; this is empirical testing, the acknowledgement that right and wrong are not clearcut, but have to be discovered within the complex interweaving of motive and action. A single standpoint is not enough: within the Doge himself, several attitudes coexist and influence him, and his fellow conspirators reveal not only varied conceptions of what they are doing, but different priorities in their scales of values, when the crucial moment of action is reached. Even the central concept of 'Venice' which is the focal point of the whole play is not a single vision, but an amalgam of the Doge's idealism—itself at once highly aristocratic and democratic—the Forty's rigid upholding of its law, and the conspirators' anarchic love for their city.

Faliero can reconcile the rebels' incentives with his own vision of the perfect state:

> You are met
> To overthrow this monster of a state,
> This mockery of a government, this spectre,
> Which must be exorcised with blood,—and then
> We will renew the times of truth and justice,
> Condensing in a fair free commonwealth
> Not rash equality but equal rights,
> Proportioned like the columns to the temple,
> Giving and taking strength reciprocal,
> And making firm the whole with grace and beauty,
> So that no part could be removed without
> Infringement of the general symmetry.
>
> (III, ii, 164–75)

On the other hand, his clandestine association with this motley group arouses his aristocratic misgivings:

> Deem'st thou the souls of such a race as mine
> Can rest, when he, their last decendant chief,
> Stands plotting on the brink of their pure graves
> With stung plebeians?
>
> (III, i, 99–102)

He is 'a Prince who fain would be a citizen Or nothing, and who has left his throne to be so' (III, ii, 209–10), but he is keenly aware of the unique dilemmas of his decision. Israel Bertuccio, the rebel leader, deserves the simple name of patriot, not he:

> . . . you act in your vocation;
> They smote you; and oppressed you, and despised you;
> So they have *me*: But *you* ne'er spake with them;
> You never broke their bread, nor shared their salt. . .
> You grew not up with them. . .
> Nor wore them in your heart of hearts, as I have. . .
>
> (III, ii, 456–9, 461, 465)

'Would that I could save them and Venice also!' (III, ii, 306): the Doge must be divided even when his mind is fixed on 'this dread duty' (IV, ii, 77), and his recoil from the means he must employ to carry it out leads him to question the whole human situation:

> Oh men! what are ye, and our best designs
> That we must work by crime to punish crime?
> (IV, ii, 167–8)

Such a crystallizing statement is typical of Byronic drama, in its effort to set forth complexity, and even more, the sufferings of a mind which encompasses all this complexity.

The play also considers the psychology of insurrection. Faliero, awaiting the signal for the slaughter to begin, and burdened with his personal role, sees also the general horror which it will unleash:

> . . . one stroke struck,
> And the mere instinct of the first-born Cain
> Which ever lurks somewhere in human hearts. . .
> Will urge the rest on like to wolves; the sight
> Of blood to crowds begets the thirst of more. . .
> (IV, ii, 55–7, 59–60)

And within the group of conspirators themselves, two readings of their activity are expressed in the hesitancy of Bertram and the single-minded resolution of Israel Bertuccio. 'Tyrannicide' is a noble ambition to the latter, an impersonal act of purification to which they are called as a 'high destiny' (85) and to which they must dedicate themselves utterly:

> We must forget all feelings save the *one*,
> We must resign all passions save our purpose,
> We must behold no object save our country . . .
> (II, ii, 87–9)

Whereas to Bertram, the same purpose must go by other names and call forth other sentiments:

> I have not
> Yet learned to think of indiscriminate murder
> Without some sense of shuddering . . .
> (III, ii, 64–6)

Bertuccio counters this reaction by showing it to be, from his point of view, merely a betrayal of their cause:

This false compassion is a folly, and
Injustice to thy comrades and thy cause . . .
    . . . all their acts are *one*—
A single emanation from one body
Together knit for our oppression!
          (III, ii, 280-1, 285-7)

The play thrives on such dialectic, which allows no concept to
be taken at its face value and no action to be oversimplified into
automatic categories of admirable or deplorable behaviour.
Bertram ultimately dooms the rebellion by attempting to save
his friend as well as Venice. Going to warn a Senator of danger,
he finds that the choice has to be made, and that his strongest
loyalty is centred on his personal life: 'then perish Venice rather
than my friend!' (IV, i, 314).

Faliero too has experienced the shifting ground of loyalty and
treachery, and at his trial by the government whose authority
should have been a limb of his own power, he hears his enemies
voice again a truth he has suffered in himself. In a last ironic
touch to Byron's pattern, the spokesman of the Forty sentences
and reproaches his sovereign:

Thou has forgot thy dignity in deigning
To plot with petty traitors; not so we
Who in the very punishment acknowledge
The Prince . . .
        thou shalt fall
As falls the lion by the hunters, girt
By those who feel a proud compassion for thee.
          (v, i, 560-6)

The whole play 'acknowledges the Prince' and extends awareness of princely responsibility; it examines the implications of
commitment to a cause or an ideal; and it demonstrates that
values such as loyalty are not ready-made, immutable abstracts,
but concepts which only take on meaning when they have been
experienced in all their paradoxical and conflicting implications.
Marino Faliero shows that the aim of Byronic drama is to animate
without coarsening the concepts which move its creator. The
total experience, the patterned structure of the play provides the
only method of evaluating them: the elements represented in
the Doge, the conspirators, the Senate, all contribute by means

of their interaction even when they are hostile to each other. The effect is rather that of a symposium than a contest, and the play embodies a sophisticated, forward-looking notion of dramatic potential.

The Two Foscari also exploits the sympathetic imagination, setting it to probe issues very close to those of *Marino Faliero*. Again we have a drama about loyalty, the demands it makes, its conflicts and disciplines, both public and personal; and again the awareness of complexity is the key to the whole treatment. Doge Foscari, like Faliero, is a figure beyond a simple division of feeling, the war of good versus bad: he suffers because of the demands of two kinds of good clashing within him, his love for his son and his devoted service to the state. The positive force of both these feelings make him what he is, and Byron portrays their intimate relationship as well as their opposition. The mystique of public duty and responsibility which drives the Doge to sit in judgment at the treason trial of his son is the more impressive because it dominates, and at the same time draws on, the intensity of his paternal feeling. In other characters, this complexity is broken down into its elements; Jacopo Foscari, though accused of treason, looks on Venice like a lover and is consumed with a fanatical patriotism which prefers imprisonment and death to exile; this exclusive passion is balanced by his wife's disregard for all but her husband—he is her Venice, and no less personal claim is admitted. This is the pattern of *The Two Foscari*: the balancing, interplay, conflict, and, in the Doge, mysterious fusion, of loyalties. As the concept takes on depth and life, more human territory is opened up, more levels of experience are realized.

Sardanapalus examines the conventional ethic of power. Its central character refuses to pursue the 'glory' of kingship as his Assyrian ancestors have understood it: if a hero is to be defined as one who 'sheds blood by oceans' (I, ii, 187), he does not seek the title, shunning the destructive role of the conqueror. He offers instead a reign of peace: but this may be variously interpreted, as the play demonstrates when it shows the idea being tested in the reality of a world which includes soldiers, rebels, and admirers of the old heroic standard.

Faliero is both patriot and traitor; Foscari puts Venice above

all, despite and because of his love for his son; and Sardanapalus is a third hero displaying a paradox. Voluptuary and idea-
list, he is a pleasure-loving being of 'sensual sloth' (70) who
rules from a desire 'to love and to be merciful' (i, ii, 276), and
the play does not deny either aspect of its hero. Byron shows
that a man may be weak and strong, his failures and his visions
springing from the same temperamental roots. Any morality is
meaningless to the Romantic mind unless this kind of complexity, the make-up of an individual, is understood and accepted.

In the egotistical and the protean mode alike therefore[1]
Byron's drama announces the advent of a 'mental theatre' as a
vital means of exploring and doing justice to such complexity.

8

In his three completed plays, Shelley provides more evidence of
the Romantic imagination's double-edged resource and of the
dramatic variety inherent in it. His comments in the prefaces
show his critical alertness to his own intentions in writing
dramatically. In her note to *Prometheus Unbound*, Mary Shelley
quotes what he says of an image he found in Sophocles, 'coming
to many ways in the wanderings of careful thought':

> What a picture does this line suggest of the mind as a wilderness of
> intricate paths, wide as the universe, which is here made its symbol;
> a world within a world which he who seeks some knowledge with
> respect to what he ought to do searches throughout, as he would
> search the external universe for some valued thing which was hidden
> from him upon its surface.[2]

Here is the Romantic text: the moral quest pursued through the
intricacies of the inner world, and Shelley's plays show him
threading the labyrinth.

Prometheus Unbound and *Hellas* are direct reports of his mental
journeys, his world of visions, ideals and hopes for humanity.
His Prometheus, he says in the Preface, is 'the type of the highest
perfection of moral and intellectual nature . . .',[3] and in line

---

[1] The unfinished *Deformed Transformed* shows signs of a new blending of the two
modes and suggests that Byron's interest in experimental drama was by no means
over in 1822.

[2] *Complete Poetical Works of P. B. Shelley*, ed. T. Hutchinson, p. 269.

[3] ibid., p. 201.

with his usual poetic intentions, this drama is aimed at those of 'highly refined imagination', to familiarize such readers 'with beautiful idealisms of moral excellence',[1] by awakening them to feelings of love, admiration, hope and endurance. He invites his readers to share his experience of the Promethean story, which acts upon the white light of his vision like a prism, breaking it down into its component colours. Shelley's Promethean drama is an act of the self-personifying imagination, in its dynamic Romantic character; like *Manfred*, it emerges from the awareness and the energies of the egotistical sublime.

So too in *Hellas*. Sparked off in the autumn of 1821 'in a moment of enthusiasm'[2] at the Greek bid for independence, it is an attempt to convey his vision of freedom, and he was doubtful of describing it as a play. It is 'a series of lyric pictures', he says; the subject can only be treated lyrically—yet it is 'composed in dialogue',[3] and so may be described technically as drama. This neatly suggests the twin compulsions upon him: he is writing out of his idealistic reactions to a contemporary event, more concerned with what it may symbolize, than with an actual political conflict; and at the same time, his views need clarifying by the use of different voices. *Hellas* is the result of the double response, and so makes its small contribution to that department of drama of which *Prometheus Unbound* is a major achievement.

Shelley's most explicit dramatic theory outside the *Defence of Poetry* occurs in his preface to *The Cenci*, and here he shows himself conscious of the two kinds of drama, and equally perceptive on the second, or chameleon, type to which he assigns this play. He composed *The Cenci* in the summer of 1819, just after the first three acts of *Prometheus*, and before the fourth act, so that, as with Byron's almost simultaneous composition of *Cain* and the historical plays, there is a probability of mutual stimulus between the two modes, reaffirming their creative interrelationship in the Romantic imagination. This juxtaposition may also have sharpened Shelley's critical insight into his activity as a dramatist, and aroused that passionate faith in the power of drama which the *Defence* was to declaim with such fervour.

[1] ibid., p. 203.　　[2] Note by Mary Shelley, ibid., p. 476.
[3] Preface to *Hellas*, ibid., p. 441.

He tells in the preface how he first saw the material of *The Cenci* as potentially valuable:

> Such a story, if told so as to present to the reader all the feelings of those who once acted it . . . would be as a light to make apparent some of the most dark and secret caverns of the human heart.

This recalls Wordsworth's intention that *The Borderers* should illuminate 'the depths of our nature', and the parallel emphasizes that it is a view common to the Romantic poets to see chameleon drama as exploratory, a deliberate means of enlarging understanding. Shelley propounds further his doctrine on the function of 'sympathy' in human life, and relates the exercise of this faculty to the moral evaluation induced by the drama's own nature:

> The highest moral purpose aimed at in the highest species of the drama, is the teaching of the human heart; through its sympathies and antipathies, the knowledge of itself . . .

He explicitly distinguishes the chameleon subjection to experience from the egotistical superimposing of self:

> I have endeavoured as nearly as possible to represent the characters as they probably were and have sought to avoid the error of making them actuated by my own conceptions of right or wrong, false or true: thus under a thin veil converting names and actions of the sixteenth century into cold impersonations of my own mind.[1]

It is unlikely he regarded so vital an expression of his mind as *Prometheus* as a drama of 'cold impersonations', but the contrast is clear; he understands that a primary characteristic of *The Cenci* must be its submission to the outlook and behaviour of the world it enters—the value comes from this. The goal of moral illumination is common to both types, but the different routes to it are clearly pointed in these statements, and also in the following remarks on *The Cenci*:

> It is written without any of the peculiar feelings and opinions which characterize my other compositions: I having attended simply to the impartial development of such characters as it is probable the persons represented really were.[2]

[1] *PS*, pp. 272–3.
[2] Peacock, July 1819; *Letters of P. B. Shelley*, ed. R. Ingpen, ii, p. 698.

Links between *Prometheus Unbound* and *Manfred* are easily found. Both have their origins in the period of daily association in Switzerland in 1816 when Byron and Shelley discussed such favourite heroes as Faust, Job, and Prometheus, together with Aeschylean drama and similar topics. Further, Shelley professed immense admiration for *Manfred*—only exceeded later by his reception of *Cain*—and it is therefore surprising that he never shows any recognition of the connections between his 'egotistical' drama and its esteemed predecessor.[1] Writing to Peacock after the completion of the third act, in April 1819, he says: 'it is a drama, with characters and mechanism of a kind yet unattempted'.[2] His claim to be original may be broadly accepted, in so far as such a play marked a new conception of dramatic potential in English practice; but this breakaway is made the more significant because it has a companion, whether Shelley realized this or not. One 'daring' drama, as the reviewers called *Manfred*, may be a freak and remain an oddity: two, independently written, announce a much more noteworthy phenomenon. If both are taken in the context of the pioneering Romantic imagination, the importance of their appearance is explained: their distinctive 'mechanism' is one way of solving the new technical problem which their whole purpose imposes on them. The two plays result from the creative pressures the poets felt in their effort to capture and render articulate the mind's attempt to know itself and its capabilities with no loss of subtlety and no deadening of power. With *Cain*, they are dramas of the moment in the English imagination when self-consciousness becomes a creative force, when the Magus Zoroaster meets his own image walking in the garden. The lyric poet now finds he needs a stage—though not necessarily a theatre—peopled with spirits and demons, located anywhere in the cosmos, and dominated by one central consciousness, his own, causing all else to be, and throwing around it the unifying illumination which is its awareness of its complex self.

Shelley wrote to Godwin that he thought his powers lay in apprehending 'minute and remote distinctions of feeling . . .'

[1] See S. Uttam Singh, *Shelley and the Dramatic Form* (unpublished thesis, University of London, 1959), where the point is discussed.
[2] 6 April 1819; Ingpen, ii, p. 688.

and in communicating 'the conceptions which result from considering either the moral or the material universe as a whole'.[1] *Prometheus Unbound* is his most ambitious attempt to exercise these powers and to find an adequate vehicle for their expression. The work is at once vast and subtle, less bold in its dramatic delineation of 'the mind, the spirit, the Promethean spark' than *Manfred*, but concerned with depicting a philosophic vision of that mind with the finer shades of its nature and qualities exposed. Shelley's sense of evil is less inward and immediate. Prometheus is oppressed by evil but his strength and self-knowledge emerge from his adamant resistance to its tyranny, whereas Manfred knows it as a powerful part of his own being—his ultimate defiance of the demons results from his intimate experience of the responsibilities, not of innocence, but of guilt. The tension is higher in *Manfred*, and much of the difference of effect stems from this.

Shelley's focus is on good, the mind freed and rejoicing in its own fulfilment, and most of his poetic resources and the new mechanisms are expended on communicating such a condition, elusive as it must be even to an imagination so attuned to the idea as Shelley's. His apparatus for conveying the darker side of the action is less original. Prometheus on his rock is assailed by 'horrible forms' (445) called 'Furies', who swoop on him like the traditional vultures. They remain comparatively simple personifications of human misery, and Jupiter is likewise an uncomplicated figure of tyranny. But from the first act, the real ambition of the drama is made apparent when the Earth says to Prometheus:

> To cheer thy state
> I bid ascend those subtle and fair spirits,
> Whose homes are the dim caves of human thought
> And who inhabit, as birds wing the wind,
> Its world-surrounding aether . . .
>
> (657–61)

These spirits arrive 'like fountain vapours' (668)—and at once the note is more rarified, the poetry gently stalking its intangible prey. As it progresses, the play penetrates further into the

---

[1] 11 December 1817; Ingpen, ii, p. 574.

'atmosphere of human thought' (676), the mind's evanescent impressions and moods. The sensation of inner life is realized without being coarsened, so delicate is the poet's method. There is in *Prometheus Unbound* the most perfect accord between what is revealed and the means by which it is done.

The dynamo of the drama is the growing realization of a vision achieved; its movement quickens as Prometheus nears his moral victory, but it is not so much this triumph in itself as the state of mind it confers which forms the climax of the play. Once evil has been jettisoned, and Prometheus unchained, the central experience of the drama is still to be staged. This throws light on Shelley's decision to add another act; it is not just the overflowing of his inspiration, Edward Dowden's lyrical 'after-thought',[1] but the logical culmination of the whole trend and nature of the play. Act III asserts that the mind is free, that love has prevailed, but it does not fully demonstrate what this state of being feels like, and it is his ability to provide such a demonstration that distinguishes Shelley's concept of drama. Act IV is a dramatic formulation of a mind simultaneously exerting, contemplating and celebrating its own power. The act is the experience of a new consciousness, as it enters its kingdom. The chorus of 'spirits of the human mind' (81), arriving 'as the flying-fish leap' (86), epitomize the sensation of energy joyfully released which is the key to the climax, and the whole structure of the act dynamically presents the inner resurrection. Shelley's egotistical drama therefore rises to an experimental attempt to capture the fullness of intellectual joy, of mental power at once exuberant and profound, without killing it and without losing the complex psychological shadings which make up such a condition.

Shelley's theory that moral illumination can be brought about by exercising the sympathetic imagination receives in *The Cenci* its one practical trial in terms of drama. This play shows some links with Byron's histories, but it is also related to the dramatic research into evil carried out by Wordsworth and Coleridge. There are differences of emphasis: Shelley is not interested in the state of remorse, the suffering of those committed to their guilt but aware of it as such; he is concerned with a different

[1] *Life of Shelley* (1886), ii, p. 298: 'a sublime afterthought'.

criminal psychology—that of the man who cultivates evil devotedly, with no drag of conscience to burden his career. He is also fascinated by the fate of such a man's victims, and by their reactions to close contact with unrelieved iniquity. But there is a common impulse in the three plays—*The Borderers*, *Remorse* and *The Cenci*—to investigate moral perversion by means of imaginative exposure to its influence.

The Cenci helps us to recognize more clearly what is happening in drama which springs from such an incentive. At high moments in the play's action Shelley leans heavily on Shakespeare, and this suggests that his creative engagement with his material is to be located not in the vivid communication of event, but in the study of the psychology which decrees the event, and reacts to it. In Shakespearean drama, of course, the two are simultaneously present—Macbeth murdering and Macbeth soliloquizing are interlocked. In the Romantic drama, however, there is a widening split between the two, and a concentration of interest on reaction rather than action. Event here serves a revelatory purpose: it may be near-symbolic action, as in the dungeon, caves and forest scenes of *The Borderers*, *Remorse* and *Zapolya*; it may be overtly mental action as in *Manfred*, *Cain* and *Prometheus Unbound*; or it may be a stress on a complex situation, as in Byron's Venetian plays and *Sardanapalus*. But all are designed to turn attention back to the minds of the persons central to the drama, because it is there that the whole motive of the work is discovered. In this experimental move, the first tentative steps are taken towards the much more confident experiments by modern dramatists. But the immediate effect of such a bias towards mental action was to foster the dramatic monologue, and this development *The Cenci* foreshadows. It anticipates Browning.

Written twenty-five years later, it could have been a companion to *The Ring and the Book*. There is a similarity in the material taken from Italian court records: the innocent victimized by the depraved; and many of the speeches of the main characters show Shelley adopting the monologue's self-revelatory, analytical technique. The drama is most clumsy where self-revelation is attempted through action or through spontaneous outbursts of emotion; then Cenci seems an ogre, Beatrice a Player-queen. But when Orsino remarks of the Cenci: "'tis a trick of this same family To analyse their own and other minds' (II, ii, 108–9), we recognize the instinct animating the whole play. Orsino reflects on the 'trick' and displays it at work in himself:

> Such self-anatomy shall teach the will
> Dangerous secrets . . .
> So Cenci fell into the pit; even I,
> Since Beatrice unveiled me to myself,
> And made me shrink from what I cannot shun,
> Show a poor figure to my own esteem
> To which I grew half-reconciled . . .
>
> (II, ii, 110–18)

The practice of analysis is typical of the almost narcissian self-awareness prevailing in *The Cenci*. The people speak to show themselves and Browning's taste for unveiling the minds of sophisticated Renaissance characters is anticipated in the speeches of Cenci himself, as the following extract will show. Camillo is merely the occasion for the speech, corresponding to the silent presence serving the same function in a Browning monologue:

Cenci. All men delight in sensual luxury,
All men enjoy revenge; and most exult
Over the tortures they can never feel—
Flattering their secret peace with others' pain.
But I delight in nothing else. I love
The sight of agony, and the sense of joy,
When this shall be another's, and that mine.
And I have no remorse and little fear,
Which are, I think, the checks of other men.
This mood has grown upon me, until now
Any design my captious fancy makes
The picture of its wish, and it forms none
But such as men like you would start to know,
Is as my natural food and rest debarred
Until it be accomplished.
Cam.   Art thou not
Most miserable?
Cenci.   Why, miserable?—
No.—I am what you theologians call
Hardened;—which they must be in impudence,

So to revile a man's peculiar taste.
True, I was happier than I am, while yet
Manhood remained to act the thing I thought;
While lust was sweeter than revenge; and now
Invention palls:—Ay, we must all grow old—
And but that there yet remains a deed to act
Whose horror might make sharp an appetite
Duller than mine—I'd do—I know not what . . .
I rarely kill the body, which preserves,
Like a strong prison, the soul within my power,
Wherein I feed it with the breath of fear
For hourly pain.

                                   (I, i, 77–102, 114–17)

In *The Cenci*'s bias towards self-expressive utterance of this kind and its uncertainty in the more conventionally dramatic scenes, the real sphere of Romantic interest and its implications are exposed. The Romantic poets' own versions of the monologue, an important aspect of this argument, I discuss in the following chapters.

9

'We want to see something that our great-grandsires did not know.' So wrote Beddoes to Thomas Forbes Kelsall in 1825, deploring the state of drama and looking for some 'bold trampling fellow' to reawaken it.[1] His opinion on all recent plays as mere Elizabethan ghosts—a 'haunted ruin' of a drama—is too sweeping, but his belief that innovation was needed falls in with the Romantic endeavour we are examining in this chapter. He speaks out of the same instinct as that working in the poets for the previous twenty years. Some trampling at least had been attempted, and more boldness was ensured for the distant future because of it. Whether Keats might have brought this future nearer must be left for our conjectural dreaming.

Although he is the most enthusiastic potential dramatist of all, Keats contributes least to the body of Romantic plays. There is *Otho the Great*, written with Brown 'under very peculiar conditions', as H. Buxton Forman says,[2] in the summer of 1819, and

[1] 11 January 1825; *Letters*, ed. E. Gosse (1894), p. 50–1.
[2] Editor's note, *Otho the Great*; *Complete Works of John Keats*, ed. H. Buxton Forman, iii, p. 35.

about 200 lines of *King Stephen*, the idea of which was also Brown's, but which Keats, eager to dispense with 'leading-strings', was working on alone.[1] *Otho*, conceived with Edmund Kean in mind and with commercial hopes, was composed as Keats and Brown sat together: the latter provided 'a description of each scene', for Keats to 'enwrap it in poetry', in Brown's phrase.[2] This went on for four acts, with Keats knowing nothing beyond the scene he was working on, until finally, setting aside Brown's plans for the fifth, he wrote it freely 'according to his own views'.[3] It is not surprising that the play does not reach any great heights; in fact it has more coherence than might be expected, and a spark of vitality at least in Prince Ludolph, its central character, which says something for Keats's powers, if he could breathe life into such a second-hand creation. He saw himself as simply the 'midwife' to Brown's plot;[4] and elsewhere referred to them both flippantly as 'harnessed' to their 'dog-cart' of a tragedy,[5] but most of the credit for what quality the play has must go to him. What Brown gave him, he took: he did not merely write blocks of blank verse, but tried to feel the life within the scene he was working on; the poetry is by no means all wooden. *Otho* was a genuine exercise in dramatic composition for him, and even in the method of enforced concentration on one scene at a time, there was something congenial to his temperament, because it demanded that complete subservience to the immediate experience which was so basic a doctrine of his letters. Obviously he would learn little about dramatic structure by such a piecemeal approach, but here again, inadvertently, the bias of the Romantic dramatist is illustrated: away from the mechanism of progressive action, towards the deep realizations of the personal situation. In the last act, moreover, where he proceeded according to his own instincts entirely, the main preoccupation is with Ludolph's disturbed mind, an attempt to portray his emotional distress and near-delirious confusion. Scene v has an elaborate stage direction describing a banqueting hall 'brilliantly illuminated and set forth with all costly magnificence'. Out of key with the gloom of the action in Act V, the

[1] Editor's note, quoting Brown, *King Stephen*, ibid., p. 147.   [2] *PK*, iii, p. 35.
[3] ibid.   [4] Taylor, 5 September 1819; Rollins, ii, p. 157.
[5] Dilke, 31 July 1819; Rollins, ii, p. 135.

lavish festal scene is ordered by Ludolph as he imposes his inner world of fantasy onto his surroundings. His guests therefore are bewildered actors in his play:

1st Knight. Grievously are we tantalized, one and all—
              Swayed here and there, commanded to and fro
              As though we were the shadows of a dream
              And link'd to a sleeping fancy. What do we here?
Gonfred.   I am no Seer—you know we must obey
              The prince from A to Z—though it should be
              To set the place in flames.

                                        (v, v, 1–7)

For a moment, the conventional is swept aside, the dramatic worlds of Pirandello or Genet become possible. *Otho the Great* is feeble enough in many ways, and it is no play to build vast claims on; but Keats was engaged with his material, he was exerting his valued chameleon skill, and he does, fleetingly, produce something wholly Romantic in his identification with a mind as it self-consciously lives out its own upheaval. Debts to *Hamlet* and *King Lear* are obvious, but this is not imitation; the poet is probing reality and illusion for himself and utilizing dramatic form to this end.

There is too little of *King Stephen* for any judgment of its quality to be made, but its existence testifies to Keats's continued desire to tackle the problems of play-writing after his first taste of them. The passion was certainly there, and the terms in which he expresses it give some of the most articulate evidence that the energy of Romanticism did not bypass drama, nor regard its composition just as an act of veneration to the Elizabethan past. In August 1819 Keats declared to Bailey: 'one of my ambitions is to make as great a revolution in modern dramatic writing as Kean has done in acting'.[1] This avowal coincides with the first venture on his own, in Act V of *Otho*, from which we may conclude that his experience of independent work encouraged his belief that he could develop as a dramatist.

His enthusiasm for Kean is characteristic. He wrote in one of his notices for *The Champion*: 'Kean delivers himself up to the instant feeling, without a shadow of a thought about anything else'.[2] He hails his own 'negative capability' here, and two years

[1] 14 August 1819; Rollins, ii, p. 139.   [2] 21 December 1817; *PK*, iii, p. 231.

later he wrote *Otho* as if he were Kean acting. Yet at the same time he confirms that a strong sense of identity is intimately related to the denial of self which this acting demands. He goes on to say that Kean 'feels his being as deeply as Wordsworth'.[1]

Now that we have traced the characteristic pattern of egotistical and chameleon work and recognized the exploratory energies of Romantic drama, we may go on to discover the same pattern and the same energies in Romantic poetry.

[1] ibid., p. 232.

III

EGOTISTICAL AND CHAMELEON: WORDSWORTH AND COLERIDGE

Poetry without egotism comparatively uninteresting.
Coleridge, *Notebooks*

He went like one that hath been stunned
And is of sense forlorn:
A sadder and a wiser man
He rose the morrow morn.

The Ancient Mariner

IN NAÏVE explanations of Romantic poetry, the poets are said to be 'expressing themselves', setting down their intuitions, thoughts and feelings, especially the latter. Even in more sophisticated critical commentary, something of this is still assumed: poetry regarded as a revelation or confession is taken to embody the Romantic approach. In so far as these ideas point to the consciousness of self in the poets, there is truth in them. But they are misleading in that they reduce Romantic work to a simple kind of unpacking. This is a most inaccurate version of Romantic creativity, the whole principle of which is not self-expression, but self-exploration and discovery. The poems are the living substance of this inquiry, the one method of scrutinizing experience without loss of its subjective immediacy. The self is indeed the starting point of such poetry, but it is also its goal, only to be known by being imaginatively grasped as it weaves the complex web of its own experience. Romantic poetry begins from a perception of the essential marriage between objective and subjective, not merely in the relationship of the world and the observer, but in the effort of self-realization to which the poetry is committed and by which it is most stimulated. The poets are alert to the complexity of the experiencing self, they regard identity not as an evident fact but as an ultimate achievement, its realized possession both the motive and the reward for creative exertion.

If we approach their poems from this angle, and with the further assistance of the material in Chapter I, there is less likelihood of our reading them in that oversimplified fashion which takes their use of the word 'I' at its face value and also ignores their dramatic bias to the extent of excluding their plays from serious attention altogether. Whether the poems seem to be direct personal statements or whether they submerge the poet himself in some way, they are creations of an imagination willing to admit mystery in the notion of an experiencing mind, and convinced that by exploring this mystery some criteria for evaluating what is experienced can be found. In each Romantic poet, there is the double mode of exploration, the self intensely contemplating and exercising its unifying subjective power, and the self indulging its Ariel-prerogative, entering into forms not its own. That Romantic poems as well as Romantic plays operate in accordance with this creative law I shall now begin to demonstrate, looking first at Wordsworth's part in the *Lyrical Ballads* experiment.

2

There is as much harm in assuming Romanticism to be merely the birth of a long expected child as in seeing it as an overnight revolution in which a complacent, unsuspecting eighteenth-century literature was murdered in its bed. For all the thoroughly documented signs of change in the preceding years, 1798 remains a date of moment. The *Lyrical Ballads* are far more than a gesture against poetical diction; in their publication the distinctive Romantic course was initiated. Their 'way of meaning' deserves the name 'epiphany', says Langbaum in stressing their 'essential innovation': '. . . the epiphany . . . is a way of apprehending value when value is no longer objective . . . [it] grounds the statement of value in perception; it gives the idea with its genesis, establishing its validity not as conforming to a public order of values but as the genuine experience of an identifiable person.'[1] They are the first poems deliberately engaged in the empirical testing of life, aware of the experiencing self as the prime factor in this process. The precision of the

[1] *The Poetry of Experience*, p. 46.

title of the volume has not been sufficiently appreciated: the ballad has indeed become lyrical, the event depends on the reacting consciousness.[1] Wordsworth himself brings this out when he observes in the 1800 Preface: 'the feeling therein developed gives importance to the action and situation, and not the action and situation to the feeling'. A momentous sentence, for here the impetus of Romanticism is to be found.

The *Ballads* show this significant orientation, and they also exhibit the two modes of Romantic sensibility. Professor J. L. Danby points out[2] that they are not straightforward 'first person' poems, and assumptions about their artless simplicity go astray here. Most of the ballads display 'an essentially dramatic self-projection', and Danby indicates their variety within this experimental form, from the monologue as in *The Complaint of the Forsaken Indian Woman* to the 'neutral narrator' reporting in *Goody Blake and Harry Gill*. In the three ballads he singles out for closer examination, *Simon Lee*, *The Thorn* and *The Idiot Boy*, he finds Wordsworth exploiting with skill the opportunities, including the ironic tone, of a 'more complex merging' of voices. They are poems with a 'dramatic-narrative' approach.[3]

In the light of my present discussion, such a finding is particularly interesting. And if Wordsworth's contributions to the volume are taken as a whole—the 'few other poems' together with the experimental ballads—we can see that he tries out in it most of the notes on the scale from chameleon to egotistical. The latter, the voice which earned him Keats's classification with Milton, sounds forth strongly in *Tintern Abbey*, and there are the 'Lines on various occasions' as lower-toned instances of the reflective self. Then, transitionally, there are the several dialogue poems: *Expostulation and Reply* and its com-

---

[1] Although R. Mayo in his important article on 'The Contemporaneity of the *Lyrical Ballads*' (*Publications of the Modern Language Association of America*, lxix (1954), pp. 486–522) plays down the choice of title by arguing its similarity with those in vogue in the 1790s, he does also admit that it was not itself used before Wordsworth and Coleridge adopted it (p. 509).

[2] In *The Simple Wordsworth* (1960), Chapter II, especially pp. 35–8.

[3] See also articles by S. M. Parrish: '*The Thorn*: Wordsworth's Dramatic Monologue' (*English Literary History*, xxiv (1957), pp. 153–63), and 'Dramatic Technique in the *Lyrical Ballads*' (*PMLA*, lxxiv (1959), pp. 85–97), which asserts that they were 'experiments in dramatic form, in characterization, and in narrative technique' (p. 86).

panion piece, both nearer the egotistical in their articulation of
the poet's moods and outlook, while *We are Seven* and *Anecdote for
Fathers* move closer to the chameleon by means of a partial
submission to the attitude of the child characters—their point of
view is active and necessary and must be realized by the poet
and the reader alike before both revert to the role of judges
drawing adult conclusions. In *The Last of the Flock* the whole
impact of the poem depends on the poet's effacing his ego, but
entering the poem as the occasion for the shepherd to reveal his
own story; Wordsworth is also the shepherd speaker, and the
chameleon change, in its basic form, has been made. *The Female
Vagrant* offers a vestigial remnant of the egotistical, yielding to
the dramatizing mode after the single line of introduction: 'The
woman thus her artless story told'; and the monologue proper—
if undeveloped—arrives with the direct entry into the mind of
the dying Indian woman, all narrative explanation having been
removed from the poem into a prefatory note.

The more complex poems, as Professor Danby rightly defines
them, are so because they are more searching experiments.
They discover the range from egotistical to chameleon, but they
also assert the close relationship of the two, their mutually rein-
forcing function in the Romantic imagination. In *The Idiot Boy*,
for example, Wordsworth is present as an urgent spectator of
the action, not so much narrator as producer, switching the
scene and setting it before the reader with direct impact:

> Why bustle thus about your door
> What means this bustle, Betty Foy?

The poem keeps this observing presence throughout, and it
serves as a sounding board for the emotions and the action being
depicted: the reader is not alone with Betty, Johnny and the
pony in the moonlit wood, he is aware of the story going on in
the mind of this semi-participant, the commentator and director.
This is most apparent when the poet steps back a little and
remarks on what does not happen to Johnny in the wood, but
the control is there throughout, and the poem is not a drama put
before the reader but a dramatically vivid experience offered to
him as it is enacted in the poet's mind. Thus, it clearly remains a
product of Wordsworth's egotistical imagination; he enriches

the poem by making the reacting mind a structural feature, insisting on the reader's being aware of a double process, of action and response, simultaneously important. *The Idiot Boy* also shows Wordsworth striving for that kind of evaluation which comes from grasping an experience in its totality. Comparatively primitive though the attempt may seem, it is an effort of the imagination which sets the course for a century's poetry.

Although this ballad does not relinquish the unifying presence of the poetic mind, it does reject the subjective limitations of self-enclosure. A poem such as *Resolution and Independence*, on the other hand, is as 'egotistical' as *Tintern Abbey*, for the person of the old man is realized as an agent bringing about certain changes and movements within the poet's mind, so that he becomes before all else an integral part of that mind. *Simon Lee* is a ballad which anticipates such egotistical writing in that the poet is primarily concerned with the result of the encounter in himself, the emotional perception which the episode releases in him. These catalyst figures are neither cheapened nor deprived of dignity by being so assimilated, but the contrasting handling of *The Idiot Boy* shows that Wordsworth was indeed susceptible to the pull of the chameleon technique as a way of offering a different kind of tribute to other human beings whose plight or character moved him, even while he remained faithful to his egotistical impulse, his own awareness of being moved. Turning on the latter, *The Idiot Boy* none the less creates the worlds of those engaged in the story, from the conflicting agitations of Betty as mother and neighbour, to the pony going his undirected way, unable to fathom 'what he has got upon his back'. And the master-stroke comes in the poem's conclusion where it triumphantly penetrates and takes us into Johnny's mental experience of the night, bringing about that shock of recognition which renders the entirely strange immediately accessible:

> The cocks did crow to-whoo, to-whoo
> And the sun did shine so cold.

The poem therefore digests a number of individual experiences in its presentation of the story, conceding that the truth of any given set of events is to be found only by the mobility of the sympathetic imagination which seeks out the reality of each point of view, the feeling of the situation to each of those who constitute it. Because it can claim, then, to be a poem resulting from the exercise of both the egotistical and the chameleon faculties of the imagination, *The Idiot Boy* shows them intimate, both rooted in the Romantic desire to feed on experience to the full in the business of self-discovery.

The Thorn also illustrates the growing imaginative need to take into account, in the process of assimilating an episode, the fact of subjective reactions. As a poem it is both more and less ambitious than *The Idiot Boy*. It does not make the same effort towards totality, but it does represent Wordsworth's most deliberate attempt to deal with an experience as it strikes a particular consciousness, not his own. A story again becomes an emotional truth, event and consciousness illuminate and modify each other. Despite the vast evolutionary distance between them, *The Thorn* looks forward to the development of the monologue in Browning's hands: a speaker and his theme inter-dependent, each a vital element for the understanding of the other, each falsified by isolation or any more objective evalua-tion. Wordsworth's poem is the crudest approximation to such exploiting of subjective relativity, but the dim perception of more adventurous possibilities are there, as the fact that he thought it prudent to give an explanatory note in his 1798 advertisement suggests:

The poem of *The Thorn*, as the reader will soon discover, is not sup-posed to be spoken in the author's own person: the character of the lo-quacious narrator will sufficiently show itself in the course of the story.

And his interest in this loquacious character as a psychological presence in the poem, colouring his story by what he is and being revealed by the experience he narrates, is further emphasized by the expanded commentary on the poem in 1800. Here Words-worth regrets the absence of 'an introductory poem' wherein the speaker could have been described more fully. Envisaging him as a sea captain retired to village life, he says

Such men . . . become credulous and talkative from indolence; and . . . they are prone to superstition. On which account it appeared to me proper to select a character like this to exhibit some of the general laws by which superstition acts upon the mind.

These statements show the imagination embarking on its policy of reaching the general only by the particular, and concerning itself with the psychological reverberations of events. And they show Wordsworth declaring himself the chameleon artist, so staking another claim for the experimental character of the whole volume.

But Wordsworth's explanation about *The Thorn* and his intentions in it perhaps also arise out of a doubt as to his success in handling the poem, not merely from his feeling that it is a work demanding some elucidation before it can be properly appreciated. His doubts, if he did have any, seem to be justified, because the poem copes only feebly with the retired sea captain:[1] the perception of what could be achieved belongs to the prose notes only and to the creative impulse which led him to try out the idea. Some imitations of garrulity are offered, certainly, and one defence for the poem's much mocked addiction to precise measurement may be found in the supposedly practical bent of the man from the sea, but otherwise *The Thorn* seizes the imagination without the mediation of the intended narrator. The poem is not a failure, except as an example of chameleon endeavour: ironically enough, it succeeds as an egotistical poem. Martha Ray is a living property of Wordsworth's, not the captain's subjective consciousness, a figure in a desolate setting with an imaginative appeal comparable to the leech gatherer. Around her shines the light of the poet's own transfiguring vision:

> For oft there sits, between the heap
> That's like an infant's grave in size,
> And that same pond of which I spoke,
> A woman in a scarlet cloak,
> And to herself she cries,
> 'Oh misery! oh misery!
> Oh woe is me! oh misery!'
>
> At all times of the day and night
> This wretched woman thither goes,
> And she is known to every star,
> And every wind that blows . . .

[1] But see S. M. Parrish on this poem for a different yet relevant evaluation of it.

But Wordsworth opens up the chameleon sensibility in 1798 just as much as he pioneers the egotistical mode. The *Lyrical Ballads* offer a full-range encounter with the Romantic imagination, hinting its potential as it begins to discover not only the strength but the variety of its resources.

3

In his Preface to *The Excursion*, Wordsworth set out the full ambition which lived in him for so long: 'a determination to compose a philosophical poem, containing views on Man, Nature and Society; and to be entitled, *The Recluse*; as having for its principal subject the sensations and opinions of a poet living in retirement'. The egotistical bias is evident from this statement; the larger view is to be arrived at by the poet's study of his own 'sensations and opinions'. The congruence of the preparatory poem—that is, the finished but unpublished *Prelude*—to this main aim needs no stressing. Referring to it as an 'ante-chapel' to the body of a gothic church, he describes it as a scrutiny of his powers, their 'origin and progress'; 'a history of the Author's mind', which he undertook to assess his readiness for creating the larger structure. Such a point of departure speaks for Romantic empiricism in general, and the egotistical pole of it in particular. But *The Recluse* itself was never written, except for Book I and that section of it published as *The Excursion*: Wordsworth's gothic church remained an ante-chapel and a sketch of the more imposing edifice.

Various reasons have been given for his failure to carry out the plan, and no doubt the actual reasons were various. But it is an interesting failure. Given the egotistical bias of the whole plan, it is difficult to see that more could have been written, after *The Prelude*, because what began as an introduction to an ambitious scheme became the scheme itself. He has done in *The Prelude* exactly what he intended to do in *The Recluse*; within the masterly realization of the stages and vicissitudes of his own growing consciousness, he has surveyed man, nature and society. Recognizing in the design of *The Recluse* the integral relationship of the philosophic conclusions with the reacting mind, in *The Prelude* he composed the poem of this union. It is no coincidence that the extant fragment of the main poem echoes the tone of *The Prelude*: dealing with the 'sensations' of his arrival in Grasmere to settle there, the joyous recognition of a desire fulfilled and of a fruitful dialogue between man and place, it offers (though not retrospectively as the preparatory poem does) evaluation through the living moment. *The Recluse*, if written, could only have extended *The Prelude*, and that, as his instinct knew, was unnecessary.

If this is accepted, how did *The Excursion* come to birth? My answer would be that, while it too overlaps *The Prelude*, it is the product of Wordsworth's imagination swinging to its other pole. There is support for this idea in his Preface to the poem where he outlines the plan for the three parts of *The Recluse*:

the first and third parts will consist chiefly of meditations in the Author's own person . . . in the intermediate part (The Excursion) the intervention of characters speaking is employed, and something of a dramatic form adopted.

The contrast made here suggests that although Wordsworth was unable to go on 'in his own person', he was able to release another type of energy by responding to the opposite mode of creation. A fair proportion of *The Excursion* was drafted at the turn of the century, when the state of intense egotistical creativity stimulated him to attempt the complementary method simultaneously.

The Excursion has points in common with Wordsworth's other chameleon researches into man, nature, and society, and its character and qualities emerge more forcefully when it is aligned with *The Borderers* and with the *Lyrical Ballads*. Aligned, that is, with the Wordsworth who deliberately tunes his sensibility to a wavelength not his own, increasing its range of experience so that he has more data for consolidation. The egotist constantly present in the Romantic exercise of the sympathetic imagination must not be forgotten, and indeed, in this poem cannot be.

Two kinds of chameleon enterprise are shown in *The Excursion*: 'characters speaking', and reported accounts of a variety of people. Thus it incorporates something of *The Borderers*, a near-dramatization of present action, and something of the ballads' technique of anecdotal commentary, lives revealed through the medium of eyewitness memory and observation. Such a range suggests a considerable vigour of poetic intention, a bid to cast the net as widely as possible. From the copresence of these two types of dramatization, and their parallels outside the poem, *The Excursion*'s aims become clearer. *The Borderers* was written as a means of illuminating a destructive psychology, an attempt to enter a disturbed mind which felt itself alien from exactly those impulses of human sympathy that a chameleon imagination cherishes; the ballads' design is to exercise the sympathetic impulse itself—they seek to bring the mind into possession of the reality of each situation and so increase its moral capital. The play therefore probes an illness, and aids understanding of it, the ballads in their manipulation of feeling offer the cure. *The Excursion* does both.

The key figure is the Solitary; he and his cast of mind are the occasion for much of the eloquent discourse on man, nature and society which occupies a great part of the poem and he is too a more dynamic centre, for to bring about a change of attitude in him is the aim of the other speakers. He gives direction and an impetus to the poem which its somewhat stately pace may obscure, but which is important. For the Solitary is an Oswald, but an Oswald on the defensive, not actively dominant as was the protagonist of *The Borderers*, imposing his view onto the susceptible young and using the weak as his tools. The Solitary does not exert power, but he moves others to oppose him and to seek his conversion. His part in the poem is to present himself as an envoy from a different and darker universe, so that the Wanderer, as beneficent sage, the Pastor, and the poet, may all realize their own concept of life, their own being, more urgently. Although the angle is changed, a process of exploration is at work here recalling *The Borderers*: the nature of light and dark are both being discovered by their contiguity. The method is experimental before it is discursive, a confrontation of mood and feelings out of which didactic discourse grows, certainly, but not to the exclusion of all else.

Wordsworth is not preaching a secure philosophy in *The Excursion*, as is implied by critics who see the Wanderer as little more than a mouthpiece for his own convinced outlook and the

Solitary as a mere ghost of an opponent, reduced to a scarcely discernible breath of argument by the end of the poem. The employment of the chameleon device of speakers signifies more imaginative unrest than this: the poet is working over that crucial period of his life, the mid-1790s, in a further attempt to realize the exact nature of what happened to him then. He was impelled at that time to write *The Borderers*, and it remains a mark of his recourse to the chameleon mode that he is trying to exorcize or master, at least to understand, painful or destructive forces. In the *Lyrical Ballads*, the poems which adopt a chameleon technique are those dealing with harsh emotional situations: the solitary death of an abandoned woman, the agitations of a frightened mother, the misery of a girl haunting a child's grave. To deal with his awareness of the 'impulse from a vernal wood', he relies on the personal lyric. Moreover, in *The Prelude*, passing quickly from analysis of his darker states of mind to his restitution, he delegates the study of what he then was to some 'less guarded' mode of utterance, as he terms it in the 1850 version (XI, 284). This suggests both the greater vulnerability of the submissive chameleon approach, and its capacity to break down experience which is formidable in its impact and radical in its effects. It is sufficient in his work of egotistical assimilation merely to record his confusions and despair. *The Prelude* plots the course of his healing mind and portrays its powers of self-restoration, its ability to reap an imaginative harvest from moods of terror or desolate gloom. But the effort to relive the crisis cannot be sidestepped—*The Borderers* must be endured, and *The Excursion* likewise:

> Time may come
> When some dramatic story may afford
> Shapes livelier to convey to thee, my Friend,
> What then I learned, or think I learn'd, of Truth,
> And the errors into which I was betrayed . . .
>
> (1805 version, x, 879–83)

The full Romantic assessment must be made. In *The Excursion* Wordsworth sets out to provide it, supplementing his play with a retrospective return to his moral shipwreck. He does not recreate this in the isolation of its original occurrence, as he did in *The*

Borderers. In the Solitary, the crisis returns in a different form: can disillusion and soured idealism be integrated with all else that the poet knows himself to be? What remains to be discovered is not whether the Solitary can be opposed by other views, faiths and moods—it is obvious to the author of *The Prelude* that he can—but whether more than this can be achieved. Whether, that is, the Solitary can be accommodated as well as answered, not merely shunned as a sinner against the light but entertained as a legitimate and even seminal state of mind, however dangerous he is as an exclusive attitude. Wordsworth discovers more fully what that 1790 phase has meant to him, both by setting in motion again his opposition to it and in allowing it to repeat its impact upon him. Only the chameleon approach gives scope for this experimental programme and Wordsworth adopts his 'dramatic story' because he needs its freedom as the essential medium for his twofold purpose. He seeks not just the way of release from the predicament of the Solitary, but the value inherent in that predicament itself. He is in this poem an exorcist, but the devil vanishes through understanding not repudiation. If we come to the poem in this way, we grasp its unique but integral place in Wordsworth's work and see it positively, as a necessary complement to *The Prelude*.

Besides the Solitary, there are three main speakers or actors: the poet, the Wanderer, and the Pastor. Of these, the Wanderer presides in the number of his speeches, in the outlook he proffers, and in his office of guide and leader towards the poet, who stands in the subsidiary role of recorder, reacting audience, and mirror of the scene. Receiving the action in this way, Wordsworth witnesses the drama of his past produced by the chameleon freedom of his imagination; his presence in the poem is one of comparative passivity, contrasting strongly with its dominance in *The Prelude*. His consciousness is diffused throughout this poem, most vividly discovered when merged in other voices. The Pastor reinforces the Wanderer, but is himself a vital instrument in the poem's development, becoming central as the Wanderer in his turn takes the role of listener.

Solitary and Wanderer are antithetical in their temperament and habits of life. The Wanderer embodies the sympathetic imagination in its most purified form, where this faculty and moral vision are identified:

> Unoccupied by sorrow of its own,
> His heart lay open, and, by nature tuned
> And constant disposition of his thoughts
> To sympathy with man, he was alive
> To all that was enjoyed where'er he went,
> And all that was endured . . .
> > He could *afford* to suffer
> With those whom he saw suffer. Hence it came
> That in our best experience he was rich,
> And in the wisdom of our daily life.
> > > (I, 361–6; 370–3)

To this serene selflessness is opposed the history of the Solitary and its embittered consequences. The Wanderer tells how, disillusioned by the deviation of the French Revolution,

> he forfeited
> All joy in human nature, was consumed,
> And vexed and chafed, by levity and scorn,
> And fruitless indignation; galled by pride . . .
> And wastes the sad remainder of his hours,
> Steeped in a self-indulging spleen, that wants not
> Its own voluptuousness . . .
> > (II, 296–9; 310–12)

The Solitary himself also tells his story, the recapitulation testifying both to the self-absorption observed by the Wanderer and to Wordsworth's magnetized concern with this particular mental career, from exultant humanistic idealism to cynicism. He speaks the 'bitter language of the heart' (III, 462) twice, in different voices, because he is engaged in a scrupulous inquest which finds its truth in the shifting of angles, not in the anonymous depersonalization of fact. What the Solitary is, is to be understood by the Wanderer's version of him, the poet's observation of him, and by his interpretation of himself: a germ of *The Ring and the Book* is unexpectedly discovered in Wordsworth.

In much of the Wanderer's discourse, the antithesis of sterile and responsive living is worked over, the Solitary's presence rendering such descriptions as the following pertinent diagnosis

76

rather than generalized didactic warning. Wordsworth beholds an experienced reality and admits it as such, when the Sage delineates the crisis of human consciousness:

> The repetitions wearisome of sense,
> Where soul is dead, and feeling hath no place;
> Where knowledge, ill begun in cold remark
> On outward things, with formal inference ends;
> Or, if the mind turn inward, she recoils
> At once—or, not recoiling, is perplexed—
> Lost in a gloom of uninspired research;
> Meanwhile, the heart within the heart, the seat
> Where peace and happy consciousness should dwell,
> On its own axis restlessly revolving,
> Seeks, yet can nowhere find, the light of truth.
>
> (IV, 620–30)

The collision of Wanderer and Solitary, each expounding his own theory and experience, precipitates the fundamental questions. As they meet the Pastor by the village graveyard, Wordsworth has reached again the weary brain-cudgelling of his youthful disillusion, and is brought before the bar of philosophic and ethical questioning. The Wanderer summarizes 'the points on which our inquest turns' (v, 480–1) for the Pastor's opinion:

> Do generations press
> On generations, without progress made?
> Halts the individual, ere his hairs be grey,
> Perforce? Are we a creature in whom good
> Preponderates, or evil? Doth the will
> Acknowledge reason's law? A living power
> Is virtue, or no better than a name?
> Fleeting as health or beauty, and unsound?
> So that the only substance which remains . . .
> Among so many shadows, are the pains
> And penalties of miserable life,
> Doomed to decay, and then expire in dust!
>
> (v, 466–78)

The gulf between the opponents lies in their answers to these questions. Such was the dead end of Wordsworth's thoughts, the point at which as he says in *The Prelude* he 'yielded up moral questions in despair' (1850, XI, 305). Here he returns to that intellectual deadlock in an attempt to realize more deliberately the machinery of its resolution, the method of transition from the negative to the positive view. He is less concerned with the conclusion that the positive is tenable than with the actual accomplishment of the change: the throwing of a bridge which the argument itself fails to create. Now we see that the function of the Pastor is not theological but imaginative and in *The Excursion*'s demand that he answer both Sage and Solitary, Wordsworth relives, but with emancipated clarity, his own evolution from Solitary to Wanderer.

In *The Excursion*'s presentation of the Wanderer, his innate possession of the sympathetic imagination is stressed; but he cannot communicate this to the Solitary. He depicts the result of its presence, not its own vivifying nature. The Pastor with his stories of his parish, on the other hand, shows the power itself as it operates. The graves of the 'churchyard among the mountains' open as the pastor surveys them, and the living experience of their inhabitants is offered to be absorbed and realized by his listeners as the only valid answer to their dilemma. Wordsworth's full apprehension of this crucial moment in the poem is conveyed in the Wanderer's invitation to the Pastor:

> The mine of real life
> Dig for us; and present us, in the shape
> Of virgin ore, that gold which we, by pains
> Fruitless as those of aëry alchemists,
> Seek from the torturing crucible. There lies
> Around us a domain where you have long
> Watched both the outward course and inner heart:
> Give us, for our abstractions, solid facts;
> For our disputes, plain pictures.
>
> (v, 630–8)

The Pastor quarries the *Lyrical Ballads* mine, exemplifying the empirical study of 'act and circumstances, that make The individual known and understood' (VIII, 17–18). He displays the way of salvation which took Wordsworth further into his own individuality in *The Prelude* and equally, towards the poems of country life of 1798. In the numerous stories recounted in Books VI and VII of *The Excursion*, the Pastor, like Wordsworth

in 1798, seeks to bring about in his hearers that emotional consequence which follows from the act of genuinely moving one's
position to another point of view. From this exercise comes the
discovery that such honouring of experience illuminates it with
the value of something intimately loved. Already at the beginning of the poem, the poet and the Sage have sketched this
process. As he is told the tale of poor Margaret, the poet remarks
on the snaring of his reactions:

> In my own despite
> I thought of that poor Woman as of one
> Whom I had known and loved . . .
>   . . . the things of which he spake
> Seemed present . . .
>
>   (1, 612–14; 617–18)

The Wanderer himself suggests the movement: 'my spirit clings
To that poor Woman'; and the poet shows the culmination of
the emotional stimulus in his final gesture: 'with a brother's
love I blessed her' (1, 779–80; 923–4). In the Pastor's fund of
stories Wordsworth reiterates his conviction that only by being
moved to react as a brother, to know and love in this sense, will
the Solitary alter his philosophic position. 'Life' cannot be agreed
on, but each hearer may be moved by the specific histories
narrated, this volume of ballads about a prodigal son, a 'gentle
Dalesman', an obsessed miner wearing his path from hut to
mine, Ellen the abandoned lover, the lonely herbalist, the
strangers of antagonistic politics who settled in the dale and
became inseparable. A community is resurrected, and the
listeners share in its experience. The mine of real life yields its
riches, and the heart of *The Excursion* is reached in these books.
The Solitary is moved by what he hears, and the last lines of the
poem indicate that some 'degree of healing' has been accomplished, but the purpose of the poem is to show the route from
sterility rather than depict—except in the Pastor and the Sage—
the outcome of the journey.

    We may well see in *The Excursion* some tension between the
abstract expressions of piety to which the Wanderer is prone and
the working of the empirical approach just discussed. But the
poem itself recognizes this and incorporates it in its whole

pattern, by means of the Pastor who is at once priest and imaginative spokesman. Wordsworth takes the opportunity to explore the relationships of poet, priest and philosopher, and the tension is part of this enterprise. The poem moreover does drive steadily on to affirm the claims of the empirical imagination. In the bid to restore the Solitary, the empirical is seen and shown to be the only way; and there is the further point of the Solitary's own contribution to the vision of the poem. In so far as his disillusion means a loss of illusion, he is not a figure of opposition, but an integrally necessary part of the poem's main movement. The goal becomes clear in the final books which, surveying the contemporary scene in English village life, brood on the theme of industrial change. The effort here, within the aura of religious and patriotic emotion, is to admit actuality in the unvarnished *Lyrical Ballads* manner; it extends, in short, the Pastor's mining of 'real life'. The Wanderer has his vision of a 'humanized society' (IX, 389) and is buoyed up by his hopes for better things, a sure faith in a dignified destiny. But the balance is kept as the breaking up of the old patterns of living is described in Book VIII; and in the force of the Solitary's astringent observations, human nature itself is denied any easy nobility. Wordsworth had to learn to see his shepherds when necessary without the light of setting suns around them, and in the Solitary's realism he re-enacts this lesson of his youthful experience, which had its place in bringing the *Lyrical Ballads* to birth. His development is portrayed in the check and balance relationship which emerges between Wanderer and Solitary, together with the crucial intervention of the Pastor between them.

The positive value inherent in the Solitary is inseparable from the shocks which blighted him, as his own narrative in Book III makes clear. Striving to preserve his exaggerated ideal of glorified humanity, battered but not wrecked by the Revolution's course, he departed for the 'western world' (III, 870), travelling far into the virgin lands in his search:

> But that pure archetype of human greatness,
> I found him not. There, in his stead, appeared
> A creature, squalid, vengeful, and impure . . .
>
> (III, 951–3)

On this final disillusion he erected his sceptical philosophy. But notwithstanding the despair of mind that resulted, he had learnt to see what creatures really walked the earth. So had the young Wordsworth, and hence the ballads of cruelty and age, swelling ankles and idiot children. To see was not enough, but it was the first essential. And so there is the fruit of the Solitary's perception in the inclusion of 'forbidding' tales in the Pastor's miscellany (VI, 662), and in the later acknowledgement that changes of circumstance do not entirely account for the miseries of some human lives. 'Soft verse' (VIII, 401) may speak of a 'whistling ploughboy' (398), but the Solitary sees his clumsy legs, his 'wide, sluggish, blank' eyes (410), his soul 'a caterpillar sheathed in ice' (419):

> This torpor is no pitiable work
> Of modern ingenuity; no town
> Nor crowded city can be taxed with aught
> Of sottish vice or desperate breach of law
> To which (and who can tell where or how soon?)
> He may be roused . . . This Boy the fields produce . . .
> . . . what liberty of *mind* is here?
>
> (VIII, 420–5; 433)

Thus the Solitary sounds though he does not disturb the Wanderer's serenity: and his force in this sense is undiminished throughout. In his tenacious fidelity to what confronts him, the calibre of empiricism is asserted; the Sceptic is teacher as well as pupil in need of reclamation.

Wordsworth therefore fulfils his promise in *The Prelude* to employ a dramatic story as a means of clarifying and assessing his period of crisis. In doing so he shows its place in his whole poetic evolution, relating *The Borderers* to the Ballads, tracing his descent into the mines of real life. He shows too the double necessity of this move: to combat the impasse of his thinking, and to reveal that the shocks he had suffered were also an awakening. It is not surprising that the most egotistical of poets should pursue his inner self so blatantly in his major chameleon exercise. Yet it is only through the release and exploratory freedom of a more dramatic approach that he could handle this area of his experience at all. And by means of it, he demonstrates convincingly that the taproot of Romantic art, chameleon and egotistical alike, reaches down to the 'solid facts', the sensation of an individual life in its vivid and unique representation of the universal round of experience from youth to age.

4

Coleridge's handling of experience in his best poetry shows him pursuing the Romantic ideal of self-realization, and responding to both creative poles. There are egotistical poems and chameleon ones in his work and some, especially in the 1790s, which are only partial attempts to manage either mode. It is useful to look first at these less successful earlier poems because of what they reveal of his instincts as a poet.

Many of his poems are best described as 'effusions', since this term indicates their general intention and their tone, and we can distinguish both intellectual and emotional effusions. Coleridge breaks into verse to give vent to his ideas when they assail him at a pitch of excitement; and also to commemorate some occasion or relationship which has stirred his feelings. The poems range from the fervid visions of *Religious Musings* (1794) —'Pure Faith! meek Piety!'—to the equally histrionic proliferation of lines to sundry deserving persons and objects: 'to a beautiful spring in a village' ('Once more! sweet stream!'); 'on a Friend' ('Edmund! Thy grave with aching eye I scan!'). Exclamatory and uncertain though this work is, there is more to be learnt from it than a patronizing glance will discover. Coleridge is more gauche in these early verses than Wordsworth ever was, but he is engaged in a genuine creative struggle.

This struggle is a search for method, and it involves an effort to bring together the two instincts of his mind, for theory and for fact. Both impel him towards poetic composition, but expend themselves in quickly exhausted bursts of writing if he merely gives them their head. Shape, direction and the generation of further import in the material is lacking in the effusion as such. But his appetite for the specific sets him on the road to more resonant creation, and leads him towards Romantic method. Crude indications of a desire for some relationship between the worlds of intellect and actuality are to be found in the presence of the Laplanders in *The Destiny of Nations* (1796).

Only incorporated into the poem to provide an instance of the innate power of even the 'rude eye' (62) in responding to nature, and as such rather unconvincing, these travel-book Lapps none the less give the poem a moment's equilibrium amid the welter of theory and capital letters, and provide a hint of anchorage for all the 'wild phantasies' (121) of the young and speculative Coleridge:

> . . . while the snowy blast
> Drifts arrowy by, or eddies round his sledge
> Making the poor babe at its mother's back
> Scream in its scanty cradle . . .
>
> (72–5)

They exist, and though they are quickly lost in 'phantasy', the brief connection of the two worlds is not a casual accident of Coleridge's imagination but an undeveloped symptom of a recurring effort. Another example is provided by the lines which not surprisingly brought ridicule on his head, *To a Young Ass* (1794). Here the poem attempts to make a bitter social criticism by means of an extension from the lot of donkeys to humanity, and there is no reason to suppose Coleridge was not alert to the ironic implications. He lays himself open to mockery not in the plan, but because he handles it clumsily. He is too literal—too factual—about his 'poor little foal of an oppressed race', its ragged coat and its mother,

> Chain'd to a log within a narrow spot
> Where the close-eaten grass is scarcely seen,
> While sweet around her waves the tempting green!

The donkeys are so well observed that their function as properties in a political attack seems only incongruous and where they are intended to administer the final thrust, they rout the idea entirely by the very force of their donkeyhood:

> . . . more musically sweet to me
> Thy dissonant harsh bray of joy would be,
> Than warbled melodies that soothe to rest
> The aching of pale Fashion's vacant breast!

Shadowy personification is no match for such asinine robustness. But the attempt to manage his point by establishing contact between the reader and two animals who can be stroked and fed and heard is indicative of his desire to employ the specific, to relate the fact and the identifiable experience to the abstract formulations of his thought. And here, the specific is more ambitiously yoked to the latter, because the whole poem is envisaged in terms of its donkeys, whereas the Laplanders do not in themselves impinge upon the ideas that surround them. However ludicrous its effects, *To a Young Ass* is a poem relevant to the creative development of Coleridge.

Where *To a Young Ass* fails, another effusion of the mid-nineties, trying a similar approach, *To an Infant* (1795), is more successful. That is, the problem of getting beyond the merely effusive to produce a work of more impact and more design is again tackled by uniting the poem of the specific with the poem of theorizing utterance, and here, the two achieve tolerant cohabitation if nothing more intimate. Coleridge moves to an observation on the infantile character of human nature in this life, but his poem begins with the lines:

> Ah! cease thy tears and sobs, my little Life!
> I did but snatch away the unclasp'd knife . . .

The crying baby seeking comfort in its mother's arms soon becomes 'man's breathing Miniature' and this reflection, 'such a Thing am I' takes the poem on to its final prayer to 'thrice holy Faith':

> Still let me stretch my arms and cling to thee
> Meek nurse of souls through their long Infancy!

The two aspects of the poem, the idea of human life and the domestic episode have come together sufficiently to give it movement and shape, and by working out this relationship, Coleridge has made an effusion into an entity. What aids him more than anything else is his choice of starting point: here we can see another element in his sense of the specific, his alertness to a moment, an immediate stiuation. *To an Infant* is a typical effusion but it is superior in its dramatic feeling for the situation, which gives it a vigorous opening to provide an impetus for the further development of the central idea. Coleridge sees here how to use not merely the fact, as with the Lapps and the donkeys, but the immediate, living fact. He might have exclaimed at the baby being saved from the knife, and its tears;

he might have meditated on human life as a period of depen-
dency, and weakness, and growth—in the mid-nineties he was
very ready to do both. But he is also coming to recognize the
imaginative rewards of combining the two, and more centrally,
to exploit the experienced, specific 'fact', preserving the reaction
to a moment's happening as an emotional and structural aid to
a poem whose purpose goes beyond this immediacy. A much
more sophisticated illustration of this growing tendency of his
mind, and a sign of where it can lead is given by *The Eolian Harp*
of 1795.

The poem begins in the familiar vein of effusion, but the
quality of the occasion, the sensuous and emotional life of it, is
central:

> My pensive Sara! thy soft cheek reclined
> Thus on mine arm, most soothing sweet it is
> To sit beside our Cot, our Cot o'ergrown
> With white-flower'd Jasmin, and the broad-leav'd Myrtle,
> (Meet emblems they of Innocence and Love!)
> And watch the clouds, that late were rich with light,
> Slow saddening round, and mark the star of eve
> Serenely brilliant (such should Wisdom be)
> Shine opposite! How exquisite the scents
> Snatch'd from yon bean-field! and the world *so* hush'd!
> The stilly murmur of the distant Sea
> Tells us of silence.
>   And that simplest Lute,
> Placed length-ways in the clasping casement, hark!
>
>   (1–13)

As the lute is set within the August evening, so the whole poem
is given its keynote by this evocation of scene, mood and object.
Coleridge goes off into his philosophic meditations—already
hinted in the parentheses of the first passage—but he keeps the
poem in contact with the initial serenity and with the 'simplest
Lute': both are transmuted into imagery for a state of mind in
which ideas visit him involuntarily. As he 'tranquil' muses
'upon tranquility' (38), thoughts traverse his brain

> As wild and various as the random gales
> That swell and flutter on this subject Lute!
>
>   (42–3)

The harp is further integrated with the meditations, when its music and the way it occurs offer him the means of reaching and expressing his intuition of life as a relationship between the responding self and all-pervasive spirit (26–33); it gives him too his philosophic climax:

> And what if all of animated nature
> Be but organic Harps diversely fram'd
> That tremble into thought, as o'er them sweeps
> Plastic and vast, one intellectual breeze,
> At once the Soul of each, and God of all?
>
> (44–8)

Far more adroitly than in the 'infant' poem, Coleridge here brings his awareness of an occasion and its properties to bear on the speculations of his ranging mind that apparently discard the world of quiet evenings, beanfields and eolian harps for their own rarified intellectual sphere. But they are, on the contrary, dependent on this localized world for their poetic existence, their disciplined development, and their emotional force: the poem has roots, and the moment depicted has become an essential part of the whole statement, tonally as well as structurally.

This is only one aspect of *The Eolian Harp*'s greater realization of the potential in the close marking of the moment. There are two people in the poem, and because Coleridge directs his words to 'my pensive Sara', the poem is modified by the immediate presence of another person. *The Eolian Harp*, in short, is a monologue; in it Coleridge has discovered the poetic opportunity provided by the relationship between speaker and listener. The material is egotistical, but it is seen from a double angle, the poet's thoughts are checked and his mood more self-consciously pointed by Sara's reactions and her mood. The tone of conversational exchange provides its own kind of movement and shape. End and beginning are brought together as the final section looks at the foregoing theological speculation through the eyes of the 'meek daughter in the family of Christ' (53), and then turns from thought to thanksgiving for 'this Cot, and thee, heart-honoured Maid!' (64), so returning the poem to its starting-point of place, mood and persons. In *The Eolian Harp*, the Coleridge of the mature poems comes into sight.

5

The poetic centre, where all Coleridge's work, mature and immature, meets is his concern with the 'reflex consciousness' and its formation—the transmuting of all 'energies and sufferings' into the further apprehension and experience of self. *Frost at Midnight* contributes to the striving for self-awareness equally with *The Ancient Mariner*; it unites *The Nightingale* and *Kubla Khan*, the *Dejection Ode* and *Christabel*. These poems form groups within this unity, of egotistical and chameleon.

Those often termed 'conversational'—*This Lime-Tree Bower, Frost at Midnight, The Nightingale*, and in its own way, the *Dejection Ode*—are all monologues clearly developed from the poems in the musing, first-person voice of 1795 and 1796, in particular *The Eolian Harp*. In this group, Coleridge exercises his powers of self-articulation. He writes egotistical poetry of a distinctive kind, though it is related to the Wordsworthian technique of relived experience. The monologue is made into an instrument for the poet to know himself in the actual moment of experience, not merely by recollection. Coleridge sustains the poem as its essential agent, the vital consciousness, by whom it is brought into being, but he is also detached as the poet objectifying this experience, which is that of subjectivity itself. He fuses the roles of monologue speaker and listener. The result is not simply soliloquy: the element of detachment is too strong for that, and the double life of the poems is precisely that consciousness of the living self as phenomenon which soliloquy—thinking aloud—seeks to play down or eliminate. Soliloquy uses the faculty of self-awareness, but it does not contemplate this faculty as it operates, and the feat of Coleridge's egotistical poems is to offer this complex of experience and consciousness. At the same time they remain relaxed conversational poems, moving with unforced changes of tempo and carrying their complexity with all the ease of occasional poetry. But their quietness should not deceive: in them Coleridge is presenting Coleridge in creative possession of the reflex consciousness.[1] In

[1] M. Schulz, *The Poetic Voices of Coleridge* (Detroit, 1963), develops a similar argument in his discussion of the 'conversation' poems, and his whole thesis is pertinent to my point of view on the poet. Another relevant and stimulating

their amalgam of sensation and observed fact, they are the fruit of his earlier groping instinct for bringing thinking and feeling into a relationship with the particular moments of life. What he dimly felt then as an aid to more potent and constructive poetic statement here becomes the *raison d'être* of the poems, because it is only through the reality of the particular that the inner life is made accessible and given form, or is brought fully into existence at all. Coleridge's method affirms Romantic empiricism and demonstrates its efficiency for meeting the concept of subjectivity head-on.

The bower under the lime-tree, the quiet cottage on a winter night, the 'old mossy bridge' where the nightingale is heard: all these are more than settings and points of departure. They are described as the occasion become conscious, Coleridge in the act of realizing himself as he is, an element in the fabric of impressions which make the moment's experience. So, as more naïvely in *The Eolian Harp*, he is at the centre and aware of his position:

> Well, they are gone, and here must I remain,
> This lime-tree bower my prison . . .
>
> Come, we will rest on this old mossy bridge . . .
>
> The inmates of my cottage, all at rest
> Have left me to that solitude . . .

The moment is dramatically caught, with an immediacy that carries the whole poem forward as an unfurling experience; and the moment is contemplated, a commentary offered by the poet for his own deeper appreciation of it in its totality—that is, with himself as participant consciousness. All three poems set up tension between the present time and place, and the free ranging of the speculative mind as it sails its own oceans, but the underlying unity prevails as their main statement. Coleridge's experience is one of counterpoint between unlocalized rumination and the individuality of the passing hour. Despite the presence of other persons, the orientation is unreservedly

discussion of these poems is A. Gerard's article, 'The Systolic Rhythm: The Structure of Coleridge's Conversation Poems', *Essays in Criticism*, x (1960), pp. 307-19.

egocentric, there is no sinking of the self and no vicarious
extension of being, just the marshalling of all resources to aug-
ment the illumination of the one significant consciousness.
Coleridge sets himself before his own imagination even as he
peoples his stage with other actors.

To show this by discussing *This Lime-Tree Bower* seems
eccentric, since the occasion for the poem is Coleridge's solitude,
he being unable to accompany his friends on their walk. But the
poem shares the walk, because Coleridge, without setting aside
the place in which he knows himself to be, brings before his
mind's eye a vision of scenes which the others are likely to visit.
The double sense of place increases the richness of the poem,
with its display of the mind's life, and it is also a device which
Coleridge uses to bring home experience in a metaphoric not
just a simple sense. By imagining other people looking at certain
scenes he knows well, he makes his own contemplation of these
places more complete, or possesses it more fully. He realizes his
own experience and such passages as the following bring about
an epiphany:

> ... and there my friends
> Behold the dark green file of long lank weeds,
> That all at once (a most fantastic sight!)
> Still nod and drip beneath the dripping edge
> Of the blue clay-stone.
>
> (16-20)

He sees for his friends, he reacts for them: and knows himself in
doing it. This mirror-recognition is sketched in another of the
apprentice poems, the *Lines to a Young Friend* of 1796, where in
forecasting the delights of the friend's 'domesticating with the
author', Coleridge imagines them responding to the landscape
together, and so realizes the more intensively his own delight in
the local scenes. It is a duplication of sensibility, which has the
effect in these more sophisticated poems, of conferring on the
poet a new mastery by extending his conscious awareness of his
being. Also, by visualizing his friends in other scenes, Coleridge
reaffirms his solitude in the bower; the poem uses their absence
as well as their presence. The poet is helped to know himself
alone, because of the withdrawal of people from him; his
identity is rendered more tangible by this kind of definition. He

experiences his boundaries, and hence his territory of awareness, the more surely because they are walking elsewhere and he is here. The poem begins with this simple and obvious point, and transforms it into a revelation of the mysteries of subjectivity.

The Nightingale is grounded in a concerted act of listening and again in this focusing of more than one consciousness Coleridge's grasp of the experience is made objectively as well as immediately real. Here the friends are present, serving as mirror-images. He finds in them his own condition, and this process is continued by another version of the mirrored self. As Coleridge recalls his experience of a whole grove of nightingales, he relives it not only as his personal memory, but again in his account of the 'gentle maid' who frequents the woods to hear and see the birds as he has done. The double image out of memory is added to the group centred on the present nightingale in the living moment of the poem, and so we have multiple reflections of the listening Coleridge, all generated by himself out of the intensity of his self-awareness in this act and situation. And finally, the almost trance-like concentration is broken by a shift of angle—but only for a last crystallization of the poet's reactions. He adds his evaluation of the experience to bring it to a final clarity. Telling a 'father's tale' of his son's response to the moon and his probable delight in the nightingale too, Coleridge distances his own experience in order to contemplate its significance; he does not really turn the poem away from himself. His hopes that Hartley 'may associate joy' with the night confirms his immediate joy and matures it to its place in a philosophy, which is the necessary culmination for any Coleridgean experience. Rather as Wordsworth regards his sister at the end of *Tintern Abbey*, as a means of reflecting and giving full articulation to earlier aspects of himself, so here Coleridge contemplates his experience-become-philosophy in depicting his son and his hopes for him.

The structure and movement of *Frost at Midnight* is a blend of *The Nightingale* and *This Lime-Tree Bower*. It shares with the latter the acute sense of self which comes on being left alone, so that the incentive of the poem is again to distinguish subjectivity and render it accessible. The flow of Coleridge's thoughts and his registering of his environment spring from this awareness and his curiosity about it. But he is not completely alone; the baby sleeps beside him, and as with the recollections of Hartley in *The Nightingale*, its presence intensifies the father's self-awareness. And by becoming the object of his thoughts and emotions as the poem progresses, the baby serves similarly to bring about a philosophical clarification, without supplanting Coleridge as the poem's centre. First aware of the child's breathing in the 'momentary pauses' of his thought, Coleridge links it with his more objective consciousness of his own presence in the scene: a rhythm of systole and diastole is suggested, as he is alternately immersed within his meditations and then emerges to watch himself so occupied. This is the pulse of subjectivity as it seeks to catch itself in the act, a quest Coleridge pursues as surely in this quiet domestic poem as in the intellectual wrestling bouts of his prose. Feeling through his son, as he did through the absent friends in the bower and his fellow listeners to the nightingale, he inherits his own experience the more completely and in offering it as a gift, he is able to know its value to himself the more fully. It is logical on all levels that the poem ends with the renewed response to the present moment, for throughout Coleridge's effort is to establish contact with himself in this moment, and to comprehend it by placing it within the context of his whole self—his past history and his intellectual universe. Aided by the sleeping baby as agent, but not as rival consciousness, he has achieved this measure of realization.

In each of these poems, then, there is the movement towards self-possession. The final satisfaction of each of them is the sense of entry into the daylight, that which was obscure and half shapeless becoming known and displayed, Coleridge experiencing Coleridge and beholding him. When in 1815 he created Andreas, he retraced the same psychological movement, and confirmed that such a process is central to his imagination.

The direct, or egotistical, approach to the development of 'reflex consciousness' reaches the end of its poetic road for Coleridge in the most candid and unsparing of his mirror-poems, the *Dejection Ode*. The paradoxical nature of this ode has been dwelt upon often enough: a phoenix rising from the ashes of imaginative life, it simultaneously affirms and denies Coleridge's poetic collapse. But the poem is a paradox in a more precise and special sense than this. It shows the egotistical Romantic arrived at his goal, and because of his success, robbed of creative incentive. Or we could say that while *The Nightingale* and *Frost at Midnight* are dynamic, poems pressing forward towards the daylight, the *Dejection Ode* is static. The poet has achieved his desired state and is face to face throughout with his own condition. Instead of the journey to self-discovery there is a steady comprehension, an enduring situation not an act of epiphany, and the creative power is handing over to the critical assessor in consequence. The vital union of subject and object which he struggled for in the early work and found in the last years of the century can no longer be sustained: the quick of the experiencing consciousness is delivered over to the scrutinizing intellect, a surrender which ironically arises out of the very degree of sensitivity he has reached in apprehending that living self.

In so far as the *Ode* records perceptions on the whole nature of consciousness, it is not of course a negative work, but merely a stage in Coleridge's lifelong effort towards understanding in this field. But there is also in it the more negative side of self-recognition as described above, and the function of the Lady as contrasting consciousness emphasizes this aspect. Like Dorothy Wordsworth in *Tintern Abbey*, she possesses what the poet has lost. No longer experiencing the immediate joy of self-contact, nor able to make his poem out of this, Coleridge recovers its force vicariously and sees it the more plainly for what it is:

> To her may all things live, from pole to pole,
> Their life the eddying of her living soul!
>
> (VIII)

Only by this image of his past self can he inject positive vitality into the poem, and at the same time, reconnoitre his present frontiers with accuracy: the awareness of what is gone from him makes clearer what remains. Similarly, the exact observation of the external scene with the movement from it to the inner world and back again—a harmony desired and thwarted each time, helps in this marking of boundaries: self and not self are distinct as present and past self, and yet a necessary intimacy is all the time realized as part of the mesh of experience that composes the moment's consciousness. Coleridge's egotistical poems lead him inevitably to the analytical clarity of the *Ode*: they are really a continuous poetic effort to reach such a peak of observation. But it is one which turns out to be, creatively speaking, above all height, and the *Dejection Ode* stands as an epitaph for his egotistical imagination.

6

Turning to the chameleon side of Coleridge's work, we find that this route to the reflex consciousness was just as instinctively undertaken as the egotistical. His incipient feeling for the monologue has already been suggested, notably in *The Eolian Harp*, and even though the bias here and in the mature conversational poems is towards the direct articulation of the poet's own identity, all help to show Coleridge's dramatic potential. Certainly the people serve him as mirrors: but in a poem where two or more are gathered together, other kinds of development are made possible. Thus fleetingly Sara in *The Eolian Harp* ceases to be the mute listener and becomes an alternative point of view—her August evening exists as well as his; the other Sara in the *Dejection Ode*, though a complementary and dependent figure, stands on the brink of offering a contrasted experience of the night, with Coleridge looking out of her eyes instead of merely recognizing a previous vision of his own by means of her; and the other listeners to the nightingale might themselves speak of what they hear and how they hear it, if he had not chosen that they silently reflect and intensify his own experience. In addition to these possibilities, there are the actual dramatic enterprises of the 1790s. The general disposition towards the chameleon mode is therefore easily established.

Then, when we look at the 1797–1802 period more closely, we see the same phenomenon occurring in Coleridge as in Wordsworth: the stimulus of their association results in a greater appetite for the chameleon mode. A greater readiness, that is, to try out the monologue and the dramatic approach, with their promise of variety of angle, a freer range of experience and hence, crucially, their extension of self-awareness. Wordsworth's response to these opportunities has been illustrated from the

93

Lyrical Ballads themselves—his attempt at character-narrative for *The Thorn*, his role of producer and commentator in *The Idiot Boy*, and as passive but affected listener in *The Last of the Flock*. *The Last of the Flock* is especially noteworthy because of its affinities with the method of Coleridge's most striking chameleon contribution to the volume, *The Ancient Mariner*. Simple though the device is in Wordsworth's poem, it is a sign of the common imaginative impulse acting on both poets at this time: the desire to be wrought upon and so to be illuminated by experience which is not their own at first hand. *The Last of the Flock* and *The Ancient Mariner* are perhaps the two extremes of poetry emerging from this desire, the one a mere sketch, the other dramatically developed and exploited far beyond the unsophisticated encounter of poet and distressed shepherd. But Coleridge's successful poem has its more primitive brethren in his own work, and they testify the more clearly to the existence of such a creative trend because of the very baldness with which they reveal it.

The Old Man of the Alps, first published in March 1798, is the doleful (and very Wordsworthian) story of an only daughter bereft of her lover, losing her mind in consequence, and ultimately drowned in a night of storm, to leave her aged father alone, apparently to wander the Alps in his misery. But the story is presented as a direct account by the old man, beginning in this way:

> Stranger! whose eyes a look of pity shew,
> Say, will you listen to a tale of woe?

Though less importunate than the Mariner, and poetically considerably more crude, the speaker employs the same tactics, and the poet makes the same choice—a story communicated as an experience, not distanced as an impersonal narrative. The relationship of speaker to listener, that is, is important, a structural device to bring about a more immediate engagement with the material by the reader, who identifies himself with the listener, and by the poet, who participates in both roles. This choice and this double exercise by the poet establishes what the Romantic demands in his poetic experience: not only the extension of his emotional range, but the awareness that he has been so extended. The method is experimental, and the result, the new state of mind, is just as necessary for a satisfactory conclusion as the initial excursion into the other consciousness. So Coleridge is at once the Old Man and the accosted Stranger, the actor and the acted upon. The poem remains undeveloped, but the duality is rather more evident in a second example, *The Mad Monk* of 1800, which begins: 'I heard a voice from Etna's side', and follows with the unseen monk's tale of love and murder. After his 'dreary plaint', the poem concludes:

> Here ceas'd the voice. In deep dismay,
> Down thro' the forest I pursu'd my way.

Coleridge thus extracts the maximum emotional content from the situation, recounting as a nightmare the monk's guilt and wretchedness and receiving this experience as the listener, moved to 'deep dismay' by what he hears. Of course these chameleon poems have their egotistical counterparts—Wordsworth in *Simon Lee* and *Resolution and Independence*, for instance, where the shift of mood and its consequence within the poet-as-listener is more central than the process of self-extension into another being. This serves to emphasize the ruling Romantic motive, the urge to self-realization; but the poets are ready to pursue it in the less obvious way as the adventuring chameleon, becoming Alpine wanderers, ruined shepherds, or deranged hermits, as well as—but not instead of—the sensitive recipients of such varied histories.[1] I would claim that one of the most significant poetical devices of both Wordsworth and Coleridge, especially at this period of their joint pioneering, is their use of an encounter and its consequences, first as a relationship of immediacy and dramatic tension between the parties involved, and secondly as a psychological event for the poet himself,

---

[1] Other instances from the *Lyrical Ballads* period include *The Foster-Mother's Tale*, published in that volume, and the long, unfinished poem *The Three Graves*, in which Wordsworth as well as Coleridge had an interest. As Schulz points out (op. cit., pp. 183–4), *The Foster-Mother's Tale* is not just a narrated life-history, but a tale told to a listener; and Coleridge's note to *The Three Graves* shows it as an experiment comparable to *The Thorn*: 'the language was intended to be dramatic; that is suited to the narrator'—he being a village sexton, who speaks 'in a country church-yard, to a traveller whose curiosity had been awakened by the appearence of the three graves. . .'.

whether he responds with chameleon identification or egotistical concentration.

The Ancient Mariner can now be seen as the greatest fruit of a prolific tree. Not at all an isolated phenomenon, it realizes the full potential of the Romantic encounter poem, handled with entire chameleon conviction, yet never sacrificing its awareness of the mesmerized listener to a simpler dramatic effect.

Its place in the *Lyrical Ballads* experiment is well known from Coleridge's account in Chapter XIV of *Biographia Literaria*: it represents the 'supernatural' class of poem, as contrasted with those rooted in subjects of 'ordinary life'. As in the latter poems, the object is to impress the experience upon the reader actively and directly: he is to feel the 'dramatic truth' of these extra-normal occurrences, and so, his emotional capacity being enlarged, his sympathetic grasp of the potentialities of the universe is to be increased. This recourse to empirical methods in order to explore qualities of feeling beyond the ordinary range should be recognized as the major event for nineteenth-century poetry that it is. It marks the moment when the Miltonic presentation of the supernatural scene gives way to the Romantic investigation of the supernatural experience, an approach which leads on to such Victorian researches as *In Memoriam*, Hopkins's *Wreck of the Deutschland*, Patmore's Eros and Psyche odes, Browning's *Caliban upon Setebos* and *Abt Vogler*. Faith in another world is neither the central, nor the starting point for this poetry: poets and readers alike share the experience of the Wedding Guest, shocked by the intrusion of unsuspected dimensions of feeling into a domestic, orderly universe. Carried out into the vast oceans by the Mariner's tale, what he learns is more about himself; by the end of the poem he has emerged from his parochial shell as from a chrysalis. This change of being is the heart of the poem, and it is the force within what is loosely called Victorian 'religious poetry'. The journey is primarily into the unfolding psyche, the discoveries those of Coleridge's reflex consciousness. A Christian may add that the goal is God, but the poetic energy of the century is generated by the Coleridgean perception that a God is the ultimate of self-realization, and this is sufficient for the creative vision. Victorian and Romantic, for all their differences, are engaged in a single effort of imagination whose strength is not yet exhausted.

The Ancient Mariner cannot be estimated justly without such an acknowledgement of its seminal character as well as of its immediate context. By 1817, Coleridge himself was increasingly aware of the poem's nature as an attempt to supply a poetic answer to a metaphysician's problem. This is shown by his placing the following quotation from Thomas Burnet's *Archaeologiae Philosophicae* as an epigraph to later editions of the poem:

I can well believe that there are more invisible than visible natures in the universe. But who shall describe their family? Who set forth the orders, kinships, respective stations, and functions of each? What do they do? Where is their habitation? The human mind has always sought after, but never attained, knowledge of these things. Meanwhile it is desirable, I grant, to contemplate in thought, as if in a picture, an image of a greater and better world; lest the mind, accustoming itself to the minutiae of daily life, should become too narrow, and lapse into mean thoughts. But at the same time we must be vigilant for truth, and set a limit, lest we fail to distinguish certain from uncertain, day from night.

Coleridge maintains that the bridge from visible to invisible is the human mind itself, in the first place because of its very ability to conceive these other natures; and further, he seeks to remove the problem of ignorance and vain speculation by exploiting the mind's readiness to assent to other kinds of conviction besides that of intellectual proof. That is, he sees the imagination as the agency which ranges beyond the 'minutiae' but which at the same time authenticates and safeguards this adventuring, because of its method of empirical demonstration. The minutiae are not abandoned. The 'dramatic truth' of experience and the full exploration of the psyche is the route he proposes as the poet's alternative to the philosopher's impasse.

With so much implicit in the poem, and its testimony that a new phase of imaginative research was begun, the success of it as a ballad is the more astonishing. But on all levels, from that of sheer story-impact to the deepest probings into reality, the relationship of Guest to Mariner is the secret of this triumph. Coleridge's handling of it gives the poem its confident narrative grip while enabling its essence, the transformation of experience into valuable perception, to be boldly, yet subtly, shown. What is offered is the actual process of strange experience being broken down, absorbed, transformed into awareness. The whole cycle of assimilation from the immediacy of the disruptive experience itself to the assessed result when it has become a part of the victim's psychological organism is simultaneously suggested. Events are at once distant and of the moment, there is an interplay of recalled, hauntingly familiar and comprehended emotion with the shock of unknown, new and violent feeling. The poem leaves the Mariner appeased, the Guest disturbed. The Guest shoots his albatross as he shrinks from the hand laid on him, and is a 'sadder and a wiser man', embarking in his turn on the Odyssey of purgation and assimilation as the Mariner arrives again at his harbour of self-knowledge.

Christabel shows signs of a complex ambition comparable to *The Ancient Mariner*, and it is, initially at least, another encounter poem, with the active presence of a narrator-observer, again, and more closely, resembling *The Idiot Boy*. The questioning voice of the latter poem, 'what means this bustle, Betty Foy?' is paralleled as 'the lovely lady, Christabel' is watched:

> What makes her in the wood so late,
> A furlong from the castle gate?

And Coleridge adds his own innovation, asking and answering in choric commentary:

> Is the night chilly and dark?
> The night is chilly, but not dark.

As Christabel encounters Geraldine, this voice becomes emotionally charged—'Jesu, Maria, shield her well'—and the cue for the chameleon operation is given, with Geraldine as Mariner to the innocent Guest of Christabel. In this poem, however, the relationship is not so purely managed, for here, Coleridge sets himself also to handle a still-developing action, and not merely to manipulate a retrospective narrative where further action is confined to the emotional evolution in the mind of the listener. Because of this, the narrator-voice, instead of holding the reader in contact with the scene and so providing one shade of response, one angle on the whole experience, must here become more

narrowly functional in conveying information. The more complicated the plot, the more is it reduced to this role, and the less
it is free to act as a creative instrument in the poet's multiple
awareness of his material. The tension of the encounter is consequently lower: the focus on the relationship of Christabel and
Geraldine is less sharp, and neither the strange seas of Geraldine's nature nor the enthralment of Christabel are explored
with that painful enlarging of sensibility which *The Ancient
Mariner* achieves in poet and reader. The poem can only be
admitted to the heights of chameleon creation on the strength
of some scenes. Its unfinished state and its increasing commitment to plot both hamper it: it lacks unity, and it threatens to
run to detail. These drawbacks in themselves underline the
character of Romantic chameleon work. First, the unity of an
experience is an essential feature, of the encounter poems in
particular. From the simplicity of *The Last of the Flock* to the
fulfilled potential of *The Ancient Mariner*, a complete movement
of mind from initiation into a new emotional proposition to its
final absorption is the hallmark. A chemical change takes place:
the individual is not as he was before, he has acquired this
experience and he now knows it as a part of himself. He must
hereafter live with it. In *Christabel*, the heroine is not accom-
panied through this testing journey: no one therefore emerges
sadder or wiser; the sea-change has not been suffered. And
secondly, the necessity for fact to be irradiated with the 'ideal
light', as Coleridge himself would call it, is brought out by this
poem's lack of that light as it progresses. Romantic empiricism
is not to be interpreted as a passive observer's dependence upon
specific, concrete material; the experiencing mind is the pivot
always, and if this awareness loses its central position in the
poems, their life is gone. Coleridge's instinct to portray the
Laplanders on their sledge, and to present a young donkey with
its mother is only a search for the best means of conveying and
realizing the thought which animates his consciousness. In the
Prospectus to *The Friend* he remarks on his 'habit' of 'noting
down . . . whatever had occurred to me from without, and all
the Flux and Reflux of my Mind within itself', and in the
creative recognition of the intimate relationship of 'without'
and 'within' his poems come into being, the egotistical *Frost at*

Midnight and the chameleon *Ancient Mariner* alike. Hence in the later narrative of *Christabel* where this relationship is weakened, the power is diminished.

7

There remains *Kubla Khan.* Coleridge's whole career, especially his way towards the central years of poetic achievement, is a revealing demonstration of the nature of Romantic effort, its problems and its successes. This is not surprising, his being the mind most intellectually aware of its vigilant preoccupation with the issues of identity and consciousness. His writing *Zapolya* and *Biographia Literaria* in close succession speaks for his continued compulsion to study the phenomenon of growth towards the 'reflex consciousness': Andreas seeking to know his name, and discovering his royalty is the creative counterpart of that account of 'life and literary opinions' which develops into a formidable exhibition of a mind turning upon itself to behold its own being. The publication of *Kubla Khan* with *Christabel* in this same period, 1816, is not irrelevant to these signs that a fresh tide of such awareness was flowing in him. His prefixed note of explanation reads like one of his habitual observations on the history of events without and processes within, and shows an active interest in the piece as a clue, a psychological specimen, even while he denies it poetic quality. As a part of his mind, a mirror of the 'ideal', that is, he accepts it; it falls in with his main line of investigation. But this is not sufficient to qualify it as a poem in his eyes, an interesting distinction, and one which points once more to the persistent effort of his imagination to reconcile 'ideal' and fact. *Kubla Khan* to its creator lacks the grit of the world and remains disembodied vision, missing the incarnation essential for poetic life. Mind is not discovered here within the realized experience: it remains known only as 'a vision in a dream'.

Coleridge's distinguishing 'psychological curiosity' from 'poetic merit' is valid at the level of the Romantic imagination we are considering. His reason for the distinction is best understood in the light of the deeper impulses of that imagination. But this does not mean that his verdict must be entirely accepted: rather, *Kubla Khan* may be regarded as the poem of apotheosis in which the creative centre, the subjective core of consciousness celebrates and confronts itself. In this sense, it is a 'pure' creative act, a feat of self-recognition by the undirected dreaming mind, corresponding to the *Dejection Ode* on the waking plane. The poem is strictly neither egotistical nor chameleon: it is the fountainhead of those twin creative streams, the strange basic experience of self from which these impulses of exploration arise. Its visionary scenes are the means by which Coleridge touches the quick of the subjective experience. We return to his statement that 'the great end and purpose of all [the human soul's] energies and sufferings is the growth of that reflex consciousness'. His creative exertion is to capture alive this process of transmutation from the turbulence of emotional experience to the peace of deepened perception. In *Kubla Khan*, the darkness and the 'ceaseless turmoil' of rock, fountain and river are brought into patterned relationship with serenity, light and calm—'gardens bright with sinuous rills', the poised and 'sunny' dome, with 'caves of ice'. The impressions oppose each other, interact, meet in reconciliation; their 'meanings' beyond this active dialogue are less important. The poem's climax is its achievement of the 'miracle of rare device' and the delight in this accomplishment is a tonal feature supporting the structural sense of an ultimate goal of repose won from an agony of passionate exertion. The psyche thus exposes in its own picture-language its travail and its rewards, the 'energies and sufferings' becoming self-knowledge, transfigured to clarity and the permanence of an inviolable possession.

The poem's final section confirms this ecstatic recognition of the profound movement of the psyche in creation, its 'deep delight' in attempting to convert the vision into form:

> . . . with music loud and long
> I would build that dome in air,
> That sunny dome! those caves of ice!

His other poems—and his prose—show him at his building; and it is fitting that *Kubla Khan*, as the vision of creative consciousness *in esse* should conclude with a shift of angle which in a simple, almost schematic, way summarizes the whole activity and purpose of that consciousness. In the last lines, Coleridge sees himself in the creative rapture, and thus the poem achieves an objective grasp of self out of its complete subjection to the direct experience of the inner life. The transition takes place in three stages. There is no subject, no consciousness reported in the poem as far as the climax of the 'miracle of rare device': here the immersion in the actual subjective vision is complete—this is the mind's 'continuousness'. Then, in the first section of the conclusion, the personal voice is introduced: this is the pivotal stage between instinctive self-experience and the full 'reflex consciousness'. Coleridge—like Andreas—is aware of himself acting and being, striving to be at once subject and object: 'I would build that dome in air'. And lastly:

> And all who heard should see them there
> And all should cry, Beware! beware!
> His flashing eyes, his floating hair!
> Weave a circle round him thrice,
> And close your eyes with holy dread,
> For he on honey dew hath fed
> And drunk the milk of Paradise.

He is seer and spectator, knowing his vision—himself—with the fullness of detachment as well as in the intensely charged immediacy of subjective sensation. To the Romantic imagination such an entry into possession of the reflex consciousness is the human apotheosis, a sunrise in the mind. It is the moment of 'holy dread'.

IV

EGOTISTICAL AND CHAMELEON: BYRON, SHELLEY AND KEATS

The Revolt of Islam was ... a genuine picture of my own mind.
Shelley to Godwin

And feeling, in a poet, is the source
Of others' feeling; but they are such liars,
And take all colours—like the hands of dyers.
Don Juan

THE WORLD of Byron's poems is the world of their hero, or, sometimes, their spokesman; setting and action and all other elements are means by which the identity of the central consciousness is made tangible and accessible. This consciousness is the poem's creative centre, and just as in the work of his fellow poets, it is amenable to discussion in egotistical and chameleon terms; in the major poems in particular, the correspondence with Wordsworth's pattern is inescapable. *Childe Harold* and *Don Juan* stand in a polar relationship as do *The Prelude* and *The Excursion*. It is too simple for us to call the one egotistical, the other chameleon, but broadly, these categories indicate the character of the poems and establish the positive connection between the two most obvious phases of Byron's career—a connection which has not been commonly accepted. The move from Harold to Juan has been labelled the swing from sentimentalist to cynic, or melodramatist to sophisticate, but it is a far more valuable and imaginatively rich development than these facile assessments allow. So indeed is Byron's whole poetic progress: with his own flamboyance he follows the Romantic route, responding to its challenge and discovering its potential equally with the Coleridge and Shelley he admired and the Keats and Wordsworth he abused.

Before approaching *Childe Harold* and *Don Juan*, it is useful to establish the underlying continuity of his imaginative life from other material. Byron as a narrative poet and author of monologues has not received much twentieth-century acclaim; the lure of the bold black eye and tortured mien of Conrad the Corsair has long since evaporated, while *The Lament of Tasso* and *The Prophecy of Dante* arouse no passionate regard. Yet Byron persistently turned to this kind of composition, and the poems are too enterprising to dismiss as pot-boilers, or the off-scourings of a brimming but casual imagination. The fact that some of them, notably the group of 'Eastern Tales' which belong to his days in London society, were dashed off without premeditation in some ways adds to their interest; this is the spontaneous response of his creative energies, betraying habitual preoccupations as a waterspout draws up the ocean depths. They, with *Parisina* and *The Prisoner of Chillon*, are the clues to show the course from the first to the second part of *Childe Harold*; and the later monologues and narratives—*The Lament of Tasso* (1817), *Mazeppa* (1818), *The Prophecy of Dante* (1819), and *The Island* (1823)—cover the move from *Childe Harold* to *ottava rima*.

Far-fetched though the comparison may seem, the Eastern Tales are Byron's *Lyrical Ballads*. As Wordsworth and Coleridge experimented with the telling of tales, the presentation and mastery of experience, so too does Byron in *The Giaour, The Bride of Abydos, The Corsair* and *Lara*. Or course he caught the fashion and gave an eager public his blend of the favourite Gothic and oriental flavours. But he was engaged in a creative struggle which makes these materials yield much more than popular novelties. The poems reveal the tension of his highly charged egotistical and chameleon impulses, and the centrality of this situation to his poetic life. His whole relation with these poems is complex. When speculation spread on the likelihood of the Giaour and Conrad being autobiographical, his comments, whether in public prefaces or private journals, were equivocal,[1] while of *The Bride of Abydos* he insisted that he wrote it as a refuge from the 'reality' of immediate circumstances, but at the same time he saw it as a revival of past experiences, involving 'observations from existence'.[2] Accompanying the ambiguity of his statements about his own part as actor as well as story-teller is his search for an angle of presentation: here

[1] See *Poetry of Lord Byron*, ed. E. H. Coleridge, iii, p. 225 and n.
[2] ibid., p. 150.

The Thorn, The Idiot Boy, The Last of the Flock, The Foster-Mother's Tale and *The Old Man of the Alps* become relevant. Byron is no more prepared to offer an impersonal account in an anonymous third-person voice than Wordsworth and Coleridge. Whether the material is in any sense autobiographical or not, the poet is intimately engaged with it; he is carrying out an assimilating operation, needing in his poem not only a narrator, but preferably a speaker and a listener, with the further possibility of dramatic enactment to the point of identification. This is the pressure of chameleon exploration, and in Byron it is intensified by the urge to master aspects of his temperament which haunt him. I shall discuss his self-brooding in relation to *Childe Harold*, but his remarks on the Tales and especially their heroes testify to his fear of powers of feeling within himself and also to a compulsion to investigate this dark ego. Thus, while there may well be no foundation in personal fact as far as the actual stories go, when he says the Tales are 'written . . . much from existence', he states the exact imaginative situation. He writes from his sense of his own being, from the 'darkest and brightest colours'[1] of his memory, not as a nostalgic and boastful tourist of the Orient, but as a Romantic poet seeking to understand himself in depth. His undoubted pleasure at seeing himself as the enigma of London does not detract from the psychological interest of the mysterious hinting in his journal, appertaining to the view that he was the cause of the fair Leila's fate: to 'describe the *feelings* of *that* situation was impossible—it is *icy* even to recollect them'.[2] Whatever 'that situation' may or may not have been, there are 'feelings' that appal and dominate. The *Giaour* and its companion pieces venture into the jungle where these passions and experiences lurk, their mission to capture and bring them forth; and their author is at once the pursuer and the pursued.

The Giaour grew in fits and starts—a 'rattlesnake' of a poem[3] —and it grew as a series of impressionistic scenes rather than as a coherent narrative. Even when finished, it has no clear sequence of events, and this is the first sign of the poet's dissatisfaction with the notion that his purpose should be to tell a tale plainly. His search for an approach offering immediacy, an experience

[1] ibid.   [2] ibid., p. 76.   [3] ibid., p. 77.

in place of a report in the *Lyrical Ballads* tradition, is revealed in the poem's complicated structure involving four 'voices'. After an introductory section of direct address from poet to reader, the story is begun by an eyewitness and incidental actor in the drama, a Turkish fisherman, but is then passed over to another observer, a monk in the monastery where the Giaour sought refuge, and finally, the pattern of speaker and listener is employed as the Giaour tells his own story to the monk. For a careless piece of melodrama, this is a surprisingly elaborate work: as an example of exploratory imaginative tactics, it is far more comprehensible.

As a result of these tactics, the Giaour's history may be chronologically obscure, but his experience is vivid. It is lit up from these several angles, and the poem is coherent because its various scenes find their centre in its hero's consciousness; there is therefore a structural logic to be discerned. The poem adopts the chameleon mode of emotional exploration, and its object is to examine the various energies, moods and qualities of the Giaour. The fisherman registers the dynamic force and violence of his presence: 'who thundering comes on blackest steed?' (180), and the monk, the 'stony air Of mixed defiance and despair' (907–8). But Byron's own position in the poem brings an additional element to it. After speaking in the tone of general mediation at the beginning, and then merging into the voices of fisherman and monk, he reappears to join the latter in the role of direct observer of the Giaour in his later years, and from this development the poem takes its final step to identification with the hero. The poet confronts his hero before he looks out of his eyes: and in so doing, he sets a pattern which is followed in the studies of this character which succeeded *The Giaour*—most markedly in *The Corsair* and *Lara*. Byron analyses the character as a man before a mirror, objectively aware of what he sees, yet intimately related to it; he beholds, and he is. As observer, he diagnoses:

> The keenest pangs the wretched find
>   Are rapture to the dreary void,
> The leafless desert of the mind,
>   The waste of feelings unemployed.
>   (957–60)

And as the Giaour, he speaks of what the observer beholds:

> The withered frame, the ruined mind,
> The wrack by passion left behind,
> A shrivelled scroll, a scattered leaf,
> Seared by the autumn blast of Grief!
>
> (1253–6)

In these early Tales, therefore, the signs of a complex egotistical and chameleon intermingling are already apparent. The hero's nature is to be contemplated and recognized as well as experienced: this is the imperative behind the growth of the rattlesnake and the repetition of the same darkly brooding personage in the succeeding poems also. But after *The Giaour*, these preoccupations are wedded more smoothly and directly to narrative progress. Stories are told in *The Corsair* and *Lara*, *The Siege of Corinth* and *Parisina*, while *The Bride of Abydos* has a story within a story. But in all these poems, the same hero is present, whether he is the dominant person, as in *The Corsair* and *Lara*, or whether his characteristics are put before us in other ways. For instance, in *Parisina*, a beautifully managed narrative with few concessions to the melodrama which weakens the others, the familiar issues of destruction and guilt are present, but shared between the two important characters of the poem, Hugo and his father Azo. Each is a chameleon creation, the sympathy of the poet being clearly involved with the predicament of both. The Giaour's violent obsessions are translated into terms of law and a more sophisticated social setting. In *The Siege of Corinth* on the other hand, volcanic passion explodes in the description of a city's annihilation, its cathedral blown apart with a 'thousand shapeless things all driven In cloud and flame athwart the heaven' (xxxiii). The hero of this poem, Alp, is recognizable as a descendant of the Giaour, and the action to which he gives his aid serves as the objective correlative of the forces within. Through all these poems runs a primary psychological problem: the tyranny of the fiercer over the gentler emotions. The stories enact the baffled realization that the strong prevail by destruction and that love is forced to give way to this. Bitterness, futile remorse, and further destruction—including self-destruction—then follow. The weakness of female portrayal in the Tales is not accounted for by assuming that the poet was content to follow the Gothic convention of pure but pallid women. It is an expression of what the problem is, and of his motives of exploration in writing the Tales, just as the repeated studies of the hero, with the shifts of angle and of method, also speak for an imaginative engagement with the material going well beyond the hope for easy success. Byron dramatizes what he has found, however obscurely and under whatever circumstances, within his own psyche. He acknowledges conflicts within himself, not just in *Childe Harold*, but in these poems from 1812–16, where the egotistical mirror-analysis and the dramatic realization of the energies involved form aspects of a moral inquisition. Perhaps in a more orthodox way than his fellow-poets, Byron is concerned with values, re-interpreting but not dispensing with the traditional Christian sense of good and evil. But his empirical approach to this problem is wholly Romantic.

2

The year 1816 is in some ways a watershed in Byron's poetic career: his mature writing dates from this period, the continuation of *Childe Harold* being the major sign that this is so. But his narrative poems show the development too, and bring out the essential connection of the later with the earlier Byron. Marking the arrival at a crisis of vision is the poem *Darkness*, a sombre apocalyptic narrative depicting the last hours of the human race. This is the inevitable step beyond *The Siege of Corinth*, expressing the ultimate negation, when 'no Love was left' and 'the World was void'. If the world is void, so too is self. The flat reporting of this poem exactly conveys the complete sterility of such a situation, the bankruptcy of those funds of Romantic creative energy which can be fed by pain, but cannot survive experience burnt to ashes. The death of poetry too is portrayed here.

But a phoenix was to rise. For the rest of his writing years, to 1823, Byron ascends from this desolation, and his course is charted by five poems which serve, like the earlier Tales, though less crudely, to reveal the movements and currents of his imagination. Four of these poems show his adoption of the monologue proper, after the somewhat tentative utterances of the Giaour and his fellows: *The Prisoner of Chillon* (1816), *The Lament of Tasso* (1817), *Mazeppa* (1818) and *The Prophecy of Dante* (1819); and *The Island* of 1823 shows an almost startling family likeness to the earlier Tales—startling that is if the idea of continuity of imagination in Byron is a novel and unexpected thought to us.

The move into monologue is an interesting aspect of his development. He chooses it as the vehicle for continuing his study of the suffering mind—what it may endure and how it realizes its suffering, becoming more fully itself in the consciousness of its own experience. The monologue offers the sense of living and knowing simultaneously, and as such it is the ideal medium for the Romantic poets. Byron's four heroes support this general conclusion and reveal at the same time Byron's individual use for the form. All four speakers are men imprisoned: two literally, Bonivard the patriot rebel in the dungeon of Chillon, and Tasso in his cell at Ferrara; Mazeppa tells of his nightmare ride strapped helpless to a horse's back, and Dante speaks as

> An exile, saddest of all prisoners,
> Who has the whole world for a dungeon strong,
> Seas, mountains, and the horizon's verge for bars,
> Which shut him from the sole small spot of earth
> Where,—whatsoe'er his fate—he still were hers,
> His country's . . .
>
> (IV, 131–6)

These monologues are therefore variations on a theme, four facets of a common dilemma. The same theme preoccupies Byron throughout *Childe Harold*, and its urgency to him is demonstrated by his having recourse to the chameleon as well as the egotistical way of exploring it. We may contrast the tormented hero of the Tales with the hero-figures of 1816 to 1819: the former's was a warped, guilty suffering, often still caught up in action of a disruptive and murderous nature. Now, the suffering belongs to the innocent, and what is being discovered is a new kind of strength, that of the mind and body enduring unbroken despite the efforts of destructive power opposed to them. Humanity is still in shackles, but in these later poems, there is a discovery of freedom. Here is the clue to Byron's imaginative history; these poems signpost his route from *Childe Harold* to the work written out of hard-won freedom, *Don Juan*.

A comparison of *The Prisoner of Chillon* with *The Lament of Tasso* will show his direction clearly, for in each poem the role of prisoner is differently regarded. In Bonivard and Tasso, the poet formulates first his intense feeling for man in chains and secondly his perception of the resource with which the bonds are resisted. The earlier poem concentrates mainly on the sensations of imprisonment, though even here we can recognize the seeds of the more positive reactions which come to fruition in Tasso. *The Prisoner of Chillon* is a poem where emotion is physically realized; suffering is conveyed in terms of worn stone, the 'dark vault' of a 'living grave', a heavy, deep, damp place made into a 'double dungeon' by being below the lake with the 'massy' weight of water 'knocking' overhead (VI). Bonivard traces the stages of his decline—periods of indifference, hallucination, moods of vision and hope, glimpses of the outer world which failed to rouse his atrophied heart. The poem ends with his observations on his state of mind when release finally came:

> These heavy walls to me had grown
> A hermitage—and all my own!
> And half I felt as they were come
> To tear me from a second home:
> With spiders I had friendship made,
> And watched them in their sullen trade
> Had seen the mice by moonlight play,
> And why should I feel less than they?
> We were all inmates of one place,
> And I, the monarch of each race,
> Had power to kill—yet, strange to tell!
> In quiet we had learned to dwell;
> My very chains and I grew friends,
> So much a long communion tends
> To make us what we are:—even I
> Regained my freedom with a sigh.
>
> (XIV)

If we remember the earlier narrative poems, there is more to these lines than the final bitterness of a man robbed of his capacity for living, worn down to a timid shadow of human individuality. The destructive demon has been tamed; the 'power to kill' has given way before a new compassion and sympathy: 'in quiet we had learned to dwell'. Only with mice and spiders, certainly, and it would probably be as legitimate to find a note of irony in Bonivard's surprise at this development as it would to feel the pathos in his condition. But by his entry into the being of this captive, descending to the nadir of the experience, Byron has won the rewards of this chameleon act: he has discovered the turning point, those fruits of submission which precede and make resistance possible. What Bonivard likewise has discovered is a capacity for self-extension: mice and spiders—equivalents of the Ancient Mariner's water-snakes—may be sympathetically contemplated, they are not merely alien, objective phenomena. Love emerges tentatively as a rudimentary power, bringing for this prisoner a small area of meaning and personal choice.

With his imagination working in this way, it is not surprising that Byron in the following year was disposed to believe the legend of Tasso's imprisonment for presuming to love Leonora, a princess. His monologue depends on his acceptance of the legend and the contrast with Bonivard is strong. Tasso's suffering is less concretely realized, there is less physical weighting to the poem, but his predicament is more precisely evaluated. He is not dominated by his surroundings as Bonivard is; he is aware of them in their influence on him and in the power of his mind and emotions to resist them. Insanity surrounds him and he knows it; sitting in a 'Lazar house of many woes' (IV), he hears 'the long and maniac cry of minds and bodies in captivity' (III),

> Where laughter is not mirth, nor thought the mind,
> Nor words a language, nor ev'n men mankind . . .
> And each is tortured in his separate hell—
> For we are crowded in our solitudes—
> Many, but each divided by the wall,
> Which echoes Madness in her babbling moods,
> While all can hear, none heed his neighbour's call—
> None! save that One, the veriest wretch of all,
> Who was not made to be the mate of these,
> Nor bound between Distraction and Disease.
>
> (IV)

III

It does not strain these lines to universalize them. Tasso's is a vision of the chafing human spirit, 'not made to be the mate of these', vividly aware of the proximity and threat of chaos, yet also demonstrating a degree of freedom and, while this awareness lasts, the power to refute what 'madness in her babbling moods' would assert, that there is no hope. Tasso repudiates madness, even though he has his moods of desperation. He has two resources: or at least, Byron's Tasso has. Another adjustment to fact the poet makes is to begin the monologue at the moment when Tasso completes *La Gerusalemme Liberata*, although the historical Tasso wrote his epic many years before his imprisonment. This is significant licence, and emphasizes that Byron is adopting dramatic voices to capture his own perceptions rather than to act as history's ventriloquist. His point here is to show one route to freedom which captivity cannot close. Creative powers defy the dungeon:

> . . . I have battled with mine agony
> And made me wings wherewith to overfly
> The narrow circus of my dungeon wall . . .
>
> (I)

Tasso has delighted in his 'young creation' and working on it has 'wooed' him 'from himself'. Its completion grieves him, yet the monologue immediately strikes again the note of defiance, resolution, and innocence:

> . . . in the innate force
> Of my own spirit shall be found resource.
> I have not sunk, for I had no remorse,
> Nor cause for such . . .
>
> (II)

His crime or his madness is to love Leonora: 'thou wert beautiful and I not blind'. This passion which caused his suffering at the same time sustains him, and the monologue develops this theme. What is communicated to us is a capacity for spiritual exaltation, a dominant condition which preserves the mind intact whatever the assaults on it and whatever the trials of the flesh. We are far from the unslain spiders of Chillon, yet the poet is moving connectedly and progressively, searching for and finding evidence for the triumph of integrity and the individual over hostile, disintegrating circumstance. Destructiveness does not necessarily annihilate, nor even in any real sense win. This is the trend of Byron's imagination in the years of the later Cantos of *Childe Harold*, and in that poem he fights his way to this position most explicitly, and egotistically. But in these monologue exercises, there is vivid and immediate testimony of what is happening. In Canto IV of *Childe Harold*, written within two months of *The Lament of Tasso*, he describes a brilliant sun-bow 'serene' amid the 'distracted waters' of a cataract (LXXII), and compares the sight to 'Love watching Madness with unalterable mien'. The line summarizes the dramatic statement of the monologue, and confirms the link of a common vision between the two kinds of poem he was writing at this time.

Continuity of vision is also apparent between *The Prophecy of Dante* and the work of 1817. Dante embodies the strength of the lover and the creative mind more positively than Tasso, and the poem has particular affinities with the sections in Canto IV of *Childe Harold* where works of art are acclaimed as victories over the despoiling tendencies of the lower nature. Man can make as well as wreck, that Canto asserts, and the 1819 monologue consolidates this position with its more concentrated method of approaching the theme through the dramatic realization of the individual situation.

Because they show such close relations with *Childe Harold*, it is evident that these monologues contain an element of mirror-writing as did the earlier studies of the Giaour-type hero. Byron's Tasso and Dante are his creations and can be more accurately defined as self-projections rather than as self-extensions, which the more outright chameleon exercises deserve to be called. But the distinction remains: the two modes of composition are employed as Byron, according to Romantic custom, develops his effort to assess humanity through his own experience. If there is in his work a particularly intricate movement and interplay between the imaginative poles, this is not surprising in view of his unique personal response to them and his reflection of their tension in his life.

He showed in *The Prisoner of Chillon*, however, that he is capable of complete chameleon submission to the imagined

experience. In *Mazeppa* (1818), he repeats this feat. This is a
poem as physical and three-dimensional as the *Prisoner*, concen-
trating on sensations of pain, shock, violent speed and animal
energy, all intermingled as these experiences are for Mazeppa.
But it is also in the line of encounter poems: there is a context
for the narrative, and a listener is a feature of the poem.
Mazeppa speaks because of a specific provocation to do so, and
his reliving of his youthful adventure is emphasized as a return
to past scenes brought about by the immediate situation, itself
dramatic in impact. The story is told to Charles XII of Sweden
during his flight after the battle of Pultowa. Worn out, the
party bivouacs for the night, and Mazeppa is invited by the
king to tell his tale. Although there is exploitation of a double
time sense, this is no Ancient Mariner rooting his chosen audience
to the spot—Charles is hoping to be soothed and relaxed by
listening, and he is rewarded: by the end, 'the king had been an
hour asleep' (xx). This is a *Don Juan* touch, a sign of the poetic
advent at this time of the ironic Byron, and it serves as a neat
parody on the favoured Romantic device of speaker working
on listener, disturbing his consciousness to a profound degree.

But the reader is not asleep by the end of the tale: the shift of
consciousness takes place in the poet and his audience, however
uncooperative the exhausted king may be in his role of wedding
guest. Further, story and context are unified, because each is
concerned with endurance and strain; the suffering of a retreating army, the helplessness of a boy tied to a stampeding horse
are both situations of trial in which more is learnt about the
human fabric.

The rhythm of Mazeppa's ride is one of death and of rebirth,
three times experienced. Punished for loving the wife of his
master, he, 'a stripling of a page' (VIII), was sent careering
across the vast stretches of central Europe, his 'bound and slender frame' (XI) merely acting as a goad to the unbroken horse.
They fly recklessly on and on over the timeless plain and through
the forest, faster than wolves, while the ropes chafe swollen limbs
and the speed is inseparable from delirium, until

> The skies spun like a mighty wheel;
> I saw the trees like drunkards reel . . .

> I felt the blackness come and go
> And strove to wake; but could not make
> My senses climb up from below . . .
> (XIII)

Then comes the first resurgence as the horse bears him across a river. This return to sensation is as vividly presented. 'Cold, numb and giddy' he feels the throbs and pangs of life coursing through him once more as the water revives him—'and with a temporary strength My stiffened limbs were rebaptized' (XIV). They gallop on, but gradually the horse's energy is sapped, and the poem again handles the dying fall. But here, the countering wave of rebirth coincides with this spent force, and Byron modulates from death to a vision of fresh life with moving success. The flagging horse takes its last strides through a new morning world:

> Up rose the sun; the mists were curled
> Back from the solitary world
> Which lay around—behind—before . . .
> . . . Man nor brute
> Nor dint of hoof, nor print of foot
> Lay in the wild luxuriant soil—
> No sign of travel, none of toil—
> The very air was mute . . .
> (XVII)

As the horse falls, 'out from the forest prance a trampling troop', and this innocent world is populated with its rightful inhabitants:

> A thousand horse, and none to ride!
> With flowing tail, and flying mane,
> Wide nostrils never stretched by pain,
> Mouths bloodless to the bit or rein,
> And feet that iron never shod,
> And flanks unscarred by spur or rod,
> A thousand horse, the wild, the free,
> Like waves that follow o'er the sea,
>   Came thickly thundering on,
> As if our faint approach to meet!
>   . . . they saw him stoop,
> They saw me strangely bound along

His back with many a bloody thong.
They stop—they start—they snuff the air,
Gallop a moment here and there,
Approach, retire, wheel round and round,
Then plunging back with sudden bound . . .
They snort—they foam—neigh—swerve aside,
And backward to the forest fly,
By instinct, from a human eye.

(XVII)

Mazeppa is a poem celebrating the free grace of physical being, and the birth of a realization of this out of impotent suffering. Its chameleon power lies in its combined apprehension of human and animal life, penetrating to the quick of each. The primary rhythm of the poem, from a near death to a renewed perception of life is repeated in the final movement, again in terms of Mazeppa's own recovery from seeming extinction. 'Chained to the chill and stiffening steed', he once more experiences the waves of darkness and the 'icy sickness' as his senses come and go (XVIII). He wakes to find himself rescued, and the vision he first sees and finds real is the human equivalent of the wild horses—'a slender girl, long haired and tall' with 'black eyes so wild and free' (XIX). He was 'brought into life again', and finally ruled the Cossacks who had saved him; so, 'Bound—naked—bleeding—and alone' he 'passed the desert to a throne' (XX). What the poem dramatizes is Byron's movement from *Darkness* to a universe where living beauty becomes valid and brings the dawn.

These seeming by-products of Byron's career provide evidence for the organic power of the Romantic imagination. Once this imagination is active, at grips with major issues, the marks of these preoccupations can be recognized in all its works; it is always vigilant, and always alert for exploration even when the poet's whole attention is not so roused. It leads him on, magnetizing certain stories for him, throwing a light round a scene visited, or history recalled. And should the poet's main effort be concentrated at one pole of his creative power, then he may operate from the other in a more extemporary, opportunist spirit. Thus Byron writes most of his dramatic narratives and monologues during the egotistical years when *Childe Harold* extends him most fully. But he makes one last excursion into the old narrative genre as late as 1823, when his chameleon gift was working to the top of its bent in *Don Juan*. There is no reason why the creative should share the same ideals of tidiness as the critical mind, and *The Island*, cheerfully, is somewhat out of place and a throwback from the critical point of view. But it is not irrelevant, and it still gives striking support to the idea of the organic imagination, and to the kind of tidiness which *is* a feature of the creative mind. Byron by 1823 is predominantly a poet of laughter, not one overwhelmed by cosmic desolation. He is neither idealistic nor cynical about human nature; he deals confidently with people of flesh and blood, and his relish for their behaviour is the result of the lifting of his worst imaginative fears, as exposed in 1816 and the preceding narratives. Love, whether as a relationship or a vital force of the personality has established itself, and is closely associated with creative power and achievement, the most lasting and hopeful things about humanity. In the earlier Tales, this was far from being a tenable view; loving became enmeshed with murder and remorse, innocent lovers wilted and died helplessly, and man's main concern was to blow up his brother as an enemy. *The Island* returns to the old situation, and sets it in accord with the changed imaginative picture. It is the happier epilogue to the desperate past and the epitaph for the Giaour-hero. But had the poems featuring the latter been mere *divertissements*, serving the moment's entertainment and no more, the idea of such an epitaph could only have bored his creator, and revival would have been pointless if not impossible. As it is, the links and changes between the old narratives and this new contribution measure that growth of his imagination which is not an indifferent turning away from his earlier narrative incentives, but an arrival at an understanding of them and the fears they expressed.

3

By reading these lesser examples of Byron's work from 1812 to 1823, we discover first that there is continuity, and secondly that there is evolution too. To concentrate on *Childe Harold* and *Don*

Juan is often to recognize only the contrast of the later with the earlier work, and consequently to miss the true relationship of these poems as well as the full coherence of his work as a whole. But the route from *Childe Harold* to *Don Juan* is logical—the former is not called a 'pilgrimage' for nothing—and the two poems are held together by a creative tension which is of fundamental importance to a real understanding of Romantic complexity. *Childe Harold* is to *Don Juan* as *The Prelude* to *The Excursion*: this is our first step in establishing the nature of the poems and their relationship. The next is to stress the distinctively Byronic approach to the common ground: he is always the showman of the movement, not in a way which reduces its preoccupations to theatricality, but with a heightened self-awareness which makes his major poems a full-scale display of the creative temperament and its demands, not merely the offspring of its activities. *Childe Harold* is the product of this heightened self-awareness while it was an insistent pressure upon him, whereas *Don Juan* springs from a more relaxed delight in it. The greater urgency of the first poem coincides with its egotistical bias: this is the poem where he meets himself face to face; and *Don Juan*'s exuberance takes the form not only of a release of chameleon energy but the contemplation of this power as well. Byron exhibits the forces that move him as an aspect of the works they create.

Within this context, the much-debated question of Byron's use of Harold makes valuable sense; and the fact that such a question exists is a sign that Romantic egotism is not a simple thing, but is bound up with creative strategy. Even in poems such as *Childe Harold* and *The Prelude* which seem to deal with their authors' own experience and to recreate their own universe and personal aura, there is no straightforward, untreated autobiographical truth. The naïveté which expects this must be laid at the door of the next, Victorian, generation, and it has led to distorted assumptions about Romanticism ever since. But because Byron is so explicit, a warning against such oversimplifying is given first in the very genesis of Harold, and then, in his vicissitudes in the course of the four Cantos.

Byron's problem in 1809 when he began *Childe Harold* was in general the problem of any young poet—how to manage his

BYRON, SHELLEY AND KEATS

material, and, in particular, the problem of the young Romantic poet, how to manage himself as material. The Cantos written at this time show him struggling with these difficulties, and solving them only partially: although Canto II is noticeably less stiff and awkward than the first, neither suggests the controlled ease of a poet who has discovered entirely how to do what he wants to do. In the search for a method, Harold was a necessary device. But the creation of him was an imaginative not merely a technical act, and Byron's refusal to identify Harold with himself is a sign that more is involved than simply dressing himself up as a Spenserian 'wight'. Writing to Dallas in October 1810, he denies 'all connection' with Harold, but half-concedes that 'parts' of his hero may be taken from himself. He adds 'I would not be such a fellow as I have made my hero for all the world',[1] and this comment may be coupled with his statement in the Preface to the two Cantos, that 'Harold is the child of imagination'. He is the child of an imagination aware of certain frightening areas of its own being; areas to be exposed and scrutinized. This attempt to actualize and if possible exorcize a mood and a force within is the underlying impulse in *Childe Harold*, and it converts a record of travel into a pilgrimage. But it is not accurate to equate the figure giving definition to this underworld of feeling completely with the poet himself. Harold may be a 'thing of darkness' he acknowledges, poetically, as his, but his sentiments outside the poem are rightly those of disavowal, and a certain horror at the proposed identification, because Harold is a distilled and selective creation; he can therefore only be a caricature of any actual person. He is a necessary piece of egotistical apparatus, a mirror-image, but a limited one of a precise function. Byron is writing of a specialized self in *Childe Harold* I and II and this somewhat uncertainly managed hero is his first answer to the problem of how to present and apprehend the more obscure and shadowy presences in the psyche. Moreover, the thought of simply being Harold is a nightmare that is to hang over him until 1816; he does not repudiate the suggestion out of any superficial irritation.

Harold feels on his brow 'curst Cain's unresting doom' (I, lxxxiii); his spirits are oppressed and cast a gloom over the

[1] *PB*, ii, p. xiv.

world. In the earliest stages of the poem, both he and his creator are probably afflicted by nothing worse than adolescence: we see the youthful outcast whom no one understands. But there is the hint of a more serious intuition of doom—in the reference to Cain, for instance—and it drives Byron to follow Harold on his journeying, watching and experiencing by this means in a way which would be beyond his control if he merely tried to speak in direct narrative. The egotistical imagination is working here with a diagram of its needs and intentions: naming and objectifying in order to encounter an area of itself with full perception. Harold is never alone in the poem, living autonomously in its action as Juan seems to do. He 'wends his lonely way' (I, xlv), sentenced, his function ordained explicitly by the poet:

> Onward he flies, nor fixed as yet the goal
> Where he shall rest him on his pilgrimage;
> And o'er him many changing scenes must roll
> Ere toil his thirst for travel can assuage,
> Or he shall calm his breast, or learn experience sage.
>
> (I, xxviii)

The 'changing scenes' of Cantos I and II do much to reinforce and to give body to the Childe's nameless melancholy: the war wounds of Spain and the miseries of modern Greece rouse him with the shock of reality from his own well-nursed sorrows. This awakening is a further problem for the poet, and we witness his gradual discarding of Spenserian idiom, suitable only for posing, and the search for a more valid mode of expression as the Cantos develop. The deeper trouble takes shape: the forebodings which Harold carries with him are proving justified. He is a figure of only too legitimate pessimism, for the world is bearing him out. The menace felt within by the poet is apparently also the dominant feature of human affairs: without Harold to set a distance between Byron and this discovery, the poem probably could not have emerged from the turmoil of subjective emotion it brings about. He is an indispensable agent in the transformation from feeling to imaginative perception, a vital means of showing the fusion of private inner symptoms with the common life of man, something otherwise beyond the apprentice poet's powers of communication.

Yet even in these Cantos, Harold's presence is fitful. For stanzas together, Byron does not depict him or allude to him at all, and the poem is not for long confined to the one method of diagnosing emotion. Clinging at first to the one obvious way of making immediate experience clearer to the view, the use of a mirror-hero, the poet learns as he goes on that the same egotistical purpose can be served by other means. He can reach his deeper state of mind, its fears and forebodings, by contemplating particular scenes and events so keenly that they reveal more than themselves, and when this happens, Harold is redundant. At the bullfight in Cadiz, for instance, Harold is not employed as spectator; the poet, aided by his chameleon sympathies, is roused primarily by the suffering of the animals, and as he perceives it, all his inchoate emotions on pain, destruction and the desperate straits of man find a centre and a shape. Here, and in several scenes in the second Canto, *Childe Harold* is discovering that it is a topography of the mind, not as well as, but at the same time as it is a European panorama. This union and inter-penetration of locality and condition flowers to give the greater achievement of the two later Cantos of the poem, retrospectively making the device of Harold seem all the clumsier. But he survives as a nominal or phantom presence, and this is neither perfunctory lip-service to the original method, nor a stubborn refusal to admit his redundancy. Harold is superannuated in so far as he proved a laborious means of converting scene into reaction, but as a symbol of one particular area of feeling he is functional throughout the poem. Byron extends his egotistical researches into the whole complex of his being, finding correlatives in the full range of Europe's geography and history, but his incentive is the initial oppressed state of mind, for which he seeks either panacea or refutation. Failing these he must confirm that the gloomy reading of life is the only one. Such a figure as Harold cannot carry the weight of the conflicts and crises; Europe itself is the field on which they are fought out, but his shadow persists, he is there to the end, because his creator is still on the same pilgrimage, that which brought this Childe into being.

In Cantos III and IV of *Childe Harold*, the pilgrimage followed is precisely that of the route travelled: from Belgium and the field of Waterloo to the cities of Italy, by way of the Alps. This is the literal, psychological and spiritual itinerary, the whole saga unfolding as Byron's contribution to the egotistical sublime.

Is there any freedom, asks this poem, or are we bound hopelessly to our warring and murderous selves? Is a great man merely one who is very skilful in harnessing these instincts, proving power to be a matter only for the battlefields of Europe, with Napoleon the immediate example of such leadership? Canto III struggles bitterly with these haunting questions; 'half mad' when he wrote it,[1] the poet finds his own condition in the vast mirror of history, and his despair clashing with glimpses of a different human potential. Waterloo, the 'place of skulls' (xviii), arouses memories of all such carnage and the grimmest reflections on the futility of these actions: 'is Earth more free?' (xix). Stanzas on Napoleon (xxxvi-xlv) and all those 'who ascend to mountain tops' are charged with the emotion of frustrated hope. There are those who seem to transcend the limitations of ordinary humanity only to fall into the tyranny bred by self-conceit—'thou wert a God unto thyself'; they propogate rather than curb 'the lust of War'. But in the idea of the effort at greatness, expressed in mountain-climbing imagery (xlv), Byron finds hope. His language shows him moved by the gesture of assertion, the defiance of the herd, and the acknowledged urge to singularity and individual initiative. The attempt to 'surpass or subdue' mankind is possible, and this is the germ of the central section of the Canto, where such an idea of a mind adventuring alone and upwards amid tempests becomes realized in the Alpine experience itself.

Also coming to tentative germination as the Canto progresses is an awareness of love as an experience which exerts some modifying power. He observes that feeling for his daughter and for Augusta has survived the turmoil which has driven him further into his Waterloo moods; and the perception that those moods are unable to dispel such emotion is underlined by his use of Harold to record the fact: 'he had learned to love . . . The helpless looks of blooming infancy', and 'in him this glowed when all beside had ceased to glow' (liv). Unassimilated here, unaccountable, the observation recalls Bonivard, living at peace with his mice and spiders. Thus Byron's experience yields faint

[1] Moore, 28 January 1817; *LJ*, iv, p. 49.

signs of an evolutionary development, and two strands prepare
to twist together: the effort to defy the worst by trying out one's
own potential, with the realization that love is not highly
perishable but curiously persistent and impervious to the working of a melancholy argument.

In the mirror of Europe, both the Alps and Rousseau, as they
are honoured in the Swiss stanzas, reflect the changing outlook.
Approaching the 'matchless heights' (lxiii), Byron, for the first
time summarizes a conflict, giving it the edge of paradox:

> All that expands the spirit, yet appals,
> Gather around these summits, as to show
> How Earth may pierce to Heaven, yet leave vain man below.
>
> (lxii)

Weighed down by his baser nature, 'vain man' is still able to
respond in spirit to a vision of 'cold sublimity'. So far in the
poet's analyses, egotistical and chameleon alike, the heavier
elements have insisted on their presence much more forcefully, but here the experience of the expanding spirit is about to
assert its validity with countering strength. Hence the stanzas of
exultation in the mountains themselves, these 'joyous Alps'
(xcii)—'the blue rushing of the arrowy Rhone' (lxxi), the 'big
rain . . . dancing to the earth' (xciii), the whole revelation of
'Sky—Mountains—River—Winds—Lake—Lightnings!' (xcvi).
A possible freedom is being defined, and as a necessary corollary,
the degree of imprisonment and its nature are also more clearly
seen. In this section of *Childe Harold*, therefore, opposing forces
emerge, replacing the single threat of overall doom. The poet in
the Alps feels himself torn: he is conscious of his mind's untram-
melled sense of kinship with the living universe in all its grandeur
and energy, but simply because of this leap to freedom, the
chains tug him back more harshly, and they are now named as
the chains of the flesh—'clay-cold bonds which round our being
cling'. He is realizing himself, as a creature of dual nature, and
while this has its own pain, it is a positive step too. The address
to Rousseau, one 'whose dust was once all fire' (lxxvi) and the
view of him as the ideal resident of these regions, bear out the
evolving concept of defiant inner power. What is stressed about
Rousseau is his appetite for misery—the 'self-torturing sophist'

(cxxvii)—and above all, his indomitable spirit as a lover. Byron's Rousseau is a symbol needed at this point to crystallize the version of human nature now tenable by the poet. The invocations to Clarens (xcix–civ) is the fulfilment of the Canto's earlier groping towards faith in love as a transforming and sustaining phenomenon. In Rousseau, feeling for nature and for human beauty, are two branches of a single inspiration, and this, despite all threats, is in him a creed to live by. Such a triumph over the clay bonds is hailed by the poet because it renders articulate his new position, his expanding spirit. Growth and advance are possible; and the Alps have yielded a vision of 'life and light' (c). The egotistical has begun to delight in itself, and to prove itself sublime.

Canto IV moves on from this point and continues the correlating of place and state of mind. The pilgrim is never the tourist, even though these Italian scenes show him reacting to some of the most obvious wonders of the country. Much of the Canto deals with experiences of art galleries and architecture, but this is the straight line of advance: after the response to natural grandeur comes the realization that the human mind is itself creative, not merely receptive. The poet discovered the enriching possibility of sympathetic contact with the universe in Canto III, and he now finally routs the fears that to be human is inevitably to be destructive and nothing else, by contemplating the man-made beauty which Italy offers him in abundance. But he is not a passive spectator here: the fourth Canto enacts as well as acknowledges creative power, and this is impressively shown in the stanzas on St Peter's in Rome (cliii–clix). It is not the building, but the experience of it which is central to the description, the effort of the mind and the senses to grasp the awesome immensity of the basilica. Each observer recreates it, embarking on an inner 'piecemeal' rebuilding which, as it stretches the faculties, reveals their capacity to encompass such a vision. Stone rises on stone, the vastness 'growing' so that the mind strives upwards as if 'climbing some great Alp', and the comparison is a precise reminder that this experience of the expanding spirit looks back directly to the crucial awakening in the mountains of Canto III. St Peter's is the monument asserting the mind's victories over limitations and threats, and it is 'all musical in its immensities', a phrase pointing the positive harmonies which now prove to be within human capability. 'Growing with its growth', the spirit 'dilates' to equal what it 'contemplates'.

Similarly and markedly in descriptions of statues—including the Venus de Medici and the Apollo Belvedere—contemplation is united to an active participation in the sculptor's achievement. The statues are carved again in words. The mind lit with ideals which it is able to body forth in works of art is one of the realities of the Canto, the poets of Italy as well as her sculptors and architects being saluted. But sculptural manifestations move him most, because this art comes nearest to his own vision as it develops. The Apollo Belvedere, 'the sun in human limbs arrayed' (clxi–clxiii) symbolizes the heights which may be scaled—he is the product of the mind in its 'most unearthly mood', made by 'human hands' yet transcending human experience in his aura of immortal grace: the statue seems to breathe with life, yet it has suffered no 'tinge of years'. The 'God of Life, and Poesy, and Light' is a 'dream of love', suggesting final perfection, vitality immune from decay. The fact that the creative mind can conceive perfection of this kind and can portray it in stone and in words exalts Byron, but the spectacle of such artistic achievement is bitter also:

> Of its own beauty is the mind diseased,
> And fevers into false creation:—where,
> Where are the forms the sculptor's soul hath seized?
> In him alone. Can Nature show so fair?
>
> (cxxii)

The heights are only scaled in art, not in life. The sun is not 'in human limbs arrayed', save in the sculptured form. Canto IV feels this truth, much as Harold felt it initially—disillusion, decay, violence and death are all to be borne: 'we wither from our youth' (cxxiv).

Yet the two points of view are both valid. Because the free powers of thought and imagination have proved themselves on the pulses, all is changed from the inevitable gloom of pre-1816. Byron, and hence man, is a creature of double, not one doomed nature. From this vision, which routs despair but admits a sense of incongruity, *Don Juan* comes to birth. In *Childe Harold*, tension remains high, yet a victory is won, and others become possible. The pilgrimage leads to the experience of the free power of the mind and the epiphany of the creative self; it is left for *Don Juan* to redeem the flesh and celebrate its emancipation also, in a full appreciation of the human compound.

4

The transition from *Childe Harold* to *Don Juan* might be described as a switch from Prospero to Ariel as hero. After his long progress towards the realization of himself as creative mind, Byron is no longer subject to intense, centripetal pressures and writes from the opposite, chameleon impulse, with a hero and a structure which exemplify the characteristics of this imaginative pole. Where *Childe Harold* showed the unwavering self-concentration of a pilgrimage towards the shrine of inner revelation, *Don Juan* presents the travels of an opportunist hero, drifting on whatever tides of adventure come his way and accommodating himself to whatever circumstances seem to require of him. Juan is chameleon hero *par excellence*, being 'all things unto all people' (XIV, xxxi); he is the poem's impulse, its soul, experiencing the world in its 'infinite variety', from shipwrecks to royal courts, from seraglios to sieges. Even if the poem is taken only at the most simple level, it is clear that Byron is not merely creating out of the chameleon instinct in counter-swing from the egotistical, but is at the same time demonstrating and displaying this instinct. Juan is the type of chameleon creation, rather than a character with whom the poet becomes identified. Aware of 'mobility' as a feature of his temperament, so too Byron is creatively aware of its imaginative potential, perhaps more than his fellow poets, despite the absence of theoretical analysis. In *Don Juan* there is in fact an effective if laconic substitute for theorizing when he observes at Canto III, lxxxvii that poets are 'liars', and 'take all colours—like the hands of dyers'. Juan is the incarnation of these Romantic self-transforming energies, as they may be more respectfully called, and his travels express the appetite for entering into the full range of experience as it passes, unschematized, irreducible, and impossible to evaluate save in terms of itself.

Don Juan is unfinished, but in a sense it never could be finished. It specializes in suggesting the continuity of life—the very flavour and sensation of experience itself, in its unlimited permutations. There are peaks and troughs, ecstatic and calamitous moments, but there is no finality. Swinburne saw this when he wrote with fine perception of 'an especial and exquisite balance and sustenance of alternate tones' and the 'tidal variety of experience and emotion' in the poem.[1] But it is not a neutral survey of society or an impartial reproduction of life; the chameleon mode is a means towards that full experimental grasp of living which is the Romantic path to evaluation, and in Byron's Juan this is not denied. For Juan is the poem's constant point of reference as well as the embodiment of mobility; in him Byron's verdict on experience is given, and it is a positive one. The satirical attacks are based on this: in a universe such as that dying in the poem *Darkness* satire can have no place. *Don Juan* is in favour of life, and its hero symbolizes a persistent beauty which exists together with the conglomerate of reality, not in opposition to it. Juan is the Apollo of *Childe Harold* turned from stone into flesh, 'a most beauteous boy' (IX, liii). He is described always in terms of poise, grace, and love, with a near-feminine gentleness and charm: 'he looked like one of the Seraphim' (IX, xlvii), 'a full grown cupid' (XIV, xli), or Shakespeare's herald new-lighted on the hill (IX, lxvi). He is 'light and airy', and his dancing evinces the 'grace of the soft Ideal, seldom shown, And ne'er to be described' (XIV, xl). In *Don Juan*'s world, therefore, with such a hero as its centre, the 'clay' of the body is no longer a curse but reveals its own beauty, becoming a 'precious porcelain' (IV, xi). The sense of rebirth and the arrival at this assertion of life out of destructive travail—recalling *Mazeppa*—is most movingly and concretely enacted in Canto II where Juan alone survives the grotesque nightmare of shipwreck. Exhausted, he is finally cast up on shore:

> At last, with swimming, wading, scrambling he
> Rolled on the beach, half-senseless, from the sea:

[1] Preface to Selection of Byron's poems; reprinted *Essays and Studies* (1911), p. 242.

There, breathless, with his digging nails he clung
    Fast to the sand, lest the returning wave,
From whose reluctant roar his life he wrung,
    Should suck him back to her insatiate grave:
And there he lay, full length, where he was flung,
    Before the entrance of a cliff-worn cave,
With just enough of life to feel its pain,
And deem that it was saved, perhaps in vain.

With slow and staggering effort he arose,
    But sunk again upon his bleeding knee
And quivering hand; and then he looked for those
    Who long had been his mates upon the sea . . .

And as he gazed, his dizzy brain spun fast,
    And down he sunk; and he as sunk, the sand
Swam round and round, and all his senses passed:
    He fell upon his side, and his stretched hand
Drooped dripping on the oar (their jury-mast),
    And, like a withered lily, on the land,
His slender frame and pallid aspect lay,
As fair a thing as e'er was formed of clay.

                           (II, cvii–cx)

He awakens to the Haidée idyll, her 'ocean-treasure' (II, clxxiii), and this rhythm is Byron's evolution in miniature: from horror and despair to a positive, living beauty. The same rhythm may be seen in Canto VIII, where Juan, amid the brutality of the siege of Ismail, comes upon and rescues the child Leila, who gazes at him with 'a pure, transparent, pale yet radiant face, Like to a lighted alabaster vase' (xcvi). All the chameleon delight of the poem is rooted in such revelations. In its shifting moods, from light to dark and back again, *Don Juan* is free from fear of permanent eclipse, thanks to the egotistical pilgrimage of *Childe Harold*.

    There is, however, a gap between the two poems, *Childe Harold* being so conscious of the limitations of physical and lower human nature. How is this tension eased, so that clay can appear precious as alabaster and porcelain? The key, as I have suggested, lies in the very recognition of the two elements. Once the idea of the human creature as mind opposing flesh is reached, the possibility of another equation, mind plus flesh, equal to the compound, man, is admitted. Byron's catalyst in bringing it about is laughter—laughter based on the perception that this combination of elements may readily be regarded as a union, incongruous but not tragic; and hence creative vision is released to work on living materials, not to yearn for the dream ideal. *Don Juan* is, and can afford to be, totally realistic, exploiting incongruity with the utmost zest. Thus Juan is seasick at the height of his pangs for his first lost love (II, xix, xxiii); and the last completed joke of the poem is a splendid illustration of the whole bias towards life in its fundamental physical reality, fused with the appreciation of the sheer comedy of the flesh. Juan, on his second meeting with what seems to be a chilling, black-cowled, monkish ghost, masters his panic and puts out his hand:

> It pressed upon a hard but glowing bust,
>   Which beat as if there was a warm heart under . . .
>
> The Ghost, if Ghost it were, seemed a sweet soul
>   As ever lurked beneath a holy hood:
> A dimpled chin, a neck of ivory, stole
>   Forth into something much like flesh and blood;
> Back fell the sable frock and dreary cowl,
>   And they revealed—alas! that e'er they should!
> In full, voluptuous, but *not o'er*grown bulk,
>   The phantom of her frolic Grace—Fitz-fulke!
>
> (XVI, cxxii–xxiii)

The previous fear was real, and *Don Juan* does not deny it. But what the poem is able to do is to 'expand' into laughter, to use Humbert Wolfe's word.[1] The same is true of its companion pieces, *Beppo*—part of the upward swing of 1817—and *The Vision of Judgment* (1821).

The narrator-voice in these poems is the Byron familiar from the letters and journals, and provides the nearest thing to a straightforward personal appearance in any of his poems, an exhibition of his everyday personality. Juan is the hero of his poem, but he pursues his career of chameleon wanderer under the ironic gaze of this other equally important presence. Prospero is relaxed, no longer introspectively embroiled; though still egotistically alert to display himself he now surveys his emissary

---

[1] *Notes on English Verse Satire* (1929), p. 132.

running the gamut of experience, seeing in him a vision incarnate. In *Don Juan*, with its complex relationship between narrator and hero, the Romantic vigilance and conscious use of imaginative excursions for purposes of empirical research are illustrated. Byron shows that chameleon activity is not a simple dramatic exercise, but a means of acquiring data, as his watchful narrator reacts and comments, exulting in adventuring Ariel yet in full control of him. *Don Juan* is a most sophisticated chameleon poem, exploiting the idea of mobility as well as employing it, and it is also sensitive testimony to the coexistence and interreliance of the two modes.

It falls to Byron, not surprisingly, to see the comic side of the habitual Romantic allegiance to two such poles in creative activity. The urge to act the 'liar' particularly amuses him, and in a suppressed preface to the first Cantos of *Don Juan*, he mocks Wordsworth's efforts in *The Thorn*. But he betrays in his caricature his awareness of the egotistical impulse which propels any chameleon flights:

The Reader, who has acquiesced in Mr W. Wordsworth's supposition that his 'Misery oh Misery' is related by the 'Captain of a small, etc.' is requested to suppose, by a like exertion of Imagination, that the following epic Narrative is told by a Spanish Gentleman in a village in the Sierra Morena . . . sitting at the door of a Posada, with the Curate of the hamlet on his right hand, a Segar in his mouth . . .[1]

Nevertheless, both modes genuinely exist and no Romantic knows it better than Byron, living and writing out of a response to both. The unity of his poetry, so long unperceived, stands clear when the working of the poles of imagination is traced in it: the changing Tales, the tension of *Childe Harold* and the freedom of *Don Juan* all reveal a dynamic progression, the gradual advance to an infinitely varied, bright, yet never impossibly cloudless imaginative world.

5

In Shelley's *Defence of Poetry* and his plays we saw that his imaginative impulses were of two kinds and that these corresponded very readily with the two modes I am discussing.

[1] First published, *LJ*, vi, appendix i, pp. 381–2.

But the two impulses are so sharply distinguished in his work that there is almost a suggestion of conflict between them, which is not the situation in any of his fellow poets. His comments frequently emphasize differences between his writings, as if the whole process of creation were altered according to which mode he adopted. He implies that he feels at ease in egotistical composition, but faces a harder kind of labour in chameleon. Where he knows himself to be creating a myth of his own mind, travelling along the maze of its passages and bringing forth the treasure he finds in its caverns, then notes of enthusiasm and confidence dominate his comments: any doubt about the reception of the poems is subordinate to his own faith in what he has tried to do. In the preface to *The Revolt of Islam* he speaks of the 'unremitting ardour and enthusiasm'[1] which he has given to the writing of the work, and in a letter answering Godwin's strictures on it, he repeats that 'the poem was produced by a series of thoughts which filled my mind with unbounded and sustained enthusiasm', and defends it as 'a genuine picture' of his own mind;[2] while in a letter to J. Gisborne, *Epipsychidion* is called 'an idealized history of my life and feelings'.[3] He expects few understanding readers for it, yet holds that it is authentic and worthy of him. Of *Alastor*, Mary Shelley says it was written as he brooded 'over the thoughts and emotions of his own soul' in a time of 'tranquil happiness'; it is 'the outpouring of his own emotions, embodied in the purest form he could conceive'.[4] Spoken of in such terms, these poems are companions to *Prometheus* with its rapturous portrayal of 'beautiful idealisms', and the bulk of his work belongs to the same family—poems impelled by his self-confident resolve to mythologize his own vision. This inner world he terms always the 'ideal', and he sees it as the life of his creative power; he can set it against that other kind of creativity which works with the 'real'. Though there is a practical, precautionary motive in a further comment to Gisborne, on *Epipsychidion*, he bases it on what he regards as the true character of his imagination—and the tone implies a negative verdict on the opposite mode:

[1] *PS*, p. 37.   [2] Quoted by Mary Shelley, *PS*, p. 155.
[3] 18 June 1822; Ingpen, ii, p. 976.
[4] Note to *Alastor*, *PS*, pp. 30–1.

The Epipsychidion is a mystery; as to real flesh and blood, you know that I do not deal in these articles; you might as well go to a gin-shop for a leg of mutton, as expect anything human or earthly from me.[1]

Mary Shelley agreed with this diagnosis to the extent of expressing her doubt on its adequacy as a creative policy. *The Witch of Atlas* is preceded by an address 'To Mary, on her objecting to the following poem, upon the score of its containing no human interest', in which he prays her to be content with a 'visionary rhyme'. Her discontent is recorded in her own note to the poem, where she argues that his dwelling poetically in his 'abstract and dreamy' world, drawing exclusively on the 'inspiration of his own soul' for his works, was impoverishing: a larger audience of readers, she thinks, would have benefited him and given him 'a greater mastery over his own powers'. But she adds, 'the mind could not be bent from its natural inclination. Shelley shrunk instinctively from portraying human passion, with its mixture of good and evil, of disappointment and disquiet'.[2]

It is interesting to find an awareness of the two poles of imagination in one who, while not in the major creative sense a Romantic, none the less breathed that atmosphere as her natural environment. Mary Shelley clearly responds also to the idea of a cooperative relationship between them: she advocates a cross-fertilization which could result in enrichment for the 'natural inclination', not the abandonment of it in favour of the other. She knew Shelley must write his ideal, Promethean poems, but she wished for more of *The Cenci*'s 'sad realities' of flesh and blood to stimulate his imaginative life to a more total response. Remarking on his 'shrinking' from the latter, she confirms the impression that his attitude to chameleon activity was less than eager.

Yet he did write *The Cenci*; and there is the far from cool praise for the dramatic sensibility in his *Defence of Poetry*. Obviously, therefore, the more dramatic approach was alive to him as a creative possibility. The implications to the contrary are not the

[1] 22 October 1821; Ingpen, ii, p. 920.
[2] *PS*, p. 383.

whole truth. If they were, then his criticism of Wordsworth in
Peter Bell the Third boomerangs:

> He had as much imagination
>   As a pint-pot;—he never could
> Fancy another situation,
> From which to dart his contemplation,
>   Than that wherein he stood.

(IV, 8)

The next verse acknowledges the egotistical gift of the poet,
combining all he sees 'by a master-spirit's law', but clearly to
Shelley, 'imagination' is hallmarked by chameleon capacity, the
submerging of self in favour of the realization of alien feelings and
circumstances. It would be strange if such a forthright esteem
were not reinforced with more creative demonstrations than one
realistic drama, even if he is conscious of a degree of straining
against the 'master-spirit' when he attempts to follow his own
precept. And there is further evidence that he was technically
interested in the exercise of 'darting his contemplation' and
making a poetic statement in terms of 'real flesh and blood'.
Recognizing always how sharply this differs from handling the
ideal presentations of the inner vision that came to him so
readily, he was not always reluctant to make the attempt.
Shelley was a highly professional, experimental poet, not only
when he fashioned 'characters and mechanism' to make possible
an egotistical poetry and drama 'of a kind yet unattempted',[1]
but when he felt the need to think out a means of coping with
chameleon writing, which was to him a problem and yet
essential to a worthy poetic life. Here, then, is his unique version
of Romantic polarity, and one poem in particular in its relation
to the rest, helps to demonstrate it.

Newman Ivey White describes *Julian and Maddalo* as a
'mysterious' poem, which has 'never been fully explained'.[2]
The mystery, as he and other commentators see it, turns on the
identity of the Maniac: do he and his story represent Shelley
himself, or an imagined character, or are Maddalo and Maniac
both studies of Byron, as G. Wilson Knight thinks?[3] Whatever
the interpretation, it is felt, as White says, that the Maniac is the

---

[1] See above, p. 55. [2] *Shelley* (1947), ii, p. 42 f.
[3] *Lord Byron: Christian Virtues*, pp. 251–3.

EGOTISTICAL AND CHAMELEON:

'real centre' of the poem, and this remains so when it is considered from aspects other than the more strictly biographical speculations. The poem seems mysterious first of all because it is different from Shelley's usual style, and such a first-hand, psychological presentation of a suffering, unbalanced mind is not the kind of enterprise he commonly undertakes. But the poem is not at all an isolated phenomenon if the context is extended beyond Shelley's works to Romantic preoccupations as a whole. *Julian and Maddalo* ceases to seem such an inexplicable peculiarity if we recognize its family likeness, in both structure and substance, to many other poems of the age.

Shelley's Maniac is brother to Marmaduke and Oswald, Alvar and Ordonio, the Prisoner of Chillon, and the Ancient Mariner, to name only the most prominent members of a sad company. The experience of oppression, always psychological and sometimes physical, is a necessary one for the growth of the Romantic imagination with its ambitious goal of a personally vital, not merely intellectual, comprehension of values. Shelley is more readily drawn to capture the sensations of victorious release, as the emphasis of *Prometheus Unbound* shows, but he too undergoes the darker experience, creating out of it his Maniac. The possible connection of this figure with Tasso has been proposed, as an alternative to the biographical view of his origins,[1] and this likely theory helps to illustrate in another way the poem's place in a common territory, drawing attention to resemblances to Byron's *Lament of Tasso*, composed about eighteen months earlier (April 1817, published July 1817). Shelley like Byron had visited the cell at Ferrara, and there was much in the Tuscan poet's history and the legends about it to rouse response in him, if not the same unqualified adoption of his cause as Byron's. But the underlying point is more pertinent: the need in both poets to depict such a situation at the hypersensitive extreme, that frontier region of experience where insanity presses close, or actually invades the mind.

A general kinship of substance therefore allies *Julian and Maddalo* with one class of Romantic chameleon research, and it

[1] R. D. Havens, 'Julian and Maddalo', *Studies in Philology*, xxvii (1930), pp. 648–653. Referred to by Newman Ivey White, op. cit., p. 558, note 29. Shelley planned a tragedy 'on Tasso's Madness': Peacock, 20 April 1818; Ingpen, ii, p. 596.

is the more explicable because of this. From the structural point of view also, it again stands out rather strangely in Shelley's work but is quite at home in the broader scene. It is an encounter poem, a monologue with speaker and listener—listeners in this case—all making up the total experience. Shelley's handling of it gives full play to this formula. Not rudimentary in the *Last of the Flock* sense, nor yet exploited for the utmost tension as in *The Ancient Mariner*, the encounter and monologue of *Julian and Maddalo* makes its distinct contribution to aid our appreciation of the Romantic liking for that structure.

As his framework, Shelley shows himself and Byron in the social intercourse of their Venetian life, with its blend of shared enjoyments, intellectual stimulus and temperamental conflict. Shelley objectifies the relationship in terms of Julian and Maddalo as his first chameleon step—an attempt to realize the experience of the two of them in this situation, to see both together, each in his characteristic attitude. He is not just changing names for superficial motives of disguise; the poem written from 'Julian's' point of view is not the same as simple first-person narration. The speaker is perceived as Maddalo is—the two participants are equally contemplated. They ride and they argue, Maddalo taking 'the darker side' (49) in viewing weakness and suffering as inevitable and out of any human control, while Julian maintains 'we might be otherwise' (172). Both are depressed, however, by the fact of such suffering, and the poem is propelled in its development by this depression and the confusion occasioned by the two interpretations of it. The Maniac is visited in his prison as the intuitive Romantic method of seeking further understanding: intellectual debate and the mere clash of opinion is sterile, and the imaginative course offers—in accordance with Shelley's own statements—a deeper moral enlightenment. Each hopes to prove and support his outlook from the Maniac's living evidence; but in the translation from the mental abstract to the individual, the argument is itself transformed. The centre is moved. What the Maniac is becomes the truth and the answer; the experience of him increases their perception of the central predicament they have fruitlessly debated—though it offers no solution to that debate. Neither Julian nor Maddalo finds ammunition for his case, albeit it was there for each of them: after the visit, their 'argument was quite forgot' (520) and they 'talked of him And nothing else, till daylight made stars dim' (523–4). This is the heart of Romantic perception, the key to their trust in the encounter and monologue poem. Entering into the nature of the individual, experiencing his being and so becoming inhabited by him: this creative expansion supersedes the theorizing of the isolated intellect, and draws together into common vision those who otherwise remain unable to reach each other across a gulf of disagreement and incomprehension. The lesson of *The Excursion* is repeated.

Shelley's poem in its detailed commentary, its full presentation of Julian, Maddalo, Maniac and their relationship, is a documentary study of the processes of the sympathetic, chameleon imagination, and the kind of knowledge which it hungers for and gains. And even more clearly than in the handling of *The Cenci*, it heralds the Browning monologue. The sense of situation, of a locale and a moment which Shelley shows here as the two confront the Maniac, is not that of drama: it is the means of initiating the backward journey, the voyage retracing the devious passages of inner life. As a vital contribution to this end, it provides the essential data of the present to counterpoint and reinforce the speaker's revelations of the past. Of all the Romantic encounter poems, with their strong encouragement to the development of the monologue, *Julian and Maddalo* is perhaps the one most clearly gestating the form's rich Victorian future.

Shelley was well aware that he was faced with a distinctive kind of composition in this poem, and one which he had to learn to handle. Unwilling though he may have been to deal with 'human passions', once embarked, he is drawn into a full engagement, technically alert and conscious of challenge; conscious too that this is another imaginative pole. Thus he writes to Ollier about the publication of *Julian and Maddalo*:

I would not print it with 'Prometheus Unbound'. It would not harmonize. It is an attempt in a different style, in which I am not yet sure of myself, a *sermo pedestris* way of treating human nature, quite opposed to the idealism of that drama.[1]

---

[1] 14 May 1820; Ingpen, ii, p. 781.

And similarly, he says, 'do not add the "Witch of Atlas" to that peculiar piece of writing'.[1] He expounds the linguistic niceties of the 'peculiar piece' to Leigh Hunt:

I have employed a certain familiar style of language to express the actual way in which people talk with each other, whom education and a certain refinement of sentiment have placed above the use of the vulgar idioms . . . Not that the familiar style is to be admitted in the treatment of a subject wholly ideal . . .[2]

The creative satisfaction of the attempt at *Julian and Maddalo* is brought out by his declaration to Ollier in December 1819,

I mean to write three other poems . . . the subjects of which will be all drawn from dreadful or beautiful realities, as that of this was.[3]

Depicting such 'realities' exerts more than a technical attraction, and other incentives also are revealed in *Julian and Maddalo*. Julian is deeply concerned with the Maniac, and the intensity of the chameleon act with its egotistical relevance is displayed in the later movement of the poem. After making the shift of centre from theorizing to sympathetic experience, the poem shows the power of the latter as something rooted and growing within the mind which has conceived it. Shelley, having created the Maniac in giving him autonomy of speech and location, now beholds him as his own creature, one whose experience is inextricably his, involving at once torment and love:

> . . . I sought relief
> From the deep tenderness that maniac wrought
> Within me—'twas perhaps an idle thought—
> But I imagined that if day by day
> I watched him, and but seldom went away
> And studied all the beatings of his heart
> With zeal, as men study some stubborn art
> For their own good, and could by patience find
> An entrance to the caverns of his mind
> I might reclaim him from his dark estate . . .
>
> (565–74)

This intimacy was not in fact pursued, the poem continues. But the creative relationship of the Romantic poet and his offspring

[1] Ollier, 22 February 1821; Ingpen, ii, p. 857.
[2] 15 August 1819; Ingpen, ii, p. 706.   [3] Ingpen, ii, p. 760.

is perfectly set out in Shelley's suggestion that he could redeem the Maniac's suffering by ever more sensitive identification with it, increasing his knowledge of its nature, a study likened in his mind to the patient pursuit of self-cultivation. If he was incarnating some 'dark estate' of his own psyche in the person of the Maniac, then the egotistical relevance of it all is more literally and directly pointed. But the same process of absorbing the unknown suffering into himself—having projected himself into it—and reaching an illuminated possession of it, applies if the Maniac represents the haunted side of Byron, or if he is an imaginative amalgam of all such distraction known to Shelley from literature or life. There is no need here to pursue the biographical argument, for the fundamental imaginative character of the poem does not depend on it. I would add, however, that if Shelley was by this dramatic means endeavouring to face more positively, not merely the general fact of human torment, but either his own or Byron's hidden anguish, a further inducement could have urged him into the poetic world of monologue-creation. He was always interested in the idea of 'double personality',[1] and he was therefore just as likely to perceive and be stimulated by the many-sidedness in Byron, as he was to feel the need to act out his sense of a personal duality. *Julian and Maddalo* may well contain the double image of either Byron or Shelley himself—or conceivably, of both of them; in their joint response to the Maniac, Julian's deep tenderness for him, Maddalo's help in giving him music, we may read an acknowledgement of the alter-ego by each of them. But as *Julian and Maddalo* is a poem and not a biographical cryptogram, there is every justification for taking it as a vision very near to the Romantic heart, the perception of the manifold complexity of the psyche, and the likelihood, and perhaps the necessity, of a man's meeting himself and first going out of himself to do so. This is the most profound level of Shelley's encounter poem, and the fruit of his chameleon adventure in which he creates not only the Maniac, but Julian and Maddalo in their vivid and moving experience of him and his pain.

With *The Cenci*, *Julian and Maddalo* stands as his only sustained venture into the realm of 'dreadful or beautiful realities', human

[1] See White, op. cit., p. 560 n. 44.

BYRON, SHELLEY AND KEATS

passions approached with the imagination exposed to their impact. Does it follow therefore that Shelley is, for all his high esteem for such exposure, a poet of strong egotistical dominance? This is only partially true. His most typical creations are the figures of his vision and above all of his intellectual passion. The world his poems frequent is an inner landscape. Yet within this self-ruled poetry there exists a lively chameleon impulse, a situation which again provides a pattern different from other versions of Romantic polarity. Shelley's poetical character springs partly from this particular alignment within his imagination: the tension set up from it is his own. Conversely, the peculiar intimacy of operation which he also achieves between the two modes underlines their cooperative function and the essential unity of their ends in the Romantic bid to assimilate experience.

Shelley's poetry never aims merely to look at and describe. Ideas are enacted in mythological form, and in his perception of the elemental and physical apparatus of the universe, his chameleon power is most fully exercised, to form a specialized area of sympathetic creativity. Bernard Blackstone in *The Lost Travellers* (1962) says of Shelley that he 'felt himself a vehicle for natural forces: his trend was towards an integration with energetic essences through which he could lose his identity and be free'.[1] This oversimplifies the ultimate goal, but it indicates well how Shelley's chameleon temperament is to be read. It conspires with his neo-Platonic loyalties, for his faith in the ideal of unity, the many yielding to the One, urges him the more strongly to deny any gulf between himself and the other constituents of the universe. What his theory desires, his imagination assists him to perform: an Ariel-like passing into the spirit of other phenomena. The *Ode to the West Wind* displays this favourite movement in action. At the outset the poet is a consciousness addressing the wind,—'hear oh hear'—and aware of his own condition as a contrast. But he at once begins to realize the life of the wind, so that it is dramatically dominant as a force before the more explicit chameleon submission of the fourth section, where his desire is to be lifted as 'a wave, a leaf, a cloud'. On the other hand, the climax of the poem comes in

[1] p. 260.

its final invocation, 'Be thou, Spirit fierce, My spirit! Be thou me, impetuous one', and this does not intensify the chameleon passion of the preceding verses, but exhibits most candidly the egotistical pull which has been latent throughout and which now triumphs with the lift to bold metaphoric identification of the wind and the creative power itself. However, this exhortation neither repudiates nor denies the previous outgoing. We have a poem rooted in the peculiar tension of the two modes in Shelley's imagination: able to give himself to the sensations of an autumn gale, becoming the victim and then the consciousness of an unconscious force, he finally recognizes it as, in metaphor, an aspect of himself, the creative potential within him. In such a process, Shelley gives evidence to support my belief that no Romantic merely wishes to 'lose his identity', or is capable of this, essential though the exercise is to his imaginative life. The quest is always to recover and discover identity, to possess it with the knowledge of possession; and in the pursuit of this mission, the territories of self are extended.

In a short poem called *An Exhortation*, Shelley links poet and chameleon. He is not concerned with the animal as I have caged it in this study, in order to study its Romantic nature; his purpose is to defend 'a poet's free and heavenly mind', but his ideas on these creatures, culled from legend as well as zoology, make a neat commentary on his own chameleon character. They 'feed on light and air', he says, on 'beams and winds', and he condenses the more scientific data into the statement 'where light is, chameleons change'. So Shelley changes, taking on the properties of light and air, winds, currents of water, fire or cloud. This is the authentically 'ethereal' Shelley, lending himself to elements which readily interpenetrate and into which he can merge to become an agent in their union, not a separate, intrusive consciousness. Liquidity, movement, 'elemental subtlety': in dealing with these effects, his imagination 'grows like what it looks upon'. If the chameleon work of *Julian and Maddalo* was an effort and a strain upon him, this other aspect of the mode was not, being an instinctive part of his full poetic nature, closely abetting his egotistical vision. In Shelley the complexity of tension and collaboration between the two poles is finely demonstrated; and for his mind, dazzled by the 'white radiance' it perceived, he provides the perfect description when he says 'where light is, chameleons change'.

6

Keats in his letters darts like a bird above the rough ground where his poems stumble and fight their way forward. The letters perceive in flashes, the poems must fulfil his precept—nothing is real until it is experienced. They are the means by which Apollo is made a god: experience becoming consciousness. The process is necessarily incomplete; its difficulty, never under-estimated in his own judgment, increased with the growing complexity of life, its crosscurrents and whirlpools of desires, ideas, people and events. But his poems written within such a concentrated span of years reveal the intimacy of chameleon and egotistical, the singleness of their ambition, with a particular clarity. Despite his classification of himself as chameleon, the poems as much as the letters show strong egotistical awareness. In the Odes he writes directly from this centre, impressing himself upon his materials and making out of them a personal universe. The nightingale and the Grecian urn are properties of his vision, annexed to his emotional need, helping to focus his own situation. This is the road of egotistical realization. But his claim to be chameleon in his responses is also borne out, and his capacity for sinking himself into the tactile, sensuous recognition of objects and living creatures is one of the most lauded of his gifts, with *The Eve of St Agnes* the prime example. In his longer poems, the effect is analogous to Shelley's work, for the use of myth to enact his own perceptions with egotistical zest is joined by smaller but most accomplished exertions of chameleon power. Only the area of specialization is different: where Shelley is elementally responsive and drawn to intangibles, Keats is attuned to the life of the earth in grass and leaf, and the sensations of skin and palate.

These are obvious points about Keats. In parts of his work he clearly exercises the chameleon faculty and elsewhere, the egotistical, and he is capable of blending the two with his own temperament's version of Shelley's method. But the main effort of his poems is to discover how to manipulate the two modes in order to exploit them to the full as the means towards the creation of identity. Egotistical cannot merely be egocentric expression, chameleon cannot merely be taking on the being of a hare in frozen grass. He tries to find a way of writing which will convey simultaneously with these enterprises the act of self-realization, for this is the justification and meaning of both of them. If we look at his poems with this ambition in mind we see them as a distinctive kind of technical exploration inseparable from the business of soul-making which is their mission and *raison d'être*. He shares the quest with his fellow poets: but he pursues it in a more directly introspective way which his youth encourages and which is intensified by the rapidity of his development.

The journey from *Endymion* to *Hyperion* and then to *The Fall of Hyperion* shows his experimental search for a way of putting himself into the substance of the poem, as his basic problem may be described; he needs to behold his experiencing self in order to achieve the vital sense of emerging identity. These poems move from the first crude attempt to what we might call blue-print success in the revised *Hyperion*. *Endymion* is an apprentice poem from this viewpoint as from all others. Each book of the poem is introduced by a preamble spoken in his own voice, with a rather engaging mixture of high seriousness and naïve excitement at his project:

> . . . 'tis with full happiness that I
> Will trace the story of Endymion.
> The very music of the name has gone
> Into my being, and each pleasant scene
> Is growing fresh before me as the green
> Of our own valleys; so I will begin
> Now while I cannot hear the city's din . . .
> (I, 34–40)

He is not content merely to tell the story—Endymion has moved him strongly and this fact must be recorded as part of the resultant work. He elaborates on this emotional stimulus in the introduction to the second book. Records of history are unfavourably contrasted with the effect on us of imaginative accounts of love and its sorrows:

... in our very souls, we feel amain
The close of Troilus and Cressid sweet.
Hence, pageant history! hence, gilded cheat ...
  ... the silver flow
Of Hero's tears, the swoon of Imogen,
Fair Pasterella in the bandit's den
Are things to brood on with more ardency
Than the deathday of empires.
      (II, 12–14, 30–4)

And so to Endymion's woes again. This is more than a tribute to romance: it is Keats noting how vicarious emotion becomes immediate and enters into the web of his experience. The process is as important as the outcome, and he recognizes it as pertinent to his story of Endymion. Although only marginally observed in these formally modelled introductory sections, his creative situation is already seeking to take its place as a feature of the poem it engenders.

Endymion and the *Hyperions* meet as Keats's attempts to mythologize his mind, to locate in such stories a repository for his own feeling and perception. He is not dramatizing, entering emotional realms otherwise foreign to him, but breathing new life into ancient forms from his own spirit. That this in itself is only a partial satisfaction to the Romantic imagination is demonstrated by the history of his efforts to write *Hyperion*. In the first attempt the story of the fallen Titans and the advent of the Olympians is simply and epically narrated. There is no preamble, and therefore, no overt presence of the mind in which the story is taking root and growing into fresh life. This does not prevent the tale from being a piece of egotistical creation but, as Byron might put it—where is Harold? As he felt the need for the reacting mind itself to be by some means actualized, so Keats's poem clearly did not satisfy its author in its plain-tale form. A dimension is missing. Late in this first version, he tries by the conventional invocation of the Muse in Book III to supply the deficiency: but this serves only as a rather jerky piece of scene shifting—'O leave them, Muse', and is no advance from *Endymion*, threatening indeed to freeze the poem in an unyielding formality which makes it impossible to depict what is desired, that is, the creator in relation to the created.

Hence the changed method of the second *Hyperion*. Here Keats is in the poem. He contemplates himself as he moves towards the point at which the story is born, portraying this evolutionary experience as a 'poet's dream'. He achieves here, first of all, an intensified version of the encounter poem so favoured by his contemporaries. As we have seen, the poets like to tell stories, to be in other situations and at the same time to receive and react emotionally to the story so lived through. Ancient Mariner and Wedding Guest, Shepherd and Traveller, Giaour and Monk, Julian and Maniac: to these we can now add Keats's meeting with his dream-self and Moneta, which is to make possible the further encounter with the fallen gods. Thus on a purely egotistical level he adopts what has in the main been a device for leading chameleon or semi-chameleon experience to an egotistical consequence. In *The Fall of Hyperion*, it is a method wholly designed to bring 'himself home to himself', as he says in his letters.[1] He observes himself in the throes of growth and developing vision, and he is the commentator on and the participant in his evolution. He encounters his enlarged perception, and he watches himself winning his taxing way to this ability to 'see as a God sees' (I, 304). At once the Mariner and the Guest, he witnesses his progress towards Moneta, his journeys into the profound oceans of experience. This recourse to dream-commentary is also, more directly, comparable to Coleridge's mirror-structure, as in *The Nightingale*, where self-realization is achieved through the reflection of experience by others; but again, Keats shows a more resolutely exclusive egotistical concentration, self-mirroring without mediators. In his second handling of the Hyperion story, therefore, Keats arrives at one way of solving the problems of the poetry of self-creation. Using the device of dream experience, he avoids the violation of poetic unity and also the awkward naïveté of *Endymion*'s introductory voice.

A similar movement, and a similar struggle to find technical answers to satisfy his needs, can be seen taking place with less arduous introspection, in the three narrative poems. As he moves from *Endymion*, and from one *Hyperion* to the other, converting his raw material into a richer substance, so he

[1] Woodhouse, 27 October 1818; Rollins, i, p. 387.

develops from *Isabella* through *The Eve of St Agnes* to *Lamia*. Each of these poems corresponds roughly to each of the egotistical works of myth, in that the method employed at the three stages is parallel, allowing of course for the differences inherent in the egotistical-chameleon contrast. For in his narrative poems Keats writes in the more outgoing spirit found in the *Lyrical Ballads* and Byron's Tales, and his problems are those of the narrator-voice, not so immediately his own as in *Endymion* or the second *Hyperion*. But his goal is the same: how to make his creative relationship with the material an interwoven part of the poem's fabric. This preoccupation is never far from his mind.

Isabella is not just 'a story from Boccaccio' recast into verse, and Keats is quite aware that his approach and the nature of his engagement with the tale is more complex than that of the straightforward ballad-monger who is merely the vehicle through whom the story communicates its own effect. As with *Endymion*, where he must set down his sense of emotional rapport with his hero's pangs, so in *Isabella* there is a naïve acknowledgement in the course of the poem that he finds his storytelling in itself an experience worthy of being communicated. To remain the window on the tale is not enough. He first shows that he has one eye on what he is doing instead of both fixed on the story when he pauses to invoke Boccaccio, asking his 'pardon' for the attempt to retell his tale, and assuring him that he is not seeking to improve on 'old prose in modern rhyme' (xx). That his is all the same a changed story, and perhaps a more difficult one to handle is admitted later, where he seems overcome by macabre emotion as Isabella delves in the forest grave:

> Ah! wherefore all this wormy circumstance?
> Why linger at the yawning tomb so long?
> O for the gentleness of old Romance,
> The simple plaining of a minstrel's song!
>
> (XLIX)

The impossibility of returning to simplicity and straight report is written into this very consciousness of having left it; the shift of centre from the story to the storyteller has irrevocably taken place. He is aware that he reacts to the 'yawning tomb' and every other situation and mood, and his whole concern is with what the story is doing to him, not the objective communication of it. Hence his dwelling on 'wormy circumstance': his emotions lead him, not Boccaccio. There is a kind of overflow of his feelings at times, giving such verses as that beginning

> Moan hither, all ye syllables of woe,
> From the deep throat of sad Melpomene!
>
> (LVI)

His inclination is to write an emotionally annotated poem, and part of *Isabella*'s awkwardness lies in his only being able fitfully to indulge, not to use this personal response to the material. The power of anonymous narration is lost because the pressure of the self-conscious storyteller is felt, but he cannot handle this presence confidently, nor is he completely committed to it throughout. The poem suffers; but it points the direction in which he must move.

That is, on to *The Eve of St Agnes* and beyond it to *Lamia*, as he goes from one *Hyperion* to the other. The role of the narrator in *The Eve of St Agnes* is that of the immediate recipient of the action. This is a stage past objective storytelling, and Keats, having shaken off the gaucheness of *Isabella*, has discovered how to use the sensitive presence of a commentator and integrate it with the scenes described. He no longer wavers between an imitation of plain narrative, and the indulgence of his own emotions with exclamations of distress to register the mood; he finds the chameleon method of disciplining and unifying the material, while keeping it related to himself. *The Eve of St Agnes* is less a story told than a series of impressions, an affair of substances and sensuous response rather than flowing action and dramatic manoeuvre, and this tactile assault of the poem makes us aware of the intimate presence of the poet. This is somewhat paradoxical, for what is forced on our attention is the quality of each detail in itself; the poet is obtrusive only by the very intensity of his submission to the effects he experiences. He is not acting as a window, but as a highly responsive organism evaluating his material before he offers it. His penetration of and fusion with the scenes evoked is part of what the poet offers us. All is quickened by the creative spirit as it takes possession of what it beholds. The effigies aching in their 'icy hoods' (II), Madeline and her 'warmed jewels' (XXVI), Porphyro's helmet-plume 'brushing the cobwebs' (XIII). These and all such are authentic acts of chameleon identification, but they confirm what Coleridge claimed of Shakespeare's protean power—that 'he remains always himself',[1] and Keats in *The Eve of St Agnes* is clearly the poem's consciousness. He finds himself in what he realizes so acutely outside himself: it is ultimately his own boundary he extends. He gives himself to his story, and it enriches his own being.

But this process, so crucial to his imaginative ambition, is merely carried out in the poem, not simultaneously assessed as the operation it is. And no less will satisfy Keats: he aims not only to become the sparrow on the gravel, but to know that he has achieved this metamorphosis. At moments in *The Eve of St Agnes*, the narrative voice is heard speaking as a witness and in this it is comparable to *The Idiot Boy* and *Christabel*. He stage-manages: 'these let us wish away, And turn, sole-thoughted, to one lady there' (V); and the poem ends with a sudden step back so that the story is set in distant perspective as well as concluded as the experience of the hour:

> And they are gone: ay, ages long ago
> These lovers fled away into the storm.
> That night the Baron dreamt of many a woe,
> And all his warrior-guests with shade and form
> Of witch, and demon, and large coffin-worm,
> Were long be-nightmared. Angela the old
> Died palsy-twitch'd, with meagre face deform;
> The Beadsman, after thousand aves told,
> For aye unsought-for slept among his ashes cold.

This is the creator consciously placing himself in a valedictory relationship with his material, but for the most part the poem proceeds by the power of its chameleon submission, active from moment to moment. Keats would have such narratives active in this way and reflexive too; his letters are sure of this, and clear on its central importance, but his poems only have time to begin the search for the means of achieving it. The second *Hyperion* is a diagram of what he wants, and all the other poems involving

[1] See above, pp. 7–8.

some kind of narrator voice coupled with egotistical vision or chameleon action participate in the quest to consummate the relationship more adequately. The attempts range from the ingenuous Endymion to the sophistication of Lamia.

He was more satisfied with Lamia than with either Isabella or The Eve of St Agnes.[1] Although it may be difficult for us to endorse this rating completely, since the level of performance in Lamia seems more uneven than that of the consistently fine Eve of St Agnes, still the poet's instinct for his progress is not to be taken lightly, and in Lamia he takes a step forward in his struggle to solve the major problems of his creative life. The narrator of Lamia receives the impact of the story as he tells it, and his control of the action is that of a mind aware of the significance of the whole experience, neither fitfully communicating a display of its emotional response by sudden exclamations as in Endymion and Isabella, nor yet merely living the scene and situation as in Hyperion the first and, with full chameleon energy, in The Eve of St Agnes. Nor is the poem diagrammatic: the blend is more subtle. Keats manages to suggest a circuit of experience which elsewhere he does not master. He combines an inwardness of presentation, the empathic movement from himself into object, with the subjective result of this engagement.

Detail is vivid as in The Eve of St Agnes—sandals 'shuffle o'er the pavement white' (I, 355), the 'cold, full sponge' is pressed on hands and feet (II, 192),—but it is never isolated in its impact. Neither are the incidents and emotions of the story. Each moment is a relative, not a self-sufficient experience, for the whole of the story dominates its parts. This is how Keats's subjective assimilation manifests itself and becomes a feature of the poetic statement: the tone of the scenes and episodes is dependent on the context of ultimate disaster, and the awareness of an inevitable progress to grief and disillusion conditions his handling at every stage. He knows more than these characters as he lives their history, and this knowledge is integrated into his narrative; he is moved with the life of the actors and their world, but he writes also as the mind which has been taught and illuminated by the story it tells. He portrays in Lamia not only the spectacle of his experience expanding by his sympathetic enactment of

[1] Woodhouse, 21–22 September 1819; Rollins, ii, p. 174.

this tragedy but the advent of the new self which is reached out of this submission. His mind is seen developing from what it feeds on, a stage further on the way to the full growth of its self-experience, its identity.

Doom hangs over Lycius and Lamia; the poet knows this from the outset and yet he learns it by travelling through their story also. He knows his verse cannot leave the lovers in their first happiness, but 'must tell For truth's sake what woe afterwards befell' (I, 394–5). He begins Part II able to generalize about the fate of love, with a bird's-eye (and Byronic) command of probabilities; but the proving on the pulses through the specific situation is the way to mature recognition, and *Lamia* captures the process of conversion from the experience as it is absorbed to the resultant perception. 'For all this came a ruin' (II, 16): this is the text, the beginning and the end of the poem, and the added dimension, modifying all the scenes and distinguishing the poem as a structure from the other narratives, which do not blend each moment's experience with the controlling realiza-tion of its fruits.

In the light of his drive for self-evolution, Keats's ambition to write plays takes on at first sight a contradictory appearance. But as his letters and the three narrative poems just discussed show, Keats's sense of his chameleon nature is the complement to, rather than the opponent of his equally intense and single-minded quest for his 'identity'. He is the final proof that to the Romantic these are polar not antagonistic urges. Undoubtedly his desire to write drama would have met head on his other passion for self-delineation, but it is much more probable that the tension so set up would have proved highly creative than that the two would have engendered only mutual frustration and stalemate. In Keats lay the seeds for a drama transformed by collision with this seemingly contrary force of egotistical energy; and in this potential development, the whole Romantic tendency is summed up. So the kind of work Keats might have produced is not entirely unknown: like his contemporaries, in their plays and their taste for the encounter narrative poem expecially, he moved towards a poetic form which involved the dramatic, the ability to be 'all things to all people', with the egocentric experience of the recording, growing, evaluating individual being. The logic of his development—hinted at in his handling of Act V of *Otho the Great*—looks to some kind of experiment in the field of monologue. Had he lived to pursue his poetic journey, his work might well have obviated the need for such a study as this which seeks to show the continuity between the Romantics and their Victorian successors. It is partly because Keats did not demonstrate the continuity fully by his own evolution that the clues in the work of the other Romantic poets have been so little understood.

Did Keats then actually write any monologues? The narrative poems I have discussed contain obvious gestures towards some exploitation of the speaker-to-listener situation—Lycius and Apollonius, for example. But on the whole, these poems explore the rather different relationship between the narrator and his story, and the former situation arises more incidentally. In his most straightforwardly egotistical poems, his Odes and sonnets, Keats comes nearest to comprehending the monologue and its opportunities. These are self-discovery poems, but they often adopt the mode of speaker and listener. The 'listener' may be a Grecian urn or Kosciusko, Fanny or Spenser, but the poem needs this other presence to provoke the poet to speak, and in this a monologue rather than a soliloquy situation is adumbrated. Keats favours direct address, finding himself brought to clarification and the illuminated scrutiny of a mood or an experience by the interaction, the implicit exchange, between him and the object or person fixing his attention. This is Romantic empiricism once more, involving that sense of occasion and the stimulating psychological shock of encounter and relationship which brings about a release of imaginative power.

In this context, Keats's sonnets show themselves to be experimental poems. He tries out ways of bringing himself home to himself, using the form as a psychological note-book containing moments of importance: strong emotion ('Keen, fitful gusts...'); perceptive glimpses of some truth he must prove to himself ('After dark vapours . . .'); a sudden discovery (*On Looking into Chapman's Homer*); or impulses within himself whose significance he feels but cannot grasp ('Why did I laugh tonight?'). In all of them, there is immediacy of experience and the ambition to master it, and the tone is that of one moved to a dramatically reverberant utterance rather than the whisper of private, inner thinking. Even where there is no other presence exerting its formulating pressures, he acts as a listener to his own speech, as in 'Why did I laugh tonight?', a sonnet written as he said 'with no agony but that of ignorance'.[1] This is a poem charged with promise for the future of his research into the best methods of handling the complex Romantic condition of a vigilant self-consciousness, refining itself as an instrument for evaluation and enlightenment.

He could not himself pursue the challenge. But with his fellow egotistical and chameleon poets, he pioneers enough territory to hand on to the poets who follow a rich, if difficult, inheritance. What they did with it, and how it looked to the Victorian critics, we may now consider.

[1] George Keatses, 19 March 1819; Rollins, ii, p. 81.

V

SINCERITY: A VICTORIAN CRITERION

the outpouring of a full heart . . .
Keble, *Oxford Lectures on Poetry*

ROMANTICISM was not an easy inheritance, but it was a misfortune of the succeeding age that to some readers and theorists, a simple, clear message about the nature of poetry seemed to be the sum total of the legacy. The Victorian poets themselves were not on the whole seduced by this illusion, but it was a threat to their work, and it has clouded the modern view not only of them but of the Romantics too. I must therefore try to clarify the Victorian situation before discussing the poetry of the age.

That Romantic poetry is engaged in self-research is one of the more acceptable generalizations about it, and if we recognize the tensions and relationships existing between the egotistical and chameleon modes, the true complexity of this process can be appreciated. Poets who seek to convert experience into realized identity and extended self-awareness are clearly not just 'speaking from the heart' for purposes of 'self-expression'. But this remains a popular conception of Romantic poetry, and it was encouraged by Victorian attitudes, as I can best show by examining a favourite term of critical acclaim in the middle and later years of the century: sincerity.

When this concept was established as a literary criterion the exploratory vitality of Romanticism became weakened and less adventurous. From a theory and a poetry which sought to create its own moral foundations by the personal testing of experience, the move, in the minds of critics and readers, was towards caution. There was a tendency for the Romantic effort at self-experience to be interpreted as an aspect of honesty, taking this

SINCERITY: A VICTORIAN CRITERION

virtue in its most limpid sense of meaning what one says, and linking it too with the more uncomplicated and conventional feelings of the heart. Thus a very constricting model for poetic quality came to be laid down. Why this should have happened is a question which goes outside my present discussion; what is relevant is to see how it depends on the Romantic shift of focus to the proving of experience on the individual's pulses, and at the same time completely betrays, falsifies and enervates that poetic development. Some comments in Romantic theory seemed to lend themselves to such interpretation; but the whole context of Romantic thought and practice was overlooked, and the two poles of the imagination—whose very existence refutes the idea of poetry simply spilling from a full heart—have no place in the Victorian critical approach. The situation is summed up by A. H. Warren's statement that 'sincerity is the ultimate test of value in all early Victorian criticism'.[1] It remained a highly-regarded touchstone for the rest of the nineteenth century, and lingered on into the twentieth, although its decline can henceforward be traced to its last resting places, the review of the minor novel and the young student's limited critical vocabulary. We may now look at the Victorian heyday of sincerity more closely for the light it sheds on the distortion of the Romantic enterprise.

2

Evidence of such distortion is given in Laurence Lerner's claim that sincerity is 'the peculiar Romantic term of criticism'.[2] It is not in fact used as a general literary term by these poets, a point which is supported rather than defeated by the one instance where Wordsworth does introduce it into a critical essay. Before the nineteenth century, sincerity was a word with religious associations, implying purity of belief and freedom

---

[1] *English Poetic Theory, 1825–65* (Princeton, 1950), p. 222.
[2] *The Truest Poetry* (1960), p. 86. Two other recent contributions to this topic of sincerity may be noted: David Perkins, *Wordsworth and the Poetry of Sincerity* (Massachusetts, 1964) and Henri Peyre, *Literature and Sincerity* (Yale, 1963). Both these are valuable studies which, however, assume or imply that sincerity was itself a term commonly used in Romantic critical writing; e.g. Perkins, pp. 31–7, Peyre, p. 136.

153

from theological duplicity, and Wordsworth's use of it keeps it closely in touch with this ancestry, for in his 1810 essays on epitaphs he employs it as a standard of judgment. He is thinking in these essays predominantly about good and bad epitaphs, not setting up the sole test for poetic quality. The verses of the 'sincere mourner', he says, however gauche in expression, are worthy of respect because 'his heart during the very act of composition, was moved'.[1] Even such a limited attempt to use sincerity as a standard is enough to reveal its dangers, but once the leash is slipped and epitaphs are replaced by poems in general, the Victorian critic is to fall into attitudes that Wordsworth himself did not intend, even though one of his own phrases becomes a motto for these attitudes. The idea of poetry as the consequence of 'the spontaneous overflow of powerful feelings' flourishes as the century advances. To Wordsworth, in the Preface of 1802, the 'overflow' only explained the final stage in the complex processes of the creative state of mind, and in the suppression of all the other stages lies the crucial oversimplification and misplaced emphasis which obscures the nature of Romanticism to its successors. A close grappling with the problems of creative integrity in a context of intense psychological exploration dwindles to a naïve desire for the poet to be sincere, offering to us the comfortable conviction that his poem springs from a heart moved to lay bare its 'real' feelings. This conviction, moreover, remains entangled with the older implications of sincerity: that it bears some relationship with spiritual values. It follows that a sincere poet is an edifying one, uttering and endorsing Christian ideals. All Coleridge's profound efforts to integrate the functioning of imagination with the act of self-knowledge, from the absolute success of the Godhead to the groping performance of the human psyche; Shelley's neo-platonic vision; Keats's tense straining after identity: these are debased after 1830 into expectations that poets shall be piously sincere.

It may seem odd to associate the iconoclastic Carlyle with such a watering down, yet a demonstration of sincerity's age of high prestige should begin with his treatment of it. The lectures *On Heroes* in 1840 use the idea as their touchstone; it is 'the

---

[1] *Upon Epitaphs II. Prose Works*, ed. W. Knight, ii, p. 158.

measure of worth',[1] insistently urged: 'Sincerity, I say again, is the saving merit, now as always'.[2] He lauds it:

. . . the eye that flashes direct into the heart of things and *sees* the truth of them . . . Great Nature's own gift . . . what I call sincerity of vision: the test of a sincere heart.[3]

This approach to sincerity carries the idea onto a plane which the Romantics did not frequent. They had no use for a talisman word, repeated, intoned, invested with power simply by rhetorical sleight of hand: 'it has . . . something of divine . . . a Voice direct from Nature's own Heart'.[4] Carlyle is not developing, but emotionalizing an idea, making out of it a mystique.

This is reduction by apotheosis, and a similar effect can be seen in his other assumptions. Sincerity is the mark of Carlyle's great man: 'I should say *sincerity*, a deep, great, genuine sincerity, is the first characteristic of all men in any way heroic'.[5] The hero listens to the 'voice of Nature' which others disregard and which he cannot ignore. Here, a Romantic principle about the artist's response to inner promptings has been inflated into a sign of personal greatness, worshipful in itself; the result again is aggrandizement, together with a much increased stress on visitations by non-rational forces. The careful Romantic soundings of the mind in creation, noting the interplay of impulse and reflection and the illumination which rises out of this as a poem are lost in a more turgid and more vague interpretation of a man's relation with his inner self. And as *The Hero as Poet* shows, the goal of verbal creation is of less moment than the hero himself, being a hero.

From the writings of Carlyle, therefore, sincerity emerges as a divine manifestation, the voice of nature, and as such it is a 'measure of worth' and of human stature. Wordsworth's minor confusions about personal integrity and artistic honesty when he discusses epitaphs are vastly magnified in Carlyle's engulfing of artistic canons in the concept of heroic personality. His rhetoric makes man and artist inseparable in a way Romanticism did not seek to assert. The effect of his adoption of sincerity

---

[1] *The Hero as Poet; Works* (Ashburton edition, 1885–88), iii, p. 76.
[2] ibid., p. 80.   [3] *The Hero as Prophet;* ibid., p. 56.
[4] ibid., p. 45.   [5] ibid., p. 37.

is to blur distinctions and to carry the idea towards cruder emotional and moral treatment.

3

After Carlyle it is possible to assume that if sincerity is present, all is well with an artist and he is doing what is to be expected of him. The unfortunate price of the Sage's stylistic power is to give the illusion that this term may stand alone, magically suggestive of an ultimate value. By his very ambition for it, he robs it of precision, so opening the way for its loose association, in lesser minds, with a more naïve view of poetic veracity and the vague sense that poets must be ethically noble, in their verse and out of it, the distinction not being important.

A glimpse of the consequences of the first of these assumptions, that poets are simple recorders of their real feelings, can be seen in Leigh Hunt's *What is Poetry?* (1844). Sincerity to Hunt has just this implication: he praises the 'greatest early poets' for their 'passionate sincerity', contrasting them favourably in achievement with moderns who are 'perplexed by a heap of notions and opinions, or by doubts how emotion ought to be expressed'.[1] This is to advocate the 'spontaneous overflow' without qualifications: and sincerity is the word to describe such natural ease of creation. Hunt is typical in his unquestioning acceptance of sincerity as a self-evident, innocent value, clearly opposed to any process of creative thinking, a position alien to Romantic theory and practice alike. The trend to flabbiness is readily discernible. Even in some of the more intellectually sophisticated perceptions of John Stuart Mill, such softened Romanticism makes its appearance. Despite his respect for imaginative work as a means of personal development, he too stresses the predominant role of emotion in making the true poet: 'what is poetry, but the thoughts and words in which emotion spontaneously embodies itself?'[2]

It may be argued that Wordsworth offered some precedent for this, in those parts of the Preface of 1802 where he somewhat rashly supports the *Lyrical Ballads* experiment by maintaining

---

[1] *English Critical Essays, XIX Century*, World's Classics (Oxford, 1947), p. 258.
[2] ibid., p. 355.

that among the people, strong feeling leads to powerful expression. Coleridge, however, sensibly refuted this generalization in the *Biographia Literaria*, and by the evidence of other sections of the Preface itself, Wordsworth certainly never supposed that poetic creation was one simple unconsidered step from the fit of emotion to its verbal communication. Similarly, Keats's 'true voice of feeling'[1] is travestied by any such interpretation; a subtle tuning of self and material is integral to his whole creative outlook.

But to the Victorian mind, the formula 'to feel is to write' was acceptable. Emotion therefore exerted a tyrannical role in ideas on how poetry was made, and how it was to be recognized and assessed, while its implications shrank to meet a domestic and conservative estimate of what constitutes human feeling and its permissible range.

Keble's Oxford lectures given during the period 1832–41 display the same assumptions and point the same conclusions. Wherever he perceives the 'outpouring of a full heart', he finds the 'heights' of poetry. The true poet writes for the 'relief and solace of a burdened or over-wrought mind'.[2] This is spilt Wordsworth: and to Keble it produces sincere poetry, the acme of creative work. But more striking in the lectures is the other aspect of the term, the link between poetry and conventional morality which makes the former into an ennobling and virtuous act, propagating right thinking and edifying its readers as the utterances of an upright soul. Keble writes as one who 'viewed all poetry on the analogy of religion',[3] but his equating of good poetic speech with moral worth as shown in the 'common talk of daily life' illustrates one reason why sincerity came to attain its high place in Victorian literary estimation: it brought poetry within the safe orbit of the ethic of respectability. Keble says: '. . . a simple and sincere mind declares itself by almost exactly the same manifestations, whether in poetry or the common talk of daily life.'[4] In all his statements on the sincerity of poets he ties creative value to the fixed standards of an

[1] Reynolds, 21 September 1819; Rollins, ii, p. 167.
[2] *Keble's Lectures on Poetry 1832–41*, translated E. K. Francis (Oxford, 1912), i, pp. 50, 53.
[3] M. Abrams, *The Mirror and the Lamp* (paperback ed., 1958), p. 318.
[4] op. cit., i, p. 68.

accepted morality and religion. Poetry as verbal artistry, let alone as an instrument for individual growth, or extended self-realization by way of voyages into alien attitudes and experience, has no place in his view:

> The central point of our theory is that the essence of all poetry is to be found, not in high-wrought subtlety of thought, nor in pointed cleverness of phrase, but in the depths of the heart and the most sacred feelings of the men who write.[1]

On felicity of expression, Keble merely observes that when a poet is writing in obedience to the sacred feelings, his verses 'do, somehow or other, for the most part, flow and fall more happily and with richer rhythm'.[2] Thus the poet is exhorted: be sincere, all else will follow. His coat is being cut out of a suiting very close to clerical grey.

Arnold makes a contribution to the cause of sincerity, in this at least showing himself in concord with other critics and with the Philistines. He puts his own stamp on the word, like Carlyle, but the result is a further canonization of it as a standard for both creation and assessment. The 'sincerity and strength' he applies to Byron is taken from Swinburne, but it becomes for Arnold one of his familiar, trusted phrases, and is the basis of his praise for Byron.[3] Moreover, he regards the moments when Byron is most strong, most sincere, as the moments when 'a higher power' took possession of him—'Nature . . . takes the pen for him'.[4] Despite the difference in critical calibre, this is near enough to Keble for a common point of view to be apparent; and the moral earnestness never far from Arnold's criticism emerges with another echo of Keble in his claim for poetry's 'high seriousness' which 'comes from absolute sincerity'.[5] This is the distinguishing mark of poets of the first rank. Again, the pattern is the same: a lack of discrimination between literary stature and personal character, assessment of poetic worth in the light of a desired ethic, with the term sincerity working to promote these ends.

Arnold is able to take the word sincerity and its value for granted, a mark of its establishment. By the 1860s, the term

[1] ibid., ii, p. 201.　　　　　　　　　　　　　　[2] ibid., ii, p. 105.
[3] *Essays in Criticism*, Second Series (1889); Everyman ed. (1964), p. 325.
[4] ibid., pp. 327–8.　　　　　　　　　　[5] 'The Study of Poetry', ibid., p. 256.

was so far from needing justification that it could be raised explicitly to the dignity of a fundamental principle for literary creation and communication. Beginning in 1865, the *Fortnightly Review* published a series of essays by G. H. Lewes called *Principles of Success in Literature*. Addressed to aspirants, these essays include much discussion of the 'great cardinal principle of Sincerity' and Lewes's remarks epitomize the trends of half a century's usage. Without pursuing the implications, he warns that 'sincerity will not give talent'—a reservation containing the dormant seeds of the term's undoing as a critical value. But it will give, he adds at once, 'all the power possible',[1] and thus he maintains it firmly in its central place. He is dogmatic: 'unless the artist has felt the emotion he depicts we remain unmoved';[2] 'he must believe what he says or we shall not believe it';[3] 'To believe in yourself is the first step'.[4] Lewes could be writing a moral guide, and indeed he starts from the proposition that 'sincerity is moral truth';[5] therefore 'sincere work is good work, be it never so humble'.[6] Writers are being exhorted simply to be honest—and to be honest simply; not to pretend, to write as they would live. Lewes does not sentimentalize, but he helps to enfeeble the concept of imaginative activity in his insistence on writing straight from the heart.

In all these supporters of sincerity, there is that tacit or explicit support for the heart at the expense of the head and the complex psyche, which is the most injurious demeaning of Romantic theory and practice. Equally misleading is the overhasty muddling of poetic and personal values, in terms of established religious and moral convention.

4

The pressures on a Victorian poet were strong: not only was this pseudo-Romanticism set up for him as the ideal, but the authentic Romantic influence lived inescapably in his imagination as well. The poetry of the age may be seen as a battlefield—and sometimes as a negotiating table—where these two

---

[1] *The Principles of Success in Literature*, ed. T. S. Knowles (1898), p. 172.
[2] ibid., 'The Principle of Sincerity', p. 89 and *passim*.   [3] ibid., p. 21.
[4] ibid., p. 92.   [5] ibid., p. 21.   [6] ibid., p. 86.

factions meet. But before I consider some poets in the light of
the general situation, there is one critic whose relations with the
sincerity-cult merit separate attention. Walter Pater uses the
term, but its implications for him and its place in the context of
his critical outlook demonstrate that in this realm of theory, all
contact with Romantic developments was not lost. Pater is a
channel through which these developments flow to vitalize the
succeeding ages. His criticism is important if the genuine line of
Romanticism is to be clearly discerned, and it is a measure of
the influential power of the majority's attitude that he himself
has until very recently been dismissed as an aesthete luxuriating
before the Mona Lisa and cherishing his gem-like flame.
Rather, he sensed the significance of his century's poetic directions with more alertness and more prophetic awareness of the
radical shift in moral sensibility which they initiated than any of
his contemporaries. He saw his inheritance for what it was
where others failed to recognize it.

In his *Guardian* review of February 1889 dealing with Wordsworth, he speaks of sincerity, but he invokes it neither vaguely,
nor rhetorically, nor as the self-explanatory *ultima ratio*. He
praises Wordsworth for

that sincerity, that perfect fidelity to one's own inward presentations, to the precise features of the picture within, without which any
profound poetry is impossible.[1]

Thus, as René Wellek says, sincerity to Pater is a term which
can mean 'faithfulness to the inner vision'.[2] In *Marius the
Epicurean*, Flavian's approach to his art is described in a way
which expands this conception, and brings out the Romantic
affinities. Flavian is aware of the 'actual world in all its eager
self-assertion', and of himself 'in his boundless animation, there,
at the centre of the situation'. His preoccupation with form
serves the purpose

of bringing to the surface, sincerely and in their integrity, certain
strong personal intuitions, a certain vision or apprehension of things

[1] *Essays from 'The Guardian'* (1910), p. 102.
[2] 'Walter Pater's Literary Theory and Criticism', *Victorian Studies*, i (1957–8),
p. 39.

as really being, with important results, thus, rather than thus—
intuitions which the artistic or literary faculty was called upon to
follow, with the exactness of wax or clay, clothing the model within.

He fosters a 'very scrupulous literary sincerity with himself',
maintaining this 'uncompromising demand for a matter, in all
art, derived immediately from lively personal intuition, this
constant appeal to individual judgment. . .'.[1] Sincerity is
interpreted here as a strenuous artistic effort to reach and
record the encounter of the individual self with the actual world
and with its own inner world, an exacting process of discovery
and specific, experiential assessments. As such, it looks directly
back to the Romantic consciousness, that sense of being 'at the
centre of the situation' with the obligation to take account of this
personal medium in the search for valid observation and
evaluation, the refusal to generalize without the conviction
brought by the immediate agency of a reacting self. Pater shows
that he grasps the realities of an active, empirically zealous
imagination, and the common Victorian desire for sincere poets
seems the more feeble for his perception.

When Pater insists on the 'personal quality' of a work of art,
he upholds the Romantic view that the creator penetrates his
material to make it his own, and so to reveal himself in the
process of bringing it to artistic life. 'Essentially, perhaps', Pater
observes in *The Renaissance* 'it is the quality which alone makes
work in the imaginative and moral order really worth having at
all'.[2] Such a statement could only be made in a post-Coleridgean
age. 'Poetry without egotism comparatively uninteresting',
records that philosopher in a notebook.[3] Pater understands this
in depth, and formulates an idea of poetry which takes the
remark as meiosis to the extent of regarding a genuinely 'objective' or 'impersonal' art as impossible: 'the artist *will* be felt.
His subjectivity must and will colour the incidents'.[4] Even
Mérimée, a writer who strives to obey his rule 'to put nothing'
of himself into his works cannot in Pater's view escape the
egocentric pull; the 'superb self-effacement' itself becomes 'an

---

[1] *Marius the Epicurean* (1892), i, pp. 110-11.
[2] 'Luca della Robbia', *The Renaissance* (1904), pp. 71-2.
[3] Coburn, i, entry no. 62.
[4] *Sketches and Reviews* (New York, 1919), p. 80.

effective personal trait'.[1] Pater recognizes a creative law which operates whatever the type of work produced: the revelation of self which Coleridge perceived not only in the Miltonic, ego-tistical writer but in the protean power of a Shakespeare, who, becoming all things, remains for ever himself. In the nineteenth century, this principle becomes self-conscious; poets, and critics imaginatively tuned to them, value the creative force for the opportunities it offers for the fullest experience of subjective being, and the fullest discovery of its potential—Mérimée's need to resolve to be 'impersonal' is a measure of the dominance of this awareness.

Pater is a critic so attuned; and he preserves another essen-tial feature of the Romantic outlook in that, while exalting the 'personal quality' of imaginative work, he does not reduce it to the mistaken simplicity of the sincerity enthusiasts. He recognizes that there is a complex phenomenon here, that when a poet is conscious of himself 'at the centre of the situation' his creative position is highly sophisticated and very far from naïvely con-fessional. The intricacies of self and not-self are involved, and there is a problem to debate, not just an emotion to indulge:

Personality versus impersonality in art:—how much or how little of one's self one may put into one's work; whether anything at all of it: whether one *can* put there anything else:—is clearly a far-reaching and complex question.[2]

This example of Pater's sensitivity may be contrasted with the brusque and matter-of-fact approach of Ruskin at the begin-ning of his essay on the 'Pathetic Fallacy' where he dismisses the debate on 'Objective and Subjective' as so much nonsense. To him these words are 'the most objectionable that were ever coined by the troublesomeness of metaphysicians', and the issue is not one that stands up to the straight gaze of common sense. He is particularly appalled at the suggestion—to Pater so resonant in its implications—that 'it does not much matter what things are in themselves, but only what they are to us; and that the only real truth of them is their appearance to, or effect upon, us'.[3] Ruskin here touches the nerve centre of his centurys'

---

[1] 'Prosper Mérimée', *Miscellaneous Studies* (1900), pp. 23–4.   [2] ibid.
[3] *English Critical Essays, XIX Century*, pp. 323–4.

imaginative life, but it arouses in him no answering excitement. This whole essay begs more questions about poetic statement than it settles, substituting a literal flat-footedness for insight into creative relationships, as pursued by Coleridge in the *Biographia Literaria*. And nowhere is there a more eloquent example of a Victorian critic failing to recognize the whole Romantic event than in Ruskin's scorn here for that 'German dulness and English affectation' which worries over the relation of the observer with the thing apparently perceived, and, more, dares to elevate the former to a position of crucial significance. Whereas to Pater, by contrast, the notion of individuality stimulates investigation and is the heart of creative life. It offers to him a key to living experience.

Here the prophetic role of his thinking becomes apparent. Where the earlier poets regarded the reacting individual as the most sensitive means of arriving at any mature evaluation, the Victorian inheritor of this outlook feels it to be not merely desirable and enriching, but imperative, the only way to make sense and capital out of a universe in flux. The Romantics proposed that 'subject modifying object' was an illuminating concept for poetry; but this grows into the more acute sense of relativity where subject is isolated with object, each percipient self alone in its shifting sea of experience. Evaluation only has meaning if it takes as its unit the given instant of response, for instead of continuity, each moment exists as a new proposition, confronted by a self likewise changing, altered by what it feeds on. Pater himself, acknowledging the necessity of this situation, maintains the Romantic appetite for it; so does Browning. Less confident reactions to it are to be found in other poets of the Victorian age, in Tennyson and Arnold, for example, but whichever spirit prevails, they all meet as those who honour their inheritance by making it their own, so neither degrading nor embalming it. As a result, they in their turn have much to bequeath.

Pater speaks explicitly of the 'relative spirit' which he deems characteristic of the time in his essay on Coleridge in *Appreciations*. He praises Goethe here for his alertness to 'every moment of life' with its 'contribution of experimental, individual knowledge'. In this essay, 'individual' clearly is a word close in implication to 'unique'; each person has his own vision, and within each life, 'every hour is unique'. The effort of modern imaginative awareness must be to grasp the truth of this fluid complexity of experience—'not the truth of eternal outlines ascertained once for all, but a world of fine gradations and subtly linked conditions, shifting intricately as we ourselves change'.[1] Pater also reveals the alternative response to this situation, and hence suggests the variety of creative work which can lay claim to a common centre. Although he maintains a Romantic enthusiasm for its opportunities, he can portray the same vision in terms which allow it to be interpreted as a predicament, an invitation to terror, or, more boldly, to anarchy:

Experience, already reduced to a swarm of impressions, is ringed round for each one of us by that thick wall of personality through which no real voice has ever pierced on its way to us, or from us to that which we can only conjecture to be without. Every one of these impressions is the impression of the individual in his isolation, each mind keeping as a solitary prisoner its own dream of a world.[2]

While so many Victorian critics were purveying a version of Romanticism which bore little relation to the reality, being at once too simple, too pompous and too tainted with the respectable virtues, Pater therefore was in touch with the vital imaginative current. He saw it as a profound movement of the whole psyche and the beginning of a more radical phase in the ceaseless human effort to carry out the injunction, 'know thyself'. He saw also that its potential was many-sided, that it offered scope for imaginative research which was free, on the one hand, to celebrate the individual's sovereignty or to savour the fortuitous conjunctions prevailing for the moment only; and on the other, to beat against the 'thick wall', or to make a close examination of this prison. He is a beam of light amid the fogs of sincerity.

But the Victorian poets are with Pater, despite the demands that they interpret the call to a difficult and intricate honesty as an obligation merely to pour out comforting, high-minded sentiments. They collaborated in the process of acknowledging the self 'at the centre of the situation' and in exploring the

[1] *Appreciations* (1915), pp. 66–8.　　[2] Conclusion, *The Renaissance*, p. 235.

growing awareness of the complexities of experience, with its repercussions for the moral faculty. That self-creation which fascinated Pater as a 'strange, perpetual weaving and unweaving of ourselves'[1] demanded and received the poet's loyalty, not always successfully and sometimes given under duress, but given with sufficient dedication to make them genuine followers of Romanticism and, in their turn, forerunners.

[1] ibid., p. 236.

VI

INHERITING PEGASUS: TENNYSON, ARNOLD AND BROWNING

> The next generation . . . will tumble and break their necks off our Pegasus, who runs away with us; but we keep the *saddle*, because we broke the rascal and can ride. But though easy to mount, he is the devil to guide; and the next fellows must go back to the riding-school and the manège, and learn to ride the 'great horse'.
>
> Byron to Moore

THERE WAS an alternative for the 'next fellows': they could refuse the gift of this spirited horse and mount a more docile animal with no fear of broken necks. They had every encouragement from their contemporaries to do so; the general criticism of the age assumed that the Romantic Pegasus was a much less formidable beast anyway, quite amenable on soft feeding and ready to answer to the name 'Sincerity'. The inability of many Victorians to do more than diminish their inheritance has led to the fallacious belief that the poets themselves did likewise, failing to take up the challenge Byron so vividly prophesied. But the poets mounted and grappled with Pegasus, applying themselves to the task of learning his strength and how to guide it. It is also true that they exulted less and feared more in doing so, but as a result, they deepened their insight into their steed's nature. Thanks to unflinching Victorian horsemanship, he came to his twentieth-century riders a more thoroughly known 'rascal', yet with his spirit unquenched.

2

After the stress on the 'black-blooded' aspect of his genius, which made him tolerable to the black-blooded modern reader,[1] Tennyson is now admitted to be a poet of great if confused

[1] See, for instance, Harold Nicolson's *Tennyson* (1923), where the poet's 'black-blooded race' (p. 35) is taken as the clue to the 'real Tennyson' (p. 69).

variety, with perhaps rather fewer unreadable areas than prejudice had assumed. But we still need to learn to see Tennyson
in a wider context: to many he remains a poet of his time in a
restrictive sense, and partly because of this narrow view his
work appears haphazardly rather than coherently various. But
if he is considered as a poet of the generation inheriting the
uniquely Romantic imaginative awareness, then his poetry
reveals itself as a vital body of work instead of a miscellany; and
once such a unity is apparent, so also is the way from Tennyson
to later poets. The question is no longer one of finding congenial
poems in a basically alien assortment, but of recognizing kinship
and hence the strong line attaching modern to Romantic. We
can understand the link most clearly by tracing the egotistical
and chameleon categories in Tennyson's career; for him as for
his predecessors, they are the two poles which provide the clue
to the nature of his creative power.

The chameleon impulse works in Tennyson with an energy
which shows a far from cautious acceptance of this mode of the
explorative imagination. He writes monologue, duologue,
dramatic narrative, and monodrama, with speakers who range
from young girls to old women, from saints to Lincolnshire
farmers, from Greek heroes to mermen. Before making any
judgments about sentimentality or melodrama we should recognize the fact of this appetite for what it is, a chameleon effort
to possess the sensation of the individual outlook, to grasp the
notion of such variety, not merely to take virtuoso advantage of
it. Tennyson follows where *Lyrical Ballads* and the other Romantic experiments led. He is stimulated as they were, and of course
with their example before him, by the need to enter the different
universe each person inhabits, whether it be dramatically
unique as in the startling perspective of Simeon Stylites on his
pillar or, more domestically so, in the kind of solitude peculiar
to old age, as in *The Grandmother*.

There are other tendencies in Tennyson's poetry which can
also be regarded as manifestations of the chameleon spirit. From
his earliest days, he likes to contemplate a subject in more than
one version, or to examine a proposition from two or more
viewpoints.[1] In his first volume, the *Merman* monologue is at

[1] It is interesting that Arthur Hallam also felt this impulse. A poem of his

167

once balanced by the Mermaid's point of view; *The Sea Fairies* of 1830 is closely paralleled by *The Lotus Eaters* of 1833; there are the two *Mariana* poems, and two versions of *The Northern Farmer*. Later, the most obvious example is the '60 years After' sequel to *Locksley Hall*, but this study of the rejected lover or disastrous courtship is a much-refracted theme, one which he explores not only in the double utterance of the *Locksley Hall* hero but in *Aylmer's Field, Love and Duty, The Lover's Tale, Edwin Morris*, and of course most fully in *Maud*. Similar relationships— seen from the feminine point of view—are at the least obliquely present in many other poems: *Dora, The May Queen, Mariana* and *Oenone*—with *The Death of Oenone*—for example. If we enlarge the theme to admit studies of marriages, or triangular situations, this readiness to work over and over the same emotional ground with different persons or circumstances is even more apparent—the *English Idylls* become a group, the *Idylls of the King* show this unity beneath their mythological costume; *Lucretius* is connected with *The First Quarrel* and *Enoch Arden, The Miller's Daughter* with *The Gardener's Daughter*.

But within Tennyson's chameleon energies, there is contrast as well as similarity with his Romantic predecessors. Words- worth was moved to realize the pain of the shepherd he met on the road, or the vision of an idiot child out in the moonlight as positive enlargements of his personal experience, and Keats followed Shakespeare in capturing the inward sensation of the snail in its dark house for the sheer pleasure of being able to don identities so remote from his own; Tennyson's motives, however, involve a far less delighted confidence in such creative exercise. For him, as well as the fascination of acknowledging myriad world pictures and endlessly unique versions of similar experience, there is a colder interpretation of such shifting variety: if, given one point of view, there exists also its opposite, then either they are equally meaningless, or at the most, of equal validity. There is also the further proposition that within a single mind, rival ideas and emotions may simultaneously exist and, if this is so, the chameleon power may take on a quality of menace, dividing

entitled 'Two ways of looking at one thing', and written in the voices of 'he' and 'she' is among those published in a Supplement to *Victorian Poetry*, vol. iii, 1965 (publications of the Tennyson Society, No. 3).

and giving awareness of division. It then threatens the individual integrity on which Romantic sorties into alien and opposed states of feeling were based, and which was in its turn reinforced by such researches. Byron acknowledged the tension undergone by the mobile and antithetical mind, but for him it opened the way to self-recognition; it did not as act a threat to a unified experience of self nor suggest grounds for a suicidal, self-cancelling alarm. Tennyson's chameleon creativity on the other hand brings this new fear with it.

His first collections of poems contain evidence of this development, evidence both innocent and sophisticated. Besides the dual exercises already noted, and the various attempts at monologues, all of which show what may be termed the healthy chameleon impulse, there are the twin poems *Nothing Will Die* and *All Things Will Die* and the elaborately titled *Supposed Confessions of a Second Rate Sensitive Mind not in Unity with Itself* (1830). The twin poems are a very youthful exhibition of cancelling thought and mood and no great weight of interpretation should be placed upon so slight an utterance. The significance lies in the sight of the apprentice poet playing with his gifts, and being led to a formula of juxtaposed yet antipathetic points of view, working out both, acknowledging both—or neither—and thus extending the chameleon range to confront such a mental situation. While the resulting poems are trivial, the instinct of the imagination which creates them is deeply rooted and permanently his, and more serious testimony to this is provided by the *Supposed Confessions*.

It has become commonplace in Tennyson criticism to descry states of conflict within the poetry, to point out the battle between 'star' and 'clod' which preoccupies him and masters his sensibility. Certainly in the *Supposed Confessions*, the speaker deplores 'our double nature' and the 'damned vacillating state' of humanity. But before the poem is used to explain the poet's world-picture, we may study it in its own character and in its psychological perceptions for the help it gives in establishing the fundamental habits of his imagination. The title shows that the poem is a stilted but very deliberate attempt to realize dramatically a confused state of mind. Whether it represents Tennyson's own condition, or his more impersonal recognition that such a duality of mind can occur is immaterial. The points of poetic importance are first, his decision to enact this situation in a monologue form so that it emerges as an experience, not merely as a commentary, and secondly, his implied judgment of the speaker's predicament: the mind is 'second-rate', and so there is an element of failure in its friction and disunity. Tennyson is at once identified with the condition and aware of it as calamitous —the first-rate sensitive mind, presumably, would not be so afflicted and would command itself as a single nature without vacillating; but such is not the human potential.

The poem is one of desperation. The chameleon mode is being exerted to express fears negatively relevant to its own powers, fears that the human mind is nothing but a moral chameleon, unable to maintain a steadfast belief or single approach to life. It is not 'fortified from doubt'. Tennyson's work from his first volume onwards therefore adds the psychology of doubt to the Romantic range. This a move from a ready identification with all manner of being to a panic-tinged discovery that such a capacity may seem only an unstable shifting from one point of view to another with a consequent breakdown of unified self-consciousness. Chameleon power thus threatens instead of complementing egotistical awareness, which is in its turn altered from the Romantic sublimity, harassed by these doubts cast on its reality. What develops is a darker vision of self-consciousness as self-imprisonment.

This complex condition and especially the latter aspect of it brings to birth Tennyson's two central poems. Both belong to the established modes, the egotistical *In Memoriam* balanced by the chameleon *Maud*, but each poem explores the same fears and voices the same dilemma of consciousness and self-awareness. Other poems besides *Supposed Confessions* herald this intensive concentration on the issues generated by Romantic poetry. Once that major movement of imagination had taken place, it could not be revoked; the Victorian poet was forced to revise, but he could not ignore the imaginative concern with personal identity, and Tennyson exemplifies the compulsive preoccupation and the effort of reorientation in poems such as *The Two Voices* and *The Palace of Art*. These poems helpfully introduce the longer works by indicating the way in which an inevitable and indeed willing acceptance of the Romantic legacy is mixed with a sense that it is a burden whose weight is only just becoming apparent.

Like the *Supposed Confessions, The Two Voices* is a revealing title. Published in the 1842 volume, this poem demonstrates first the ego-threatening disintegration which is one aspect of chameleon versatility. The one voice suggests, the other opposes suicide; both are credible, both speak with authority, and the mind gives itself to each, yet as it does so the case for the negative voice is more insistent simply because there seems to be no firm entity which through sheer confidence in its own existence could rout the hints that prized individual being is as nothing. The chameleon mind can entertain the notion of self-annihilation, and thus makes such an event more probable:

> 'No compound of this earthly ball
> Is like another, all in all.'

> To which he answered scoffingly;
> 'Good soul! suppose I grant it thee,
> Who'll weep for thy deficiency?

> 'Or will one beam be less intense,
> When thy peculiar difference
> Is cancelled in the world of sense?'

> I would have said, 'Thou canst not know',
> But my full heart, that worked below,
> Rained thro' my sight its overflow.

Keats's passionate faith in the evolving of a distinct identity, and the determined quest of Andreas in *Zapolya* to find himself, seem distant from this agonized acquiescence in the prospect of ultimate anonymity. Yet the one opens the way to the other. Tennyson has not retreated, his horror arises because he assents to the view he has inherited, that there is a high value in the unique self, with its powers of extending and realizing its nature more fully in all its acts. Now such abilities appear as self-division, and the capacity to become other than one self is transformed to a nightmarish premonition of non-being.

Even in *The Two Voices*, however, it is clear that one reaction to the horror and one way of diminishing its force is paradoxically to endure the full experience of all voices. For the poem is Tennyson's *Ancient Mariner*.[1] It is an encounter poem, and it brings about the enlarging participation in another person's universe. But where the Mariner leads the Wedding Guest into strange seas and imparts to him the secrets of imaginative sympathy, here it is the world of the Wedding Guest which works upon the anguished Mariner and brings him to the spontaneous chameleon impulse. 'It is the Sabbath morn':

> On to God's house the people prest:
> Passing the place where each must rest,
> Each entered like a welcome guest.
>
> One walked between his wife and child,
> With measured footfall firm and mild,
> And now and then he gravely smiled.
>
> The prudent partner of his blood
> Leaned on him, faithful, gentle good,
> Wearing the rose of womanhood.
>
> And in their double love secure
> The little maiden walked demure,
> Pacing with downward eyelids pure.
>
> These three made unity so sweet,
> My frozen heart began to beat,
> Remembering its ancient heat.
>
> I blest them, and they wandered on:
> I spoke, but answer came there none:
> The dull and bitter voice was gone.

These lines have been much abused. Modern readers accept the 'bitter voice' in Tennyson as poetically authentic, but they deny the validity of his attempts to convey a more positive state of mind. There may still be insufficient detachment from Victorian society to free scenes like this one from the stock response of repugnance. But if we adopt a view of the poem which allows

[1] Resemblances are noted by C. de L. Ryals, *Theme and Symbol in Tennyson's Poems to 1850* (Philadelphia, 1964), p. 120.

us to be aware of its mechanisms as a whole, and its Romantic ancestry, then a more just reading becomes possible. Without assenting to Victorian ideas of family life or of piety, we may acknowledge the fundamental rhythms working upon Tennyson here. *The Two Voices* provides a paradigm of his imagination. *The Palace of Art, In Memoriam,* and *Maud* all in their different ways follow the same movement from a self-concern which has become paralytic to a recognition of the value of losing the ego in order to find it. *The Two Voices* helps to make it clear that the Romantic chameleon impulse of *Lyrical Ballads* and all encounter poems works profoundly and freshly in Tennyson. He is led to investigate the implications of relationships more than his predecessors had done and so to make, in *Maud,* a more deliberately experimental incursion into the chameleon mode, and to fashion in *In Memoriam* a new kind of egotistical poem.

The Palace of Art prepares the way for *In Memoriam*. It allegorically presents the Victorian egotistical vision, as *The Two Voices* depicts the two sides of the chameleon. In this poem Tennyson first recalls the sublimity of mood which is found as the self inherits its patrimony, serene in its independence: 'my soul would live alone unto herself In her high palace there'. This is the stage of 'God-like isolation' and might be a comment on the exultant confidence of *The Prelude* where Wordsworth dwells in his palace in a spirit of eager self-discovery. But Tennyson next records how the splendour passes, to be replaced by terror and a sense of isolation far from serene:

> Deep dread and loathing of her solitude
> Fell on her, from which mood was born
> Scorn of herself; again, from out that mood
> Laughter at her self-scorn . . .

> A still salt pool, locked in with bars of sand,
> Left on the shore, that hears all night
> The plunging seas draw backward from the land
> Their moon-led waters white . . .

> Back on herself her serpent pride had curled.
> 'No voice', she shrieked in that lone hall,
> 'No voice breaks thro' the stillness of this world;
> One deep, deep silence all!'

> Shut up as in a crumbling tomb, girt round
>   With blackness as a solid wall,
> Far off she seemed to hear the dully sound
>   Of human footsteps fall.

The palace is also a tomb: Victorian fear sobers the Romantic glory. Again, it occurs not because the Romantic view is rejected but because it is so readily adopted. The first stanzas of *The Palace of Art* exulting in the citadel are as eloquent as the later verses tracing the metamorphosis of an ego turning back on itself, growing tormented and haunted by its autonomy. But the stress now falls on the torment. Being sovereign of a personal universe also means being sentenced to solitary imprisonment and, faced with this crisis, Tennyson gives his allegorical version of what is to be the central drama of *In Memoriam*: the effort to to conquer the darker implications by abandoning the palace for the cottage among other dwellings, thus inviting emotional exchange, the self experienced in terms of relationships. The departure from the palace-prison closely parallels the movement of *The Two Voices*, and leads again to straightforward chameleon resolution, but it is quite clearly also an attempt to preserve the egotistical vision. The palace towers are still loved, still seen to be 'lightly, beautifully built', and they are not to be destroyed. Tennyson reaffirms the delight in realized personal identity, enthroned and in control of its world, which imbues all the regally-toned assertions of Romantic poetry and drama.

3

In Memoriam is *The Palace of Art* translated from stylized formality into the emotional welter of life. Its natural context is Romantic egotistical poetry, and above all, it stands in close relation to *The Prelude*. Both poems record the 'most intimate subjective experience' of their authors; each is rooted in 'deeply personal analysis',[1] but in the contrasts of reaction and approach which the poems offer, the changing fortunes of the egotistical vision are well marked. The key to Wordsworth's poem is his perception of the principles of growth and organization, his sense of a self which is manifested in the interworking of

[1] J. H. Buckley, *Tennyson: the Growth of a Poet* (Massachusetts, 1960), p.108.

experience and consciousness. Tennyson's poem springs from the opposite perception—that the self may be a victim instead of an overlord, wrecked by experience it cannot master or assimilate, its whole integrity jeopardized. Where Wordsworth could rejoice autocratically in the palace of himself, Tennyson is dependent on the mirrors of emotional relationships to reach any fulfilment of self-recognition—whether joyous or desperate. It is no accident of circumstance that Tennyson's major response to the egotistical pole of his imagination was aroused by the death of his closest friend and the ensuing mood of elegy.

Whatever miscellany of experience came to Wordsworth, he found it transformed into organic unity by the process of assimilation within his mind, a mind revealed and known by this very activity; *The Prelude* re-enacts, it does not create this sense of significant order and interconnection. It is a song of himself with a music inaudible to Tennyson, who is not engaged in demonstrating assimilated and ordered experience but in making the initial effort to master what assails him as the near-chaos of self, emotion and event. In his poem, the egotistical vision is on trial. Self remains central: all that happens, all that is will be drawn into potential relation with it, but there is no certainty that it can work creatively upon this material, nor therefore that it can come to that illuminated knowledge of its own nature which is *The Prelude*'s chief sublimity and triumph. *The Prelude* is epiphanal; *In Memoriam* a crisis of faith in personal validity.

The contrasts between the two must not, however, be taken as verdicts against Tennyson and in Wordsworth's favour. *In Memoriam* faces its crises and in doing so opens up new areas for the egotistical imagination to colonize; it demonstrates what usually goes unrecognized in the work of Victorian poets, that is, the fruitful acceptance of Romantic pioneering, not in a spirit of unadventurous gratitude, but with an explorative energy of its own. The two generations for all their differences of mood and method share a fundamental instinct of imagination, the younger recognizing the affinity and accepting the responsibility of it. Section XLIV of *In Memoriam* gives an explicit illustration of the Victorian readiness to study consciousness and the phenomenon of self-awareness:

The baby new to earth and sky,
   What time his tender palm is prest
   Against the circle of the breast,
Has never thought that 'this is I':

But as he grows he gathers much
   And learns the use of 'I' and 'me',
   And finds 'I am not what I see,
And other than the things I touch':

So rounds he to a separate mind
   From whence clear memory may begin,
   As thro' the frame that binds him in
His isolation grows defined.

Here the changed temper of the egotistical idea is apparent in the poet's choice of the world 'isolation' to convey the growing conviction of individual being. And the sense of self is reached not by gradual and welcome evolutionary processes but as a consequence of shock, the loss of a sheltering love. *In Memoriam* conceives all such 'rounding to a separate mind' as a more bitter repetition of the natural emergence from childish security. There is a need for remedy rather than rejoicing here, and the connected lyrics of grief, bewilderment, and love struggle to overthrow the menace of the situation. The poet faces the most un-Wordsworthian fear that the lone self, so exposed, is without meaningful identity in the universe. Only at the end of the poem after the series of lyrics scrutinizing the sensations of the isolated creature, has he reached assurance that it possesses within itself the vital powers of consolidation, the creative mastery of its own condition. Tennyson travels painfully to end at the point where Wordsworth began, and in his triumph sounds a note of exhaustion: 'not in vain, Like Paul with beasts, I fought with Death' (CXIX). The death so repulsed brought a spectral encounter with self, 'mine own phantom':

   And on the depths of death there swims
   The reflex of a human face.

                          (CVII)

The self-awareness which Tennyson fights to convert from negative horror to positive power is not the same as the sense of a

totally independent personal identity celebrated by Wordsworth. As 'isolation' only became evident because of an
emotional amputation, so equally it is fought by an awareness
of self in association with another person. The energy of *In
Memoriam* springs from its feeling for relationship. The subjective
consciousness is always approached by an emotional route, love
for another, and thus the Wordsworthian sovereignty of the
individual is modified. Love is established as mediator. 'I dream
a dream of good And mingle all the world with thee' (CXXVIII) is
the poet's way of announcing the perceptive moment of victory,
and by it he shows also the direction of the effort throughout.
Tennyson depends on the agency of love to restore his world and
to render his enforced recognition of distinct identity tolerable.
He moves necessarily towards the apotheosis of Hallam, and
this creative act of love is self-creative also, redeeming the
phantom. As he writes in the Epilogue, half rejecting his songs
of misery,

> Regret is dead, but love is more
> Than in the summers that are flown,
> For I myself with these have grown
> To something greater than before . . .

Is this then a retreat or an advance from the Wordsworthian
heights? It involves both. A retreat, because to Tennyson the
mind alone with itself is and remains cause for panic, not
creative joy. His use of child-imagery in conveying his experience
of the 'sole self' is eloquent: 'a child in doubt and fear' (CXXIII),
'an infant crying in the night' (LIII). 'Be near me' (XLIX) is his
plea from beginning to end. The poem demonstrates that the
lone self is a threat which may be countered, but not denied, and
so it reduces the Romantic exultation at ruling freely in the
kingdom of one's individual universe. Yet, on the other hand, in
moving down from the rarefied regions of the egotistical sublime
Tennyson has passed through a valley of lonely fear to reach a
different height with a positive vision of its own. He has rescued
the egotistical as an ideal by submitting it to the experience of
love and discovering that a coherent, personally valid universe
emerges from such a surrender. He opens up the whole area of
relationships as he explores the way in which the fully-grown

self may achieve its identity by means of emotional commitment.

But *In Memoriam* retains a hint of fearful limitations even within the success of its effort to overthrow panic. In the poem's double sensibility, the Victorian imaginative situation is epitomized. Accepting the policy of the self as evaluative centre, Victorian poets learn to fear and to bear it, to face the responsibilities it brings and to pursue its implications beyond the initial vision of a splendid autonomy.

In Memoriam with its sustained lyrical quatrains in a unitary voice demonstrates the more strained Victorian position at the egotistical pole; *Maud* with its flexible rhythms presents it in the chameleon mode. Tennyson's general appetite for the latter is one of the most obvious signs of the Romantic legacy to him. But *Maud* shows more than the 'delight of the chameleon poet', indulging himself with feats of self-transformation. A poem motivated by pressing need, by a crisis of consciousness and the search for a way out, it registers the shocks of the palace turned gaol, and faces the 'dark corners' of the walled-in mind as authentically as the poem of elegy and self-debate. The chameleon powers were welcomed by the Romantics themselves as instruments for exposing the various nightmare regions of the psyche—in *The Ancient Mariner*, *The Borderers* and *The Prisoner of Chillon*, for instance—but here the Victorian poet finds more urgent and more surgical work for them. He probes the very problem of identity, seeking to understand the terror of the proposition as it now appears: that to be wholly alone with oneself is not the crown of life but the point of ultimate breakdown, leading even to the final loss of that prized self-consciousness.

There is no bolder effort in nineteenth-century poetry than Tennyson's monodrama; his choice of manic-depressive hero and the technical resources he expends in realizing the extremes of heightened feeling which are at once garish and hyper-sensitive, show an imaginative courage that has won too little praise. His pleasure in performing the poem, together with its melodramatic aspects have helped to obscure its real enterprise under applause for its virtuosity or mockery at its posturing. Yet if we place it beside *In Memoriam*, the pattern of the

Romantic imagination emerges impressively once more, emphasizing that *Maud* is wholly serious.[1] Here, as so often in Romantic
work, a major exertion at one pole of the imagination is followed
by recoil to the other and a reworking of similar themes with
undiminished energies.

Both poems centre on love for another person. *Maud* underlines my point that Tennyson's contribution to the poetic study
of self is to carry it into the sphere of relationships. The hero of
the monodrama is not a grotesque invention fathered by the
sensationalist fiction of the age, but an authentic and revealing
product of the Victorian poetic imagination, and this is only
surprising if we hold too genteel a concept of that imagination
—and of *In Memoriam*. In the violence of *Maud*, and the course
of its action, there is a desperate sounding of *In Memoriam*'s
hard-fought victory, its faith in the power of emotional commitment to release the individual's potential resources. The hero of
Maud is from the outset palpably in the grip of the *Palace of Art*
nightmare, living as a prisoner of haunting memories, 'raging
alone' as his father 'raged in his mood' (I, 14) and painfully
aware of the suicidal propensities within him. He cannot get
away from his brooding, and the world exists only in terms of it,
until, through his requited love for Maud, he breaks out. But
this experience of love is not the sustained communion of *In
Memoriam*, reknitting after the fracture of death; it is a precarious
moment of harmony, an interlude soon irrevocably shattered.
Tennyson undergoes in *Maud* the disaster of love found only to
be destroyed, the bitter process of reversion to the mind entomb-
ed after the ecstatic discovery that there can be freedom. The
personality as it reacts to love is, however, central to each poem,
and each hero places the same high valuation on his emotional
condition, regarding it as the force which liberates him, releasing
his capacity for a more creative self-awareness.

> But if I be dear to some one else,
> Then I should be to myself more dear.
>
> (xv)

---

[1] Recent research into possible biographical roots for *Maud*—R. W. Rader,
Tennyson's Maud: the biographical genesis (California, 1963)—which intends by this
means to raise its claims to serious study seems to involve something of a throwback to 'sincerity' confusions.

Although the hero of *Maud* only knows love as a passionate collision of brief duration, ending in violence and exile, he provides the dramatic counterpart to *In Memoriam*'s finely graduated lyrical analysis of prolonged stages of feeling. The highly-coloured action, the pathological pitch of the emotion, is the exaggeration of the magnifying glass, not the excess of crude or exhibitionist writing. The hero is hysterical, the poet is not. He subjects himself to extremes of behaviour without losing artistic control, seeking the salvation of the self-conscious mind by following it through the most acute symptoms of its condition. In the later sections of *Maud*, he pursues chameleon realization into the madness which follows upon the calamitous end of love and hope. The imagery of barrenness and burial descriptively used in *The Palace of Art* now takes on dramatic life. The hero, engulfed by insanity, is lost within himself, reduced to the horror of 'living death' and exposed to the torment of a completely sterile subjectivity:

> Dead, long dead.
> Long dead!
> And my heart is a handful of dust,
> And the wheels go over my head,
> And my bones are shaken with pain,
> For into a shallow grave they are thrust,
> Only a yard beneath the street,
> And the hoofs of the horses beat, beat,
> The hoofs of the horses beat,
> Beat, into my scalp and my brain . . .
>
> (XVII, I)

With their ironic sense of bustling activity a yard above the head, these lines offer the black reverse of the Romantic vision: self captive to self.

Thus the nineteenth-century imagination endures the hazards that its enlarged horizons and explorative licence have brought it. Tennyson in both his major works continues to adopt the Romantic approach even while he finds that individual sovereignty can mean destructive isolation. His task is to vindicate the two modes of self-realization rather than exhibit them as given, positive resources. *In Memoriam* works forward to experience the egotistical achievement of imposing order on its universe; at the conclusion of *Maud*, the hero is only released from his nightmare by his discovery that participating in the world of others can re-establish a more tolerable sense of his own identity. He is thankful to 'mix [his] breath with a loyal people shouting a battle-cry' (xxviii, 3) and finds relief in the knowledge, 'I have felt with my native land, I am one with my kind' (5). The dread he thrusts away here—that of the pariah-self, cut off and unreachable—is to patrol the frontiers of imagination from this time onwards. Tennyson in the last movement of *Maud* has been abused or laughed at for jingoistic naïveté, but the point he makes is one close to the heart of the modern imagination. The chameleon mode here as in *The Two Voices* recognizes its value as a defence, a refuge, and a reassuring means of self-awareness, combating the plight of the imprisoned ego.

To the Romantic, the chameleon energies rejoiced in their own power, as did the egotistical; for the Victorian, as the whole venture of *Maud* shows, the tone has changed to a thankful recognition that chameleon power can be turned against the horror of isolation. The poet can learn through exercising it that he is 'one with his kind' and this is a lesson he must now set out to learn, it cannot be pre-supposed. Love takes on a new importance as the way out from self which paradoxically provides the surest route to creative contact with it and the most concrete assurance of positive identity. Again, we see that the need to oppose an entirely daunting prospect generates a distinctive Victorian development of the Romantic vision.

4

If any poem of the Romantic age foreshadows Tennyson, it is *The Excursion*. This poem offers a model where *The Prelude* can only stand as a unique monument to the bright dawn of poetic self-commitment. Wordsworth's Solitary fathers the alienated Victorian hero, and the tactics employed for his salvation anticipate the mid-century poetry. The one hope for the closed and aloof mind of the Solitary was to prove him 'one with his kind', and to engage his sympathies with the humble experience of ordinary lives. The tales told in *The Excursion* displayed and

sought to promote the chameleon response, because Wordsworth knew its absence to be gravely injurious.

This hinterland is important in helping us to understand the
relationship of some of Tennyson's verse tales and idylls to the
deepest currents of his imagination. He writes out of the knowledge that he is Solitary as well as Pastor: he is able to participate in the variety of life around him, yet at the same time he
needs to be convinced that such contact, such enlargement, is
possible, since he knows keenly too the isolated mind. Tales such
as *Dora*, *Aylmer's Field* and *Enoch Arden* are equivalents of *The
Excursion*, sponsored by Tennyson's capacity to respond to the
material, and sharing with *The Excursion* fine moments of concrete detail, yet showing him struggling also with the conviction
of its otherness, his detachment from it. The monologues, by
contrast, show the chameleon Ariel, free and unshadowed by
such tension.

The tales betray the double angle of the poet's approach by
their stilted tone; the narrator's voice remains obtrusive, the
emotional situations being filtered through this presence which
neither yields to the scenes nor yet dominates them, but merely
broods upon them rather heavily. Readers often attribute the
uneasiness of the poems to sentimentality and ludicrous action,
which indeed are present. But they are symptoms of a more
fundamental awkwardness: the material is neither autonomous
nor ruled by the independent perceptions of the narrator. It
cannot speak for itself, for he is not given fully to it, but neither
does he stand clear in genuinely creative commentary which
would add the dimension of a narrating personality to the poem,
one sympathetic to the story and persons, yet with his own
response to their history.

Wordsworth as narrator in *Lyrical Ballads* made capital out
of his awareness of himself as commentator; Keats was ready to
learn how to do so. In Tennyson's *Aylmer's Field*, there is a token
attempt to set up a three-point view of the story, that of the
actors, the poet, and his narrator:

> Here is a story which in rougher shape
> Came from a grizzled cripple, whom I saw
> Sunning himself in a waste field alone—
> Old, and a mine of memories—who had served,

> Long since, a bygone Rector of the place,
> And been himself a part of what he told.

But there is no consequence to this structural gesture. The story proceeds in the inhibited narrative tone of *Dora* and *Enoch Arden*, and like them it falls back on the emotional attitudes of Victorian popular literature. That chameleon shift of centre which realizes feeling and situation freshly and vitally is not achieved, partly because an unredeemed Solitary stubbornly persists in the poet's imagination, and he can only persuade himself that contact 'with his kind' has been made by a show of what passes conventionally for emotion and human behaviour. The cult of sincerity can be discerned here too, helping to confuse easy tears with the penetrative sharing of pain and grief. On the other hand, the Solitary is half quelled by the very impulse to narrate these sad events, and cannot speak as himself, or render his lonely observation of the story articulate, although the strong closing lines of *Aylmer's Field* suggest a reciprocity between the action and the narrator, in their fusion of scene and mood to make a final comment of more powerful symbolic effect:

> And where the two contrived their daughter's good,
> Lies the hawk's cast, the mole has made his run,
> The hedgehog underneath the plantain bores,
> The rabbit fondles his own harmless face,
> The slow-worm creeps, and the thin weasel there
> Follows the mouse, and all is open field.

It is not coincidental that the most animated and convincing section of this part of Tennyson's work is his handling of Enoch Arden in his desert-island isolation and, more poignantly, on his return to his vanished home and a worse solitude. The poem veers towards monologue and centres on the solitary mind, forced back upon itself. Here is the *Maud* theme again, but tried out, with true chameleon instinct, in terms of a different temperament; the poet is once more researching into the trials and resources of the individual in his universe. After looking on the family happiness his presence could only destroy, Enoch feels the force of his resolution not to intrude:

> He therefore turning softly like a thief,

Lest the harsh shingle should grate underfoot,
And feeling all along the garden-wall,
Lest he should swoon and tumble and be found,
Crept to the gate, and opened it, and closed,
As lightly as a sick man's chamber-door,
Behind him, and came out upon the waste.
And there he would have knelt, but that his knees
Were feeble, so that falling prone he dug
His fingers into the wet earth, and prayed.

Without wholly surmounting its temptations, the poem achieves an inward grasp of Enoch: the Solitary within the narrator finds his mirror, and there is no longer such a barrier between the poem and emotional reality.

Tennyson's relative failure with some of his narrative material underlines the import of Romantic developments in this sphere of poetry; as Keats also found, the storyteller must now be a presence in his story. He can no longer be the anonymous reporting voice. If he is to be avoided as a speaker in the poem, then the monologue is the answer—the full exertion of chameleon power. But if the narrator is admitted, he must be acknowledged, exploited, and his implications grasped. The observer's view of a situation is a crucial part of it, whether he is drawn into the scene or stands in counterpoint to it. The poem must be made out of the imagination recognizing its creative obligations to the given scene or person. Their full existence depends on the engagement of the storyteller with his material, and a worthy nineteenth-century poem is the result of this coalescence taking place within and becoming part of the poem itself.

Tennyson, using his inheritance of subjective awareness so resourcefully and boldly in his major work, tended to falter at this most sophisticated of the Romantic innovations. His narrative work is unsure, despite its attempt at fidelity to *The Excursion* ideal; while his venture into conventional history plays only serves to illustrate that the concept of drama as well as narrative was irreversibly changed by Romanticism. Whatever their failures in their plays, the Romantic poets did not leave their deepest imaginative instincts aside when they turned to dramatic expression, and no later poet-dramatist can afford to ignore the lessons of their work. But when Tennyson wrote plays, late in his career, he reverted to the Elizabethan convention and except for brief moments forgot his nineteenth-century self, with all its fruitful tensions of egocentricity and protean experiment. The results, although actable by an Irving, are intrinsically lifeless. Such failure is illuminating in our effort to locate the imaginative nerve-centre of the century. And this effort is positively assisted, as I have shown, by the main part of Tennyson's work from beginning to end. In particular, his full release of power, egotistically and in monodrama, displays the energy of a poet seeking to bear his formidable responsibilities, with a maturing recognition of what is being demanded and discovered in the new imaginative explorations.

5

In Tennyson's poetry, the isolation indicated by Pater's phrase 'the thick wall of personality' becomes an experience. It is explored through a spectrum of implications, from neurotic panic at such incarceration, to triumph over fear in the conviction that the 'solitary prisoner' can establish vital contacts and so construct his 'own dream of a world', not desperately, but in creative fulfilment. When we turn to the poems of Matthew Arnold we remain in the same post-Romantic territories; for Arnold too, the self 'at the centre of the situation' dominates and conditions all his work. But his reading of this fate is more uniformly sombre than Tennyson's. Arnold is more frightened and more passive, regarding self-consciousness as a burden to be supported, and in his poetry the Romantic inheritance is felt as a legacy of unmitigated doom rather than an opportunity; or at the most, as a Janus gift. But it *is* felt—it is not evaded or softened; the tone of lament in Arnold shows that he comprehends his obligations, however painfully they strike him, and he undertakes to write out of his position as unhappy but acquiescent heir. Even his attempts to escape are the gestures of an imagination knowing its fate too clearly—the reflex impulses of shocked recognition, and the emotion of his poetry springs from this not from the hope of reprieve.

From whichever viewpoint Arnold confronts the issue of self-awareness, he finds in it a guarantee of pain and travail. Pater

kindles to the subtleties of a personal universe of 'fine gradations', and the evanescent coincidence of unique percipient with
unique perceived, but Arnold is dismayed by man seen as the
'plaything of cross motives and shifting impulses, swayed by a
thousand subtle influences, physiological and pathological'.[1]
The outcome to his mind is disintegration, the breaking down
of consciousness into a 'plurality of fugitive, superficial selves',[2]
moments without coherence. He turns the coin of Pater's vision,
but both writers link the Victorian with the twentieth-century
imagination by such reflections on the complexity of the
experiencing mind when it seeks to establish a notion of its
identity by empirical means. And despite his horror, Arnold
equally with Pater acknowledges the profound movement of
sensibility which has brought about what he sees as a crisis. The
old order has changed, and Arnold is one of the first to announce
and to define the essentials of the 'modern spirit'. The threat to
sustained consciousness and the stable view of self has, ironically
enough, come about precisely because that self and consciousness have become the testing centre, the ultimate arbiter.
Goethe's crucial contribution to the European mind, Arnold
says, has been to put 'the standard, once for all, inside every man
instead of outside him'.[3] That this move may lead straight to
calamity haunts the poet Arnold even while as a concept it
invigorates his prose: 'the standard' so established may prove
to be based on shifting sand. As man takes on the responsibility
of his experience in a new sense, he may find himself not even the
sum of his moments of awareness, but prostituted to each instant
as it passes. Depending so fiercely on the concept of self, he is
unable to realize or possess it. At the end of this road is the
possibility that creatively the self may not exist, as Empedocles,
hopeless besides his crater, knows.

Arnold approaches the crater by the two routes of egotistical
and chameleon awareness. He accepts the migration of the
spiritual centre and gives his allegiance to the 'standard within',
whatever his mistrust and foreboding. But his fear of the situation far outweighs his eagerness for its fruits. The confidence of

[1] Quoted from Arnold on Montaigne by J. Hillis Miller, *The Disappearance of God*
(Massachusetts, 1963), p. 214.   [2] loc. cit.
[3] 'Heine', *Essays in Criticism*, First Series (1865); Everyman ed., p. 113.

the egotistical sublime is as remote from him as the delight of Keats exulting in the chameleon power to create Iago and Imogen. The two modes exist for him as for his predecessors, but for Arnold they are instruments of creative pain, the scourges of imagination rather than its opportunities.

He belongs more obviously to the egotistical party. Monologue does not feature largely in his poetical work, although it is not absent. J. Hillis Miller remarks on the painful effort it cost Arnold to break down 'the safe barriers of cold solitude',[1] and much of the poetry reflects his egocentricity and uses it. But this solitude itself is 'cold', and the whole egotistical endeavour is taxing and formidable. Hillis Miller summarizes: 'He wants to make poetry as much as possible a matter of assimilation and control rather than of diffusion and sympathy, though the process of taking the world into oneself . . . also seems to him a cause of suffering and effort'.[2]

In Arnold's egotistical poetry, part of the strain arises from his inability to think of his own consciousness as merely distinct and unique, free to make a world in its image. Where to Wordsworth there was the gift of individuality in a knowable universe, to Arnold there is only the sentence of isolation in a world which resists assimilation. The sublime egotist found himself in his perceptions: the universe returned him richly to himself. But for the 'naked mind' of Empedocles, subject recoils upon itself in the shock of a rebuff. 'The world is from of old' (I, ii, 181), and the prestige of human consciousness is not sufficient to subdue it. From such failure, Arnold's sense of himself is wrought. The universe offers him no creative mirror but a blank surface, and in consequence his self-experience takes on an element of blind and restrictive horror. Although Arnold's is not a poetry exploiting ironies, it is generated by his recognition of one profound irony of modern life: that self-consciousness equals self-alienation. Empedocles laments the 'dwindling faculty of joy' (II, 273) and diagnoses his sterility of consciousness as a self-awareness which is 'nothing but a devouring flame of thought . . . a naked, eternally restless mind' (II, 329–30), and such is the predicament of Arnold's egotistically moved imagination. The mind is 'preying on itself' (I, i, 157).

[1] op. cit., p. 245.   [2] ibid.

It is, however, the more committed to the poetry of egotism precisely because of its appreciation of its own nature. This leads as with Tennyson, to poems of 'two voices', the 'dialogue of the mind with itself' in Arnold's phrase (Preface 1853). The tension is higher in Arnold, because Tennyson suggests an incipient chameleon energy in his arguments and contrasted views; the calamity of self-division seems less inhibiting to him. The threat of disintegration forces Arnold to poetry: an identity located in the factions of personality is at once his despair and his reward. In his poetry the psychological nerve of the 'iron time' of 'doubts, distractions, fears' (*Memorial Verses*) is touched, and its true centre, the individual's agony of self-experience, is revealed.

His one expansive display of the nakedly suffering egotistical consciousness is *Empedocles on Etna*. This work is the *Manfred* of the Victorian imagination, and might also be more sadly named *Prometheus Rebound*. It performs for its creator the same task as the Romantic egotistical plays, offering him the means of direct access to his inner situation, and its similarities with the earlier plays provide further evidence for the continuity of imaginative response and method in the nineteenth century. So too does the closely related *Dipsychus* by Clough. Empedocles lives entirely within his own being; the setting, action and other persons reflect and help to define that being, just as the Alps and the spirits of *Manfred* or the intangible presences of *Prometheus Unbound* captured the exact shades of their heroes' sensibility. Arnold's 'mental theatre' is bleaker, but it is a stage made familiar by Byron and Shelley, of paramount importance in the attempt to match vision with method and to devise adequate equipment for exploring the new lands.

For this Victorian hero, the 'root of suffering' (i, i, 151) is in himself. His story is not one of resistance to destructive forces which he can overthrow by endurance. Manfred and Prometheus both discover the power of inner freedom by their energy of defiance, their refusal to be what it seems they must submit to being. They impose their terms and achieve apotheosis. So indeed in his more sombre arrival at his suicidal destiny does Empedocles; he experiences his potential to the full. But his fate is to bear 'the burden' (i, ii, 128) of himself in all its weight and

so arrive at a true estimate of his capacity. There are no opponents to be fought in *Empedocles on Etna*—no particular areas of
the psyche to be realized, assessed and overthrown. Empedocles
is not surrounded by fiends, tyrants, spirits of ill-will and temp-
tation: in contrast with the earlier works of the mental theatre
the starkness of Arnold's scene comes home most forcefully.
His hero is reduced to the worst of solitudes, the inescapable
meeting of self with self. The creative springs of the egotistical
situation are dry in a charred waste of being. Repudiating his
laurel-wreath, Apollo's 'votary' cries that he has been 'enough
alone' (II, 219–20) and he asks, 'who will fence him from himself?' (212); the crucial gift of awareness has betrayed its promise.
Here is the sole fiend on Etna, and it proves more impervious to
exorcism than any menace haunting Caucasus or Alps, until
ultimately, by inexorable logic, suicide appears to be the one
rite of release. On his way to this conclusion, Empedocles
surveys the obverse of egotistical creativity—a kind of parody of
that vision: 'I read In all things my own deadness' (II, 321–2).
The contact and response is gone; he mourns the distant
sublimity of *The Prelude*'s harmonies of self and universe and the
reciprocity of *Childe Harold*:

> Oh that I could glow like this mountain!
> Oh that my heart bounded with the swell of the sea!
> Oh that my soul were full of light as the stars!
> Oh that it brooded over the world like air!
>
> (II, 323–6)

In the Romantic egotistical plays, the forces opposing the
heroic centre represented destructive powers, but we find an
eloquent change in Arnold's drama where the opposing quality
is that of 'life and joy' (II, 321), embodied in the fresh lyric voice
of Callicles. He is heard as a remembered but severed consciousness, the poignant knowledge of what is gone, the emotion being
stressed by the contrast of the green and sunlit lower slopes
where Callicles sings and the dead wasteland of the crater's lip.
Empedocles hears the 'sweetest harp-player' (I, ii, 13) as his
past self, recognizing in the deprivation of his present state the
nature of creative joy with its exultant interplay of self and world,
when the assimilative soul may 'brood over the world like air'

and be filled with light. Such a dual awareness—of what has been as well as what now is—is typical of Arnold's outlook, and we may see it as the peculiar state of the Victorian imagination in its relation to the Romantic, as well as his personal hallmark.

The final plunge into the crater shows the poet accepting rather than rejecting Empedocles' plight, we must conclude: for Arnold has followed the logic through and his hero affirms his commitment to the 'deep-buried' self, though he dreads the 'imperious lonely thinking-power' to which he feels himself reduced and enslaved (II, 371–91). Empedocles has his Promethean moment in this grimmer test of his integrity. He has tried not to fail his ideal of living 'in the light' of his 'own soul' (393), and the manner of his dying seeks to substitute no other philosophy. Desolate though the drama is, it is a document which looks into the heart of the egotistical imagination and does not flinch from its desperation, nor wish its discoveries unmade. The poetry of experience is vindicated not dishonoured by the decision of Empedocles; and in Callicles' requiem, Etna blossoms into a new Olympus.

Yet it remains Etna too—the egotistical vision cannot return to its springtime and there is no rebirth for Empedocles. Arnold may well have shocked himself in the remorseless candour of his imagination's self-mirroring, a reaction which could have played a part in his critical censure of the poem in 1853. But before we turn to other aspects of his attitude, there are several further points about his egotistical poetry to notice.

The theme of isolation takes a Tennysonian course in Arnold's work outside *Empedocles*. Following *In Memoriam*, he considers human solitude most deeply in the sphere of relationships and in a questioning of love. His answers are not close to Tennyson's, but in both poets, the moral pressures on the Victorian imagination are made apparent. Enisled in the sea of life, those of the mortal millions who not only live alone but realize it are paradoxically dependent on their experience with others in their effort to articulate their condition. In *The Buried Life* Arnold sees the lovers' situation as the one hope for a true revelation of the well-springs of personal being, the 'genuine self'. The common plight is a frustrating awareness that though this self exists, it remains theoretical and out of reach:

> . . . hardly have we, for one little hour,
> Been on our own line, have we been ourselves . . .

The 'buried stream' instead of sustaining life as an irrigational force is experienced only as a strong desire for contact with such a force, and Arnold illustrates here the onset of a dichotomy of self which in one sense cripples, and in another matures, the egotistical imagination. He sounds the emotional keynote of Victorian sensibility as it grows familiar with its painful kind of self-seeking. But in *The Buried Life* love is held to be a possible means of restoring the consciousness to its deeper self—'when a beloved hand is laid in ours',

> A bolt is shot back somewhere in our breast . . .
> And what we mean, we say, and what we would, we know.
> A man becomes aware of his life's flow . . .

At best, however, 'this is rare', and it is a more fragile moment of self-possession than those Tennyson ascribes to the action of love; indeed *The Buried Life* begins as a monologue in which the initial situation is a rift between the lovers. The poem in its emotion is more one of pleading hope than assured faith in the operation of mutual feeling. In *Dover Beach* also, the appeal to love—'let us be true to one another'—comes as the desperate cry of one caught in a vision of opposite import, where the odds are against such an aid to survival.

Arnold as a love poet in fact confirms rather than dispels the sense of egotistical isolation. Even in *The Buried Life*, the richest reward of love it seems is only self-recognition, not the revelation of the beloved, and thus Arnold's view of love fulfilled rather chillingly meets his poems of lament at love's failure. The Marguerite and Switzerland poems centre on the observation 'we mortal millions live alone', and it is clear that the breakdown is not an unexpected blow to the poet: his grief is not that of shock, but an acknowledgement that, given the 'salt estanging sea' (*To Marguerite*) as our element, it must be so. Arnold in these poems feels his cautious way into an important new field needing imaginative reconnaissance. The whole ethic of relationships is now coming into question. Viewed from the one side, love is the only hope for each solitary prisoner; from the other, it can offer nothing but a more acute knowledge of that imprisonment and a more intensive suffering, the 'longing like despair' as 'lovely notes' sound from shore to inaccessible shore. Victorian poets (as well as novelists) begin to investigate the alternatives of emotional experience and so prepare in their turn a legacy for their successors.

In the conduct and structure of his poems too Arnold shows himself to be at the nerve-centre of the mid-century egotistical imagination. He favours the poem of occasion as much as Coleridge, with place more frequent than person as his point of departure—Rugby Chapel late on a November afternoon, a lake on a June night, a 'deserted, moon-blanched street', the 'track by Childsworth Farm'. As apparatus by which a mood is established, these descriptive openings are important and they are for the moment imbued with the feeling of the poet, but Arnold's tendency is to withdraw from them as the poem proceeds, as he discards the listener in *The Buried Life*. He suggests retreat into himself, unlike Wordsworth and Coleridge who made the immediate—or the distant—universe their own. They were central and magnetically dominant; Arnold does not exert such power. Locality and occasion fade into the background as the voice of the poet pursues its reflections. His self-communings display the island-isolation he broods upon, and the quickening solitude of Coleridge in lime-tree bower, or midnight silence, where the experiencing mind knew itself in its absorption of the scene, is lost. In poems such as *A Summer Night*, the technique of withdrawal from the immediacy of place and time, the inability to sustain creative contact with it, is inseparable from the theme. Here, the particular experience of moonlight in an empty street modulates first to other remembered moonlit scenes, and then from the particular altogether, as the poet meditates on the unchanging contrast of 'calm moonlight' and the 'unquiet breast'. In the gulf between nature and man that the poem discusses, Arnold shows why he does not, and cannot, write another *Frost at Midnight*. He finds himself in feeling the boundaries which separate him from the universe, not in exploiting the joyous sensation of subject making object its own self and mirror. Similarly, the pastoral Arnold who numbers the fritillaries and observes the detail of the gold-dusted snapdragon is far from the Coleridge who sees the bright eyes of the nightingales. The one notes meticulously what is not himself, using his sight as a precise instrument carrying information across a distance and hence emphasizing again the separateness of thing from observer, while the other exploits the moment of creative surprise and recognition, when perceiver and perceived coincide. There is a vitality in Coleridge which Arnold cannot emulate. He offers instead more ghostly cadences as the music of the egotistical imagination, and the courage of one facing solitude become isolation.

This view of where Arnold stands in relation to his predecessors may also be illustrated by his version of the encounter poem. In their development of the monologue, the Victorian poets profited greatly from those experimental Romantic poems. But with Arnold, *The Ancient Mariner* pales into *The Scholar Gipsy*: his encounters are with phantoms or, more simply, the dead, and hence constitute a further instance of his bias not only towards the plain egotistical mode, but towards this seen as a state of isolation and withdrawal. Many of his poems are elegies as well as elegiac in tone: for example, *Rugby Chapel, Thyrsis, Memorial Verses, A Tomb among the Mountains*. The other person of the poems is therefore dumb and inactive. Arnold encounters his conception of Clough, or Wordsworth, or his father. He is not acted upon by another presence, and the poems therefore remain further studies in the lonely process of self-discovery, the egotistical in contact with nothing more than its own version of another sensibility. The movement of Romantic encounter poems is more dynamic, out from the egotistical and then back again, with speech and life both given and received in the poems' shift of centre. Arnold performs no resurrectional feat in his elegies, nor is he extended, his awareness enlarged. The Gipsy has not made him a sadder and a wiser man, but like the remembered dead, passively serves to focus further direct egotistical meditation. The persons chosen by Arnold for these shadow-encounters neither alarm nor master their summoner, nor can they pass across his boundaries, fixed and formidable as these are. We can sum up the change which has befallen the self in Arnold's work by observing simply that now it cannot, in the Romantic sense, be encountered.

6

Small wonder, therefore, that the major part of Arnold's poetry is resolutely egotistical. There is more to consider, all the same, in his attitude towards the chameleon pole of the imagination. He is aware of its pull even if he is more readily attracted to the other. More exactly and characteristically, he is aware of the particular pains attached to chameleon effort, and also to the poet's fate of being swayed by two contrasting forces. This difficulty, one time the Romantic delight, gives Arnold his version of the two voices (*Stanzas in memory of the author of 'Obermann'*):

> Ah! two desires toss about
> The poet's feverish blood.
> One drives him to the world without,
> And one to solitude.

The two desires, for the Romantic poet, reacted upon each other in a fruitful interplay and collaboration; their tension likewise stimulated rather than inhibited creative energy. But in Arnold's phraseology, here and in an equally explicit passage in *Empedocles on Etna*, it is clear that there is conflict between the two. The world is a retreat or refuge from the burden of self, but the reverse is also true, and we find feverish unrest where once there was reciprocal power. Empedocles addresses Apollo:

> Where shall thy votary fly then? back to men?
> But they will gladly welcome him once more,
> And help him to unbend his too tense thought,
> And rid him of the presence of himself . . .
> And haunt him, till the absence from himself,
> That other torment, grow unbearable;
> And he will fly to solitude again,
> And he will find its air too keen for him,
> And so change back; and many thousand times
> Be miserably bandied to and fro
> Like a sea-wave, betwixt the world and thee,
> Thou young, implacable God!
>
> (II, 220–32)

Absence from self here is negative. Keats too complained of the pressure of other people's identity, yet at the same time he recognized in it the chameleon opportunity; for Arnold, at his Empedoclean extreme, this does not follow. He did outside *Empedocles* recognize the chameleon act as a creative exercise, only to recoil from its demands, as J. Hillis Miller remarks: 'Arnold fears such a loss of his self-possession, and goes out of himself with great reluctance'.[1] His early poem *The Strayed Reveller* faces this method of imaginative research, and articulates his fear of it. The Reveller, flushed with Circe's enchantments, touches without effort the vision of the Gods—the 'bright procession Of eddying forms' takes possession of him. His hysterical, drunken state is contrasted throughout with the level-headed, controlled calm of Ulysses, this in itself being a tacit criticism of the mode of vision the Reveller expounds. Admittedly his condition is only a caricature of the chameleon sensibility, as the Reveller acknowledges. He perceives the godlike nature of the capacity to view and know all manner of men, and, as a divine attribute, the joy of this power. But for human poets to acquire insight into life in all its variety from 'the Indian on his mountain lake' to 'the merchants on the Oxus' stream', serene, detached contemplation is not enough. Neither can the intoxication of a moment supply the power, though it does show the Reveller what the price is. His superficial acquaintance with such vision is enough to suggest its awesome responsibility, its moral weight, and to suggest also the consequence, that to possess it is to be subject to great suffering:

> These things, Ulysses,
> The wise Bards also
> Behold and sing.
> But oh! what labour!
> Oh Prince, what pain!

They endure the agonies of all humanity. The gods in allowing them to share their surview, extort the maximum fee: to earn their title 'wise' the bards shall 'become what [they] sing'. This, the poem implies, is a more formidable feat of endurance than the steadfast reiteration in all circumstances of the claim 'I am Ulysses', for it means suffering the fates of all, dying the deaths

[1] See above, p. 187.

of many. The Reveller here sums up the tasks that the nine-teenth-century imagination takes upon itself: it aspires to a godlike status in its conviction that through submitting itself arduously to its full capacity for experience, it can arrive not only at an illuminated evaluation of that experience, but at a new height of self-apotheosis. Such a labour is too much for the Reveller; but even if his creator too shies away from chameleon commitment, the poems show that he recognizes and does not underestimate the enterprise.

In his 'sad lucidity of soul' (*Resignation*) therefore, Arnold the poet voices the travail of imagination as it grows in under-standing of its situation. He distinguishes the two poles as two kinds of pain, both taxing the poet's resources to the full. The bias of his temperament leads him to explore the egotistical rather than the chameleon suffering, the mind preying upon itself, rather than becoming what it sings, but there is no escapism in his poetry of isolation.

The dialogue between critic and poet which dogs Arnold's career but which was crystallized in the Preface of 1853 is expecially interesting when looked at in the light of his unmis-takable fidelity to Romantic principles despite their apparently inevitable decline into darkness and dismay. His theorizing reveals the extent of his imaginative involvement by the effort it makes to haul him back from such a fate. *Empedocles* was the occasion for an explicit attempt to call a halt. Since that poem is extreme in its egotistical study, this is logical. Recoiling from the barren crater of Etna, Arnold constructs his defensive argument, denying the work true poetic power, first because it is concerned with a situation where 'there is everything to be endured, nothing to be done', and secondly because it is centred in the poet's consciousness, the state of his own mind. Against such an example of 'modern' writing, he sets approvingly what he con-ceives to be the Greek principle: the impersonal delineation of an action significant in itself. In presenting such a stark opposi-tion, he emphasizes that the nineteenth-century poetry of self-realization was a new and bold departure, with its fully con-scious incorporation of the poet into the poem. He could, as in the Heine essay of 1863, acknowledge the current trends without panic; but in 1853 he had reason to view them less urbanely when his creative participation in them led to the grim finale of *Empedocles*, and so revealed to him the risks of these explorations. He makes his bid for withdrawal in the face of Empedocles' suicide in particular; but he confirms the inevitability of the new situation in the very weapons he uses to oppose it. Declaring that it cannot be because it never has been, he exhorts the poet 'to prefer his action to everything else',

so to treat this, as to permit its inherent excellences to develop themselves, without interruption from the intrusion of his personal peculiarities: most fortunate, when he most entirely succeeds in effacing himself, and in enabling a noble action to subsist as it did in nature.

But the modern critic not only permits a false practice; he absolutely prescribes false aims.—'A true allegory of the state of one's own mind in a representative history', the poet is told, 'is perhaps the highest thing that one can attempt in the way of poetry'.—And accordingly he attempts it. An allegory of the state of one's own mind, the highest problem of an art which imitates actions! No assuredly, it is not, it never can be so: no great poetical work has ever been produced with such an aim.

He goes to on cite *Faust* as being the work of 'the greatest poet of modern times' yet 'defective', judged 'as a whole . . . as a poetical work'. The verdict comes through all his remarks, in their own despite: the very recognition that the poet does not automatically efface himself, that self-effacement is an ideal to be aimed at and strained for, sounds the requiem of impersonal art in the old sense. The cause is never so clearly formulated as when it is lost. Yet Arnold's protest is at the same time part of the mid-century clarification of the demands of the new developments, and a warning against belittling them.

He is opposing the involvement of self in the poetic work, and the chameleon act as well as more obviously the egotistical is repudiated here, a point which becomes clearer from the poems Arnold tries to write in accordance with his 1853 thesis. They help to confirm that the nineteenth-century chameleon exertion is a part of the process of self-discovery, not merely a synonym for straightforward dramatic creation. Neither the narratives *Sohrab and Rustum* and *Balder Dead*, nor the 'classical drama' *Merope* are in the Romantic tradition of drama and monologue.

They are remote from the encounter poems and the experiments of *The Borderers* or *Remorse*, and they stand as monuments to the past not as living forms of the nineteenth century. We find only narrative without the quickening spirit of self-conscious protean energy, and figures in dead imitation marble—Coleridge's stone peaches. As formal poetry, *Sohrab and Rustum* is successful and a moving situation is surveyed with tact, but unlike *Empedocles* it generates no shock of discovery. These are products of a castrated imagination, exposing the impossibility of the 1853 theories for nineteenth-century poems. The creating consciousness cannot be left out of account—whether it shows the egotistical or the chameleon side of its nature, it must preside. Its attempted suppression leads, not back to the heights of classical achievement, but down to lifeless, copyist art. *Biographia Literaria*, demonstrating the creative spirit's fusion with its materials, and its essential presence within its creation, cannot be unwritten. Still less can the primary incentive of the modern imagination be denied: the desire to illuminate the subjective experience. If Arnold looks askance at it all with a part of his critical self, this only shows how seriously he takes it. And otherwise, as a critic and above all in the authentic impulses of his creative self, he shows his serious recognition by his commitment to the new route. He makes it his own as he records the suffering inflicted on those who follow it.

7

The old naïveté of a God's-in-his-heaven Browning has now virtually faded from the critical scene, and if he still wears the tag of optimist, it is as a tattered relic rather than a legend fresh and clear. Yet there are ways in which it may even now serve a useful purpose, indicating a rough and ready truth about his poetry in contrast to that of Tennyson and Arnold. Outworn as a term applicable to the substance of his work, it does suggest what is distinctive in this Victorian poet's attitude to his Romantic inheritance. Where Arnold is tense, often appalled at the lonely route the imagination must follow, and Tennyson is similarly haunted by the nightmare torments which the isolated self may be forced to endure, Browning finds cause for creative rejoicing. He is the son most like the Romantic father, the poet most directly descended from the early nineteenth-century excitement in surveying a new imaginative prospect. At the same time, he is truly of the second generation not the first, in that he too can be vividly aware of the 'dangerous edge'. Its threat is a facet of his creative personality: but it is there less as a burdening fear than as a challenge.

He is also strongly aware of the powers of creativity within him, recognizing their force and their attributes. His early work, in which he strove to grasp and direct his powers, provides striking evidence of this perception and I want therefore to look particularly at this phase of his career. Even in apparent incoherence, or the seeming abandonment of certain paths, his apprehension of, in particular, the two governing poles of imagination emerges unmistakably. In fact the terms egotistical and chameleon are more obviously useful in discussing Browning's early career than they are anywhere else; their relevance needs no pointing and the patterns and compulsions they suggest are manifest in the course of his work, from *Pauline* (1833) and *Paracelsus* (1835) by way of *Sordello* (1840) and the dramas to the first groups of 'dramatic lyrics', and the full monologue.

The terms are additionally helpful as a safeguard against oversimplification. Their relationship, as I have emphasized, is essentially complementary; a poet may move from one pole to the other, recoil from one to be ruled by the other, but fundamentally he remains where he was. Browning is no exception to this, though the conventional outline of his career implies something of a dichotomy between its stages. It is suggested either that John Stuart Mill's verdict on the 'morbid self-consciousness'[1] of *Pauline* so shocked the young poet that he resolved never again to expose himself to such criticism, retreating from 'personal' utterance and finding his poetic courage restored only by the dramatic voice; or, if not seen in quite such a simple light, his switch from the long, introspectively inclined poems of his youth to the monologues is still regarded as in some ways a withdrawal, a repudiation of subjective brooding in favour of

[1] Mill's criticism is quoted in *A Browning Handbook* (1935), W. C. DeVane, p. 43, and is also reprinted in *Robert Browning: A Collection of Critical Essays* (1966), ed. P. Drew, pp. 176–7.

more extroverted interests. There have of course always been
readers of the monologues who take them merely as somewhat
oblique revelations of the poet's own philosophies and feelings,
and to this extent oppose the dichotomy hypothesis, but such
interpretations owe more to the influences of the sincerity criterion than to a shrewder perception of continuity in the poet's
work. The problems of such an identification of speaker and
creator are ignored and the true relationship of poet to poems is
no more apprehended at this level than it is by the dichoto-
mists.

Each point of view has its grain of validity: but each needs
the other, and each must be relieved of its superficiality if
Browning's imagination and its movements are to be understood. Even at his most egotistical, Browning recognizes the
strong pull of the opposite mode; it is the resulting high tension
which gives his earlier poetry its character. Yet it is not the
tension of conflict—the chameleon pressure is an aspect of the
egotistical, part of its way of realizing itself, not a counterforce
seeking to reduce or extinguish the poet's self-awareness. By
appreciating this situation we can begin to determine the nature
of the three long poems *Pauline*, *Paracelsus* and *Sordello* and to
recognize their close kinship; and if we keep it in mind, we can
see the plays and the first dramatic poems taking their place in a
coherent pattern of imaginative expression as it works itself out.
Browning experiences not the restless and uncertain winds of
youthful ambition, unsure of their prevailing quarter, but the
full force of the Romantic gale asserting itself with uncommon
vigour.

In *Pauline*, the central intuition of Romanticism is explicitly
set forth, and motivates the whole poem:

> I am made up of an intensest life,
> Of a most clear idea of consciousness
> Of self—distinct from all its qualities,
> From all affections, passions, feelings, powers . . .
>
> (p. 9)[1]

In isolating the 'clear idea' in its essential character, Browning proves himself not 'morbidly' but creatively self-conscious.

[1] References are to page numbers of the Everyman Browning, i (1833–44).

He is roused by the concept of personal identity, which is a condition not to be confused with narcissus impulses. And in this same passage, he points to the double nature of his awareness: its egotistical magnetism, its chameleon urge. This consciousness is linked, he says, first,

> . . . to self-supremacy,
> Existing as a centre to all things,
> Most potent to create, and rule, and call
> Upon all things to minister to it . . .

and secondly, to the twin yet opposite need—a 'principle of restlessness', 'which would be all, have, see, know, taste, feel, all'. 'This is myself', a dually-operating consciousness: the Romantic situation is nowhere more succinctly stated. *Pauline* is a poem of youthful crudity certainly, but its recognition of the fundamentals of the contemporary imagination is confident, and its acceptance of them shows Browning already committed to his mature poetic course.

Paracelsus likewise speaks the creed of the nineteenth-century poet. He is fired with excitement at the vision which brought Wordsworth and Coleridge to the *Lyrical Ballads*, as he utters his conviction that

> Truth is within ourselves; it takes no rise
> From outward things, whate'er you may believe,
> There is an inmost centre in us all,
> Where truth abides in fullness . . .
>
> (I, p. 46)

In most lives this centre is obscured, unrealized, unreachable through the opacity of material living; but those who seek to know their being must orientate themselves towards the inner world:

> . . . '*to know*'
> Rather consists in opening out a way
> Whence the imprisoned splendour may escape
> Than in effecting entry for a light
> Supposed to be without.

In the family of which Manfred is a progenitor, and Empedocles an embittered son, Paracelsus takes his place, daring all for the adventure of self-discovery, the quest for the knowledge of the 'inmost centre', which may involve the cosmos yet prizes and trusts above all its own integrity. The 'poetry of experience' is pledged and honoured in Browning's early works.

Depending upon the 'most clear idea' of self, poetry of this kind is ruled equally by 'the principle of restlessness' as *Pauline* points out. In *Pauline* and *Sordello*, the close connection between the empirical philosophy and this principle is demonstrated, again showing Browning's grasp of the mechanics of his imagination. The sense of self is dynamic: it demands ceaseless extension of its experiential range if it is to reach its goal of full self-knowledge. Knowing involves totality of contact, not selected angles of study; and apprehending the reality of light includes enduring darkness. The Romantics in their poems and plays discovered their values by such comprehensive and first-hand research, and before Browning himself embarks on this pursuit, he depicts the minds which are driven to it with a vivid appreciation of their need. This defines further the nature of his subjectivity in the early years. Thus, in *Pauline*:

> I cannot chain my soul, it will not rest
> In its clay prison; this most narrow sphere—
> It has strange powers, and feelings, and desires
> Which I cannot account for, nor explain,
> But which I stifle not, being bound to trust
> All feelings equally—to hear all sides . . .
>
> (p. 17)

Such is the route to discovery, to valid assessment. And in *Sordello*, there is a more passionate and truculent challenge to exclusive, self-discounting standards of evaluation, in terms of the inclusive and self-grounded processes:

> I feel, I am what I feel, know what I feel
> —So much is Truth to me—What Is then? Since
> One object viewed diversely may evince
> Beauty and ugliness—this way attract,
> That way repel, why gloze upon the fact?
> Why must a single of the sides be right?
> Who bids choose this and leave its opposite?
> No abstract Right for me . . .
>
> (VI, p. 337)

Sordello can speak out clearly and definitively when it will, and here it proclaims 'the relative spirit', that crucial perception which is to condition all Browning's poetry. The tone is not Pater's, yet in the pregnant question—'who bids choose this and leave its opposite?', we look on to the vision of the later critic. The modern situation as seen by Browning is close to Pater's view, and both find much positive stimulus to creativity in their version of the Romantic universe.

From the three large-scale poems of the early years, therefore, Browning's sense of the contemporary imagination emerges as a far from tentative awareness. He is moved to show the 'most clear idea of consciousness', as it works dynamically within Paracelsus, Sordello and the speaker of *Pauline*, and he balances these depictions of the subjective mind exploring itself, making and testing its egotistical universe, with an equal insistence on the 'principle of restlessness'. From these poems, it is impossible to doubt that Browning is strongly drawn from the first to the chameleon mode, as a means of extending the search for a deeper grasp of identity. In the years from *Pauline* to the completion of *Sordello*, he comes to recognize the complexity of the concept of identity more acutely and this is reflected in the structure and handling of the poems.

To describe even *Pauline* as a simple outpouring of Browning's personal faith and passion is misleading. It is a much more stage-managed poem than such an assumption allows, being the poet's first attempt to try out a speaker revealing his own consciousness. One step away from strict egotistical commitment has already been made, for the hero of the poem is not Browning speaking in full rapport with the first-person utterance, but 'Pauline's lover'; he breaks into his speech only when a relationship has been established and the rudiments of a speaker-listener situation sketched: 'Pauline, mine own, bend o'er me . . .'. A sense of dramatic presentation stirs in Browning even in his most evidently subjective poem.

With the next presentation of a mind engaged in self-research, we find the listener has multiplied into four persons and the form of the poem is explicitly dramatic with scenes and divisions into five episodes. But the work is much nearer to a set of monologues than a play: Paracelsus is the focal figure through-

out and the scenes and other persons exist simply as opportunities for him to continue his egotistical revelations. Again, the
provocation to speech and analytical report is devised as a
necessary condition of the hero's pursuit of himself. Compared
with *Pauline, Paracelsus* also takes a step nearer the chameleon
mode in that a particular person is featured and time and
place are historical. But the incentive of the work is still egotistical, that is, Browning merely beholds in Paracelsus his own
'fierce energy', the 'irresistible force' (I, p. 37) driving him to
prove his soul, to experience what he really is. The poem is an
egotistical portrait of chameleon ambition, the study of the mind
dedicated to knowing itself, and grasping the value of the outgoing effort in bringing this about:

> . . . God is the PERFECT POET
> Who in creation acts his own conceptions . . .
> (II, p. 65)

This Coleridgean thought summarizes the *Paracelsus* stage of
Browning's career: a time of intense self-consciousness engen-
dering a fund of energy which sees its way of release in the
'restlessness' of chameleon experience, this in its turn to renew
and enhance the creator's awareness of his being. The concept
rather than the deed moves him during the 1830s; but the deeds
in the shape of the monologues yet unborn, are already promised
and conceived in the egotistical portrayals of imagination as it
beholds itself.

Sordello continues in a more complex way what *Pauline* and
Paracelsus initiate. In this abstruse work, Browning penetrates
further into the thickets of the phenomena of self-realization.
Again he is analysing the concept of self and its creative implications rather than setting out on his imaginative journeying.
Given the strength of his creative energies, as acknowledged in
Paracelsus, it is not surprising that *Sordello*, refusing them release
and insisting on further scrutiny, all but chokes its own utterance.
Admittedly he writes out of obsession with the twofold potential
of imagination, but he arrests its processes through the very
intensity of his desire to see what it does and how it does it. The
poem's turgidity should not be dismissed as a joke or an aberra-

tion; it is an extreme example of the self-conscious imagination turning on itself.

A recent article by R. R. Columbus and C. Kemper entitled 'Sordello and the Speaker: A Problem in Identity'[1] underlines the nature of the poem and offers a way into its difficulties by accepting them as essential to it. The poem is knotty with the effort of self-comprehension and the attempt to study its own intricate relationship with the creative impulse. Or it is like an elaborate arrangement of mirrors in which the poet regards himself simultaneously. The techniques of encounter poem and monologue are included within a more complex whole, for Browning deliberately arranges the frame of a speaker and an audience as the context for Sordello's story. He as poet surveys the mechanics of the device he is to employ so often, breaking down the role of self-revelatory speaker into two persons, the Speaker and Sordello; while the part of listener is formalized and emphasized as an audience, a group waiting to hear a story and to learn the nature of Sordello by way of the narrator. Browning himself is a member of the audience, for he contemplates what Columbus and Kemper call the 'complex and pliant'[2] interplay between the Speaker and Sordello, seeking to behold his own creativity as it conceives a person and yet simultaneously discovers itself by this activity.

To put the complexities another way, Sordello seeks to know himself, and so too does the Speaker; the latter's method of research is to tell Sordello's story and feel it coming alive because it is his own experience becoming manifest. The poet both enacts and watches this procedure. Thus Browning presents a construct of the Romantic imagination, without diminishing its complicated working. The critics' concept of sincerity is exposed as ludicrously inadequate when we recognize that only by such formidable machinery can a poet, remarkably aware of the needs of his imagination, portray its character and bring it home to himself. In the opening lines of the poem he shows the Speaker making his decision to remain in the poem, to be a creative presence not an invisible dramatist who leaves Sordello alone on the stage, and in this explicit decision Browning demonstrates the essential lack of autonomy which marks the

---

[1] *Victorian Poetry*, ii (1964), pp. 251–67.   [2] ibid., p. 259 (note).

dramatis personae of Romantic works. They exist as egotistical mirror-persons, or they are chameleon creations whose function is to carry their creator over his supposed boundaries and allow him to stake out the new ground which his protean energies have thus annexed. The Speaker cannot efface himself because he 'ostensibly dramatizes the development of Sordello's soul, but in fact he dramatizes his own . . . creative-intellectual predicaments. He dramatizes Sordello's losses of identity because he himself is seeking identity.'[1] So, even more, is the poet who perceives and creates both of them. In *Sordello* therefore, 'what Browning captures is the reflexive activity of consciousness concerned with itself',[2] using the structure of the poem to experience this demanding activity even as he exerts himself to produce it. The ambition of this is prodigious: Browning is unique among nineteenth-century poets in trying to scale the craggiest heights of imaginative, psychological and epistemological perception all together in a single poem. The opacity of the result is scarcely surprising; but while its wisdom may be doubted, the honour of the attempt remains.

Despite the overall darkness which so often threatens readers of *Sordello*, it is nevertheless possible to see that Browning recurs throughout to the two modes of imagination, and that their existence is to him the vital characteristic of the powerhouse of creation, the means by which the mind struggles on its way to reach its own identity. Sordello in his dilemmas and conflicts reveals the alternating tugs of egotistical and chameleon forces, while the Speaker in being cast as Sordello's interpreter himself participates in knowledge of such rhythms. The whole poem throbs with awareness of these energies, yet never unleashes them.

Sordello both as poet and man of action is acutely conscious of his own being in relation to other people—his audience, his supporters, his enemies. The chameleon experience is repeatedly described, in its genuine manifestations, its specious forms, and from the points of view of its dangers and its rewards. Some examples will illustrate this and also help to show how inescapably linked the rewards are with the ultimate goal of self-realization:

[1] ibid., p. 253.   [2] ibid., p. 263.

> ... I may find a thorough vent
> For all myself, acquire an instrument
> For acting what these people act; my soul
> Hunting a body out; obtain its whole
> Desire some day!
>
> (I, p. 227)

At his first attempts to be a poet,

> ... he took
> An action with its actors, quite forsook
> Himself to live in each, returned anon
> With the result—a creature, and by one
> And one proceeded leisurely equip
> Its limbs in harness of his workmanship.
>
> (II, p. 245)

There is an over-glib success in Sordello's constant display of a power which, though it develops his soul 'a thousand ways' becomes too much a versifier's knack and does not draw upon nor lead him to his deeper self. Man and poet do not harmonize, 'the complete Sordello, Man and Bard . . . was gone' (II, pp. 247–8). Only in egotistical self-communing does he 'expand to himself again' (II, p. 254), and in revulsion from being dyed in all the colours of the world, he perceives the ideal as it must be— not submergence, but a sense of immutable central identity, developed by protean exercise:

> To need become all natures yet retain
> The law of one's own nature . . .
>
> (III, p. 256)

The experience of incarnation in other forms is imperative, a necessary process for that nature's evolution:

> ... I must, ere I begin to Be,
> Include a world, in flesh, I comprehend
> In spirit now . . .
>
> (III, p. 260)

The egotistical centre is shown in its more dubious character in the context of the world of action. Sordello as leader

> ... only cared to know
> About men as a means for him to show

> Himself, and men were much or little worth
> According as they kept in or drew forth
> That self . . .
>
> (IV, p. 293)

But its real implications are again illustrated by an image in the next book:

> A healthy spirit like a healthy frame
> Craves aliment in plenty and, the same,
> Changes, assimilates its aliment . . .
>
> (V, p. 313)

This is a common thought in the poem—an immense appetite for experience, to be converted into self-experience:

> This life to feed my soul, direct, oblique
> But always feeding!
>
> (VI, p. 335)

At the beginning the two poles are set out as contrasts of temperament. There are those who reveal

> A need to blend with each external charm,
> Bury themselves, the whole heart wide and warm
> In something not themselves . . .

And their opposite,

> . . . a class that eagerly looks, too,
> On beauty, but, unlike the gentler crew,
> Proclaims each new revealment born a twin
> With a distinctest consciousness within
> Referring still the quality, now first
> Revealed, to their own Soul; its instinct nursed
> In silence, now remembered better, shown
> More thoroughly, but not the less their own.
>
> (I, p. 220)

In Sordello and his story, Browning strives to show the two 'classes' as the systole and diastole of the poetic temperament, both working to create and illuminate that sense of identity which alone can provide the grounding for trustworthy evaluation of experience. Columbus and Kemper emphasize that the goal is evaluation of this kind when they state: 'Sordello the

Existentialist intensely lives the story being told in the poem while the Speaker telling it tests the value and the meaning of the story both from Sordello's imagined point of view and from his own.'[1] And Browning, I would add, depicts this being done even as he himself carries out the whole 'existentialist' experiment. Such are the deep waters which *Sordello* attempts to navigate, and it shows how preoccupied Browning was in these years—he began working on *Sordello* in 1833—with the complex issues of the imagination.

8

In all the poems of intensive contemplation, chameleon power is held in check. It is only recognized, its nature analysed. However, the poems I have so far discussed are not the only works of Browning's early years, and in the pattern of his writing in the 1830s, a familiar Romantic phenomenon once again appears. In the midst of the extreme tension of his egotistical researches, he recoils to the other pole and begins to practise as a chameleon poet—a beginning which involves discoveries of both a positive and negative character, and contributes to his overall knowledge of his poetic situation. Most prominent, from the point of view of length at least, is the play *Strafford*, written for Macready in 1836, and representing an effort in strong contrast to the main preoccupation of the time, *Sordello*. As Browning's Preface shows, he turned to dramatic composition as a change and a refreshment from the taxing demands of the latter. Describing *Sordello* here as 'a poem of a very different nature' he expresses doubts on the success of his attempt to 'freshen a jaded mind by diverting it to the healthy natures of a grand epoch'. The main reason for his doubts seems to be that *Strafford* is a play 'of Action in Character rather than Character in Action'—a criticism which anticipates much that can be said on Browning as a dramatist, and which at once places him in the context of the Romantic drama with its stress on the realization of an inner world as the main incentive to the whole work.

The failure of *Strafford* would seem to be that Browning, although he perceives where his interest is really centred, seeks

[1] ibid., p. 254.

to preserve too faithfully the conventions of five-act historical drama, which are not able to cope with the less orthodox dramatic concept he has in mind. That is, the poet sees the fundamental link between his Strafford and his Sordello, Pauline and Paracelsus: what moves his imagination is the idea of the 'development of a soul', the processes of self-development and discovery. *Strafford* is a switch of angle, the projection of himself into another being in whom such activity is taking place, and to this extent is a genuine exercise of chameleon art. But at the same time, it is, in nineteenth-century terms, a crippled attempt because the machinery adopted, the successive presentation of historical scenes, forces other, more external considerations upon him, and the poet's concern with the central sensibility conflicts with them. Wordsworth and Coleridge in their plays freed their imaginative powers, relatively speaking, by their use of near-legendary stories and natural settings; while Byron's historical dramas succeeded at least in centring firmly on the personality of the hero, using symbolic effects to enrich and weight the action, so that the sense of costume drama and documentary purpose was helpfully undermined. Even so, as I concluded in Chapter II, the traditional was not really the most feasible form for the Romantic ends. In so far as they worked out new forms in *Manfred* and *Prometheus*, or adapted the Shakespearean model to their more inward purposes, they created living works; but limitations remained.

So with Browning's attempts at orthodox drama: *Strafford* shows that it is not the way for him, and the same conclusion follows from a reading of his other plays too. The speeches of the characters *are* speeches, with a formality of utterance into which the poet fails to breathe individual life; and in the manoeuvring of plot, the impact of person on person, Browning also fails to convince us that he deals with anything but declaiming puppets. *The Return of the Druses* with its peppering of 'asides', and *A Blot in the 'Scutcheon* where death solves all, illustrate the stilted nature of these works. They lack essentially any feeling that the characters have sprung from their creator: he pulls their strings from a distance, but he is not himself a part of their being. The monologue, on the other hand, gives him the chance to bring about such a union. There is no better illustration of what Romantic dramatic creation really involves than Browning's failure in his plays and his success in the much greater creative intimacy of the monologue.

It is relevant too that in the plays themselves, he moves away from the genre of historical tragedy, and in *Colombe's Birthday*, his last stage work, the theme is one of a search for identity—faintly echoing Coleridge's *Zapolya*—with Colombe discovering her real situation as Duchess and woman, external action and other characterization being subordinated to the processes of revelation. Once self-consciousness is in some way established, as a desire or an attribute, then the circuit between the poet and his creation is complete and, paradoxically enough, the character takes on his own reality, not because he is autonomous but because he is the focal point of a deep imaginative concern.

In the monologue situation, with speaker and listener, or speaker implying listener, the issue of self-awareness is central and offers the poet the chance to enact a role without sacrificing the full subjective realization of the identity as he explores it. Already in the 1830s, Browning is discovering that his way is the monologue, even as he wanders in the blind alleys of stage drama. As his egotistical poems reveal, his need to explore all forms of life, to savour 'all feelings equally' and try out the inclusive philosophy—'why must a single of the sides be right?'—amounts to a craving appetite: 'this life to feed my soul'. As J. Hillis Miller sees it, there is violence in his hunger, a 'violent instinct of self-aggrandizement which would know all things, and, knowing them, become them'.[1] Once more, the egotistical depths of the passion driving him to 'realize all forms of life',[2] are confirmed. *Pippa Passes*, however, speaks for the sheer creative zest of this desire, the holiday delight of leaving oneself to play out 'fancy's fullest games':

> For am I not, this day
> Whate'er I please? What shall I please today?
> Tomorrow I must be Pippa who winds silk,
> The whole year round, to earn just bread and milk:
> But, this one day, I have leave to go
> And play out my fancy's fullest games;
> I may fancy all day—and it shall be so—

[1] op. cit., p. 91.   [2] ibid., p. 95.

That I taste of the pleasures, am called by the names
Of the Happiest Four in Asolo!
                                        (Prologue)

Yet in the irony of Pippa's naïve ignorance of the real state of
the lives of those she deems happy and which he then displays,
Browning underlines the difference between the mere day-
dreaming of fancy and the arduous incarnation into the reality
of others' experience which is the poet's chameleon task. His
ability to perform it may be freedom, but in its omniscience it is
a far from frivolous entertainment, involving encounters with
all beings as they are to themselves, whatever their state of
madness, wisdom, or suffering, and whatever their fate or
predicament. Of all ways of finding self, the way of yielding to
other identities is the most daunting. In his commitment to it,
Browning acts with Keatsian gusto and resolution. But while
the two poets share equally the vision of chameleon power, the
Victorian goes further as a practitioner, fulfilling the ambition
of the earlier poet by extending 'the idea of sympathetic imagination from natural objects to other people',[1] although he is also
of course following the precedent set by the other Romantics
who had in their various ways already begun this extension.

Porphyria's Lover and *Johannes Agricola in Meditation* were the
earliest of his monologues, appearing in the *Monthly Repository*
for January 1836, and these two poems, together with other early
examples such as *Soliloquy in a Spanish Cloister* and *My Last
Duchess* are sufficient to show how firmly he grasped the opportunities of the form from the first. Like their successors, these
poems achieve what they attempt. Self-revealing, the speakers
are more exposed than they know, and their creator lives their
lives and perceives their nature, his perceptions sharpened by
the act of taking on this identity. Entering in so that he may
understand, the poet is not effaced, but on the contrary discovers his own resources in his full control of the other's
experience.[2]

[1] ibid., p. 106.
[2] In his essay introducing the supposed 'letters of Shelley' in 1851 (reprinted
Browning Society 1881), Browning describes the work of the 'subjective' poet as
'the very radiance and aroma of his personality' (p. 7). Although the essay opposes
the 'objective' poet to the 'subjective', the categories of egotistical and chameleon
are recognizable in it, for Browning envisages the ideal as the copresence of both

The monologues practise with tireless energy what is preached in the self-regarding researches of the three long poems. They exert the creative power which in *Sordello* is prized as the way to consummate the experience of self, and they strive to fulfil the ambition previously formulated in *Paracelsus*:

> . . . God is the PERFECT POET,
> Who in creation acts his own conceptions,
> Shall man refuse to be aught less than God?

Such is the context, then, in which Browning's most characteristic and most discussed poems can be profitably placed. It helps to show that admiring him merely as a dramatic poet, intrigued by human nature, or praising him as a ventriloquist are both inadequate ways of assessing what he does in the monologue. He is a poet seeking for as total a sense of life as possible, never content with one angle or one possibility but confident that truth is only to be apprehended when numerous other propositions or characteristics have been taken into account. Adventurous though he is in pursuing dramatic challenges, his creative centre remains egotistically fixed, not in the sense of a man using all his creations as mouthpieces but because it is the urge to self-discovery which drives him ceaselessly out of himself, making him a continual explorer of possibility, at a level deeper than that of the 'philosophizing' so frequently attributed to him. He speaks not out of what he knows, but in order to realize the experiencing self, and so to fashion a mode of evaluation empirically acceptable because it does not seek to abstract and codify, but to work from the coalescing of active response with living event. Where there is judgment, it emerges out of the matrix of a whole situation, with different viewpoints appreciated. Condemnation or approval arise out of comprehensive knowledge, and both are tempered by the central persons being so intimately realized that our vision of them is more like our way of knowing ourselves than an objective assessment. The evil of the Duke of Ferrara is also felt by the reader as the force of aristocratic pride in the passion of its convinced faith; with del Sarto we feel most the pain of failure

---

kinds of creativity within the same poet—'the perfect shield' with its 'gold and silver sides' (p. 8).

admitted; what Porphyria's lover, Agricola, or Caliban depict is received as their truth and becomes ours, before we go on to assess the extent of their delusion.

The Ring and the Book is the logical extension of the shorter monologues with their quest for the totality of an experience. In many of them sufficient is given to the reader for us to amalgamate the various versions of a situation: we see not just del Sarto's experience, but that of his wife and her 'cousin'; not only that of 'any wife' but 'any husband' too; we see James Lee's view; Gandolf's as well as that of the rival about to join him in St Praxed's church, and so on. Certainly, an overt judgment on persons and events is announced in *The Ring and the Book*, but the poem needs all its versions of the story in order to give meaning to that verdict. The court's and the Pope's pronouncements are nothing but pieces in the mosaic, completing the pattern perhaps, yet not in themselves making it. The effort towards understanding which the poem makes leaves the detached judgment for its last and least crucial act. Structurally, the poem puts off rather than advances to the legal conclusion, and its climax is not single but recurs in the arrival of each actor or spectator at his special sense of the story's significance. Browning shows here on a large scale, as he does countless times on a small, that his vitalizing inspiration is a grasp of relativity: first, in seeing that the truth of each set of circumstances depends on the individuals who live in and react to these circumstances, and, further, in recognizing that creative use of this insight must involve the poet with the poem, so that it incorporates the perceiving creator as an element in its make-up. The reacting consciousness is produced as it were, as the first actor, with the account of the poet's finding the Yellow Book. Such self-commentary, describing the creative work on the raw material looks back to the probings of the early long poems, but here Browning succeeds in presenting himself as he would handle any of his people, in focus, and known simultaneously from within and by contemplation.

9

Increasingly, if less subtly, self-presentation features in Browning's later work of the 1870s and 1880s. As yet this stage of his career is scarcely charted, and it is outside the scope of my discussion to study it comprehensively. But we may notice here that it yields a common characteristic, which suggests at least that he continues to pursue a coherent and imaginatively logical course. The late poems differ from their predecessors only in their structural technique; their central preoccupation with the activity of the creating self as it confronts its material looks straight back to the poet of *Sordello* and the 1830s, although the poet is now more relaxed and clearly enjoys presenting himself as narrator figure.

It is not a decline to a less disciplined art of telling stories after 1870. *Fifine at the Fair* (1872) is sufficient proof that his control can still be firm and that his chameleon power is unweakened. But in this poem a changing technique is apparent, in that the speaker makes use of the immediate scene and situation as a creative springboard for his attempt to read himself, and to illuminate, for her benefit, his relationship with his companion. A Don Juan figure, the speaker is fired by the urge fundamental to Browning—a 'hunger both to be and know the thing I am', striving to reach the 'inmost real' (CIII). Wandering through the Fair, he takes its opportunities for making the step from outer to inner reality, the scene of masquerades and side-shows expanding to thoughts on Venetian festivals, modulating by association into Schumann's musical carnival; and so the poem evolves, always transmuting the world of actuality into the vision of the inner being. The movements of the mind become known to itself as scene becomes thought. Browning pursues imaginative association here with a bold anticipation of modern methods, but the generating power of the poem is the hero's search for himself, and the unfolding of his self-expressive universe as the means towards this goal.

Browning's attitude to person, event and situation from the beginning is rooted in his desire to command them all as part of himself so that areas of his being otherwise inaccessible can take on a tangible reality. In the late poems on Balaustion, there is a simple acknowledgement of the important intimacy of the teller and the tale. Where *Fifine at the Fair* shows a speaker converting the scene in which he moves into a deeper sense of his own perceiving self, *Balaustion's Adventure* (1871) turns on the

Plutarchian situation of a girl retelling Euripides' *Alcestis* to save herself and her companions from slaughter by their Sicilian captors. She is the necessary medium through whom the play is presented; she offers her version of it, so that what exercises Browning is not *Alcestis*, but Balaustion's *Alcestis*. He reveals her by showing how the play has become hers. In such explorations of the creative role of narrator—tried out again to a lesser degree in *Aristophanes' Apology*—Browning finds a poetic structure extremely congenial to him.

When he repeats the idea in his own person during the later years, he combines it with an informal ease of manner which should not blind us to the serious purpose of the poems. A major example of the final development of his art is *Red Cotton Nightcap Country* (1873), where there is a landscape through which the speakers move and from which a narrative is built up. Again, the story is not enough in itself: it is wedded to the needs of the one who tells it, his desire to prove a case, to convince his companion that all is not what it seems, and more centrally, to Browning's desire to witness himself in the act of animating the story's raw material, infusing it with his own power so that it lives for him to behold. Beside this feat, merely to narrate a story, however gripping or macabre or exhilarating, is nothing. He is consistent in this belief throughout his career. That the nature of creativity is still to the forefront of his mind in 1873 is indicated by a passage in *Red Cotton Nightcap Country* where he strikingly depicts the essentially self-creative urge impelling the artist, with its result that the created work gives an illuminated vision of that subjective force:

> Yet is there not conceivably a face,
> A set of wax-like features, blank at first
> Which, as you bendingly grow warm above,
> Begins to take impressment from your breath?
> Which, as your will itself were plastic here
> Nor needed exercise of handicraft,
> From formless moulds itself to correspond
> With all you think and feel and are—in fine
> Grows a new revelation of yourself,
> Who know now for the first time what you want?
>
> (1)

The Two Poets of Croisic shows the same device, Browning surveying himself in the situation where he comes to the creative moment, in this instance one of resurrecting characters of the past. The occasion of such creativity is a part of the process, the late poems suggest, as they seek to watch and savour as well as perform the act.

In the later stages of his poetic life as in the earlier therefore, Browning stands out as one who takes to himself with immense vigour and delight his Romantic legacies. The energy with which he pursues his egotistical researches, responding to both poles of imagination readily and profoundly, speaks for a confident outlook more nearly kin to the early pioneer excitement than to the contemporary mood of Arnold and Tennyson —and Clough—in their more painful recognition of the self voyaging alone. But it would be misleading to leave this contrast unqualified: Browning is a poet of his time and he incorporates into his work a sense of the individual's isolation as well as the joys of a sovereign freedom conferred on the personal consciousness.

This point we can approach through the poet's religious sense, which is far less crude than most of the critical comment it has received. A valuable perception on the theme was at once made and missed by Rupert Brooke when he remarked in a letter to Violet Asquith: 'Did you ever notice how the Browning Family's poems *all* refer suddenly To God in the last line. It's laughable if you read through them in that way. . . It shows what the Victorians were.'[1] This piece of Edwardian flippancy does indeed offer a clue to 'what the Victorians were'. Notwithstanding its exaggeration, it points the way to a phenomenon of Browning's poetry which reveals his participation in the mid-century trends of imagination. Far from invoking the name of God as the comforting solvent of all distress and mystery, Browning can contrive to lift a poem to a climax of unanswered question and pregnant silence by means of an allusion to God. A simple example is the conclusion to *In a Year*:

> Dear, the pang is brief.
> Do thy part,

[1] December 1913; Christopher Hassall, *Rupert Brooke* (1964), p. 426.

Have thy pleasure. How perplext
Grows belief!
Well, this cold clay clod
    Was man's heart
Crumble it—and what comes next?
    Is it God?

It is the question which matters, that arrival of a human being
at the brink of speculation after the breakdown of all the
securities of experience; and such is the universe in which
Browning and his people live. They are creatures of Godot
rather than God, awaiting evidence, expecting revelation, yet
acknowledging that precisely this condition is their life and all
they have. Browning's *Caliban upon Setebos*—a central monologue
from this point of view—exemplifies the situation with peculiar
vividness, as it builds Caliban's universe wherein Setebos is a
power because the monster can only create in his image a god
which then determines his behaviour:

'Thinketh, such shows nor right nor wrong in Him,
Nor kind, nor cruel: He is strong and Lord,
'Am strong myself compared to yonder crabs
That march now from the mountain to the sea;
'Let twenty pass, and stone the twenty-first,
Loving not, hating not, just choosing so . . .
As it likes me each time, I do: so He . . .

'Conceiveth all things will continue thus,
And we shall have to live in fear of Him
So long as He lives, keeps His strength . . .

The poem remains one of self-discovery, and such is the God of
Browning's poetry: an absent, unknowable, perhaps non-
existent, idea which is at the same time a force, a scourge and
goad to compel the effort of self-recognition. It is the name in
which monster and human realize their solitude with themselves,
their impulses and resources, or lack of resources. We recognize
here the whole pressure of the enigmatic, silent universe experienced by the other poet-inheritors of the autonomous consciousness; they learn what they can from their own exertions,
piecing together their own morality and nature out of the
inescapable doom of self-reliance.

The irony of the conclusion to *Porphyria's Lover*—'all night long we have not stirred And yet God has not said a word!'— works on several levels. But saliently, the final introduction of God in his silence reverberates back through the poem to increase its eloquence, stressing further that we behold a world of entirely personal morality and self-dependent interpretation of events, a world in which the lover-murderer is happily enclosed. He has made it, he sustains it, it is unshakably valid for him. He is God in his own creation. That this poem is one of the 'Madhouse Cell' pair reminds us of the nightmares of *Maud*, the menace of each man in a sealed box of self with no communication and no way out from what can be a subjective hell, self-made, self-destroying. *Agricola* too, its companion poem, anticipates *Caliban upon Setebos* as it shows the speaker industriously working on his image of God, entirely caught within what is in essence a vision of himself. Less menacingly but still consistent with this use of the idea of God, Ben Ezra, Blougram, and Abt Vogler all fashion their own being, realizing themselves with an energy the greater because they invoke the silence beyond and gladly name it God.

Even in poems where God is not explicitly named, Browning's sense of climax is commonly a point of unfulfilled expectation or speculation, an arrival at the silence, where simply because the edge is consciously reached, no more is to be said. A poem is finished by this situation, not left broken off, for the speaker and reader are forced back more urgently on what has gone before, what can be known because the ego has experienced it and so found a reassuring mirror for itself, a kind of completion. In the poem *The Guardian Angel*, for example, the speaker, not knowing the whereabouts of his friend, relives their joint experience of a picture by Guercino and so makes contact with him. The poem ends

> My love is here. Where are you, dear old friend?
> How rolls the Wairoa at your world's far end?
> This is Ancona, yonder is the sea.

The impact of the final line rises out of the strong feeling of contrast, the vague unknown distance suggested by the sea, juxtaposed to the firm local point 'this is Ancona', wherein certain experiences are safely possessed and evaluated. The personal, self-created world against the unfathomable surrounding void: such a vision haunts the Victorian Romantic. But certainly in Browning's work, the self so isolated, clinging to its small island of consciousness and mastered experience, tends to seem an opportunity more often than an occasion for panic.

Summing up, we can say that the idea of relativity in all its aspects excites rather than intimidates him, driving him on to embrace as near to a totality of opinions, experiences and personal landscapes as possible. Different points of view do not bring dismay but a willing acclaim of the notions of subjective multiplicity and inclusiveness. Opposites too do not cancel each other out, but are welcomed as equally valid with no fear that anarchy and a collapse of values must inevitably follow. The chameleon appetite holds no threat for Browning; indulging it, he exhibits the richness and promise, not the gloom, of the Romantic world-picture. His optimism is not of a sort to be reproached for its shallow outlook. It is based squarely on acceptance of an empirical, even an existential attitude. Self-awareness is the only guide, the study of the 'single soul', the concentration on 'the single life' and its capacity, the only means towards wider evaluation or more general knowledge. He is content, like 'Artemis prologuizing' to 'await, in fitting silence, the event', and to rise by imaginative effort to his climax of anticipation, which is at the same time a result of revelation rather than a preparation for it, a silence of culmination more than promise.

As they wait on God or Setebos, gazing out to sea or into the past, alone with themselves, the people of the monologues stand at the moment of epiphany. In repeatedly bringing about this victory with an unflagging and joyous release of energy, Browning fulfils his ambitions of the 1830s. He is free to announce with all the assurance of a fully incarnate being: 'I truly am, at last' ('Reverie', *Asolando*).

VII

CONCLUSION:
MASKS AND ANTI-MASKS

Life's quick, this kind, this keen self-feeling . . .
Hopkins: *St Winefred's Well*

Ille.   By the help of an image
I call to my own opposite, summon all
That I have handled least, least looked upon.

Hic.   And I would find myself and not an image.

Ille.   That is our modern hope, and by its light
We have lit upon the gentle, sensitive mind
And lost the old nonchalance of the hand . . .
Yeats: *Ego Dominus Tuus*

To PURSUE the functioning of the two modes egotistical and chameleon in detail into the poetry of the twentieth century is not my aim. But the possibility of such a pursuit is nevertheless an important part of my argument.

The essential affinity between nineteenth-century and modern poetry is a common theme in current criticism, and in my discussion of the Romantic and Victorian cult of self-exploration and deep egocentricity I have tried to demonstrate the key place of the Victorian imagination in linking modern to Romantic. But we should not ignore the point that modern poetry declared its revolt against its predecessors. That gesture of independence cannot simply be dismissed as an illusion.

In his 1917 statement that poetry should be not the expression of personality, but an 'escape' from it,[1] Eliot joined T. E. Hulme in calling for new directions, for a poetry which was not emotionally indulgent but concentrated on depicting the 'exact curve' of the object in a style at once 'dry' and 'hard'.[2] These views are intended to be repudiations of nineteenth-century work. Hulme wrote from an idea of Romanticism which saw it

---

[1] 'Tradition and the Individual Talent', *Selected Essays* (1951), p. 21.
[2] 'Romanticism and Classicism', *Speculations* (paperback ed., 1960), pp. 126–32.

grounded in unhealthy feeling, while Eliot regarded self-display and the 'turning loose' of emotion as assumptions about the nature of poetry inherited from the previous century. Yet Hulme's plea for an intensive realization of what is perceived necessarily depends on the theory of individual perception and implies that poetic seeing is the fruit of a particularly vital—and personal—act of cognition, and his position therefore looks back to Coleridge and the Romantic universe where subject and object coalesce in mutual illumination. Similarly, Eliot's poetry makes it clear that he is concerned with the issue of personality, as distinct from the mere exhibition of it, in a way which coincides with and develops from Romantic and Victorian conceptions of the imagination, and not at all in recoil from them. It is now possible for us to appreciate the ironies of the early twentieth-century situation, wherein the leaders of poetic theory and practice derived much of their energy out of their conviction that they were rebels, while in fact they remained in profound contact with the two generations of poets they purported to despise.

Of course the impulse to make a new start was a symptom of exhaustion in prevailing modes: the Romanticism of Edwardian and late Victorian times was degenerate. Or rather, the real nature of Romanticism had become confused by the cult of sincerity to such a degree that the full vitality of the century's poetry was choked and had grown increasingly difficult to detect. Essentially, the movement of modern revolt was a rejection of the doctrine of sincerity and its implications as they had emerged in Victorian criticism and contemporary readers' assumptions. By overthrowing a dominant and popular view of poetic activity, the pioneers were, without knowing it, clearing the way backwards as well as forwards. They were making contact possible once more with the genuine springs of nineteenth-century poetry, and recharging the imagination as an evaluative force, involving self-exploration in depth. Creativity was being disentangled from the crippling bondage of being regarded as a species of naïve autobiography, primarily emotional and 'true to life' in the most superficial sense. It had not been the major poets of the nineteenth century who saw it in such an unsophisticated light; their work was not emotion turned loose, nor a parade of personality, and theirs are the efforts of self-comprehension which are renewed, however unwittingly, in the apparently hostile attitudes of post-Edwardian poets.

Unseated from its pre-eminence, however, is the term sincerity. To be used in modern criticism, it has to be carefully qualified or subjected to investigation. Thus Hulme wrote of sincerity 'in the accurate sense',[1] meaning the exactitude of the poet's vision of his subject, and I. A. Richards moved a discussion of the term and idea of sincerity towards Confucianism.[2] The standard can no longer exist autonomously and unquestioned, and its old prestige as the ultimate mark of poetic power is gone.[3]

2

The attraction of Hopkins for poets and readers of the post-1918 world is often attributed to the originality of his technical achievements, and his segregation from his age has been in consequence much stressed. Yet in his work, the continuity of modern and nineteenth-century preoccupations is really exhibited: he attracts because he is essentially of his time, and his vision is recognized for what it is by his twentieth-century reader, though it might well have been missed by his sincerity-blinded contemporaries.

His poetry feeds on the concept of self, and even more, of 'selving': that is, the process of consciously achieving identity. The fact that for him such a process is God-directed and God-initiated helps to demonstrate how distinct this kind of self-awareness is from any more superficial state of selfishness or merely sterile introspection. Although he is theologically unique among the poets of his century, Hopkins, in the nature of his creative drive and his goals, is representative not a maverick. He fuses a chameleon passion with an egotistical single-mindedness, seeking to realize all things inwardly and fully while discovering his own 'inscape' the more intensively, as his heart 'stirs' for

---

[1] ibid., p. 138.   [2] *Practical Criticism* (paperback ed., 1964), pp. 280-91.
[3] For an amplified discussion, see my article 'Sincerity: the Rise and Fall of a Critical Term', *Modern Languages Review*, lix (1964), pp. 1-11.

what he contemplates and becomes. The immediacy of self-experience is to him the central wonder in the human universe, the starting point from which all must begin. That he speaks of his 'selfbeing' in terms that recall Keats in their sensuousness is no coincidence:

. . . my selfbeing, my consciousness and feeling of myself, that taste of myself, of *I* and *me* above and in all things, which is more distinctive than the taste of ale or alum, more distinctive than the smell of walnut leaf or camphor, and is incommunicable by any means to another man (as when I was a child I used to ask myself: What must it be to be someone else?) Nothing else in nature comes near this unspeakable stress of pitch, distinctiveness, and selving, this self-being of my own . . . searching nature I taste *self* but at one tankard, that of my own being.[1]

The child's question is the question of the Romantic chameleon temperament, and Hopkins's context shows how rooted it is in the keen apprehension of the unique self. The effort to communicate the incommunicable 'self-taste', the pondering on other selves, both lead to further realization of the central identity which quickens all else and to which all must be referred back again: Hopkins and his fellow nineteenth-century poets share this stimulus to creativity.

The Wreck of the Deutschland illustrates the link, in its refusal to be content with an objective narrative account of the nuns' drowning. Following Keats in his thinking on *Hyperion*, Hopkins finds it imperative to be present in his poem as an experiencing consciousness. He erects a structure where his spiritual vision and psychological crises are related to the shipwreck and its consequences, as Keats confronts his inner condition in witnessing the suffering gods. The poem is reflexive, an egotistical mirror-work. Action is modified by the mind beholding it and the coalescing of the two is part of the poem's nature, not merely of the circumstances of its genesis.

For the Jesuit poet, all leads beyond itself, the sense of the individual being to him inseparable from the 'infinite I AM'. Coleridge's phrase is particularly suitable, for Hopkins shares with him the beliefs that such an ultimate concept only confirms

[1] 'Comments on the Spiritual Exercises', *Poems and Prose of Gerard Manley Hopkins*, Penguin edition, ed. W. H. Gardner, pp. 145–6.

the pivotal role of the self-conscious mind, and that the search
for the fullest possession of the latter is the route to the Godhead,
offering the sole experience of this which is humanly attainable.
Hopkins has a clearer formula of given values than his fellow-
poets, yet he too relies on the processes of imaginative self-
experience as the means of vitalizing them and so making them
wholly valid and potent. Systems of theology and philosophy
react upon the hypersensitive membrane, 'that inmost self of
mine',[1] with its response that transforms all notions and actions
to self-knowledge: 'what I do is me'.[2] The enlightening extension of such subjective recognition is the touchstone for Hopkins as for his Romantic predecessors, his contemporaries, and
those later poets whom he joins as a companion familiar for
reasons which underlie and influence his 'modern' use of words.

Although, like Browning, Hopkins displays the vigour of his
Romantic inheritance rather than its burdens, he is in some
ways recognizably the fellow of Tennyson, Arnold and Clough—
his kinship with the latter extending to their common fate of
enjoying a twentieth-century instead of a contemporary esteem.
The self-taste could turn sour for Hopkins as for other Victorians
and he too has his black poetry:

> I am gall, I am heartburn. God's most deep decree
> Bitter would have me taste: my taste was me;
> Bones built in me, flesh filled, blood brimmed the curse.
> Selfyeast of spirit a dull dough sours. I see
> The lost are like this, and their scourge to be
> As I am mine, their sweating selves; but worse.
>   ('I wake and feel the fell of dark . . .')

Hopkins in the Terrible Sonnets articulates a specialized fear,
self divorced from God. But the dread of such isolation is alien
neither to the torment of Maud's lover enclosed in his own
consciousness nor to the loneliness of islands in Arnold's sea.
Therefore he is a poet of his time, despite all that marks him off.
Behind him lies the same imaginative hinterland as that affecting all Victorian poets, and if he brings Romantic energies to
work on Victorian despairs, he pursues the empirical path being
beaten out by those around him.

[1] ibid., p. 148.   [2] 'As kingfishers catch fire . . .': ibid., p. 51.

These characteristics of Hopkins move his modern audience. Recent generations of readers have recognized not just his verbal freshness, but his passionate fidelity to the perceiving self and the 'exact curve' of his experience, with the intensity of his chameleon powers serving the quest—one of duty, as he saw it— for deeper self-realization. Identity was the concept that quickened him and his poetry strives to incarnate the idea. In acknowledging the stature of Hopkins's imagination, we in this century have acknowledged our own needs; we have also accepted the authentic Romantic tradition as a relevant and animate poetic force, however loud the voices crying its obituary.

3

Clear evidence for the Romantic survival can be found in the persistence of the two modes of creativity in our poetry. Imagination still responds to the two poles, setting up new patterns and tensions and finding its individuality in obeying the same constant law. We see this saliently in Eliot and Yeats, for each is egotist and chameleon, yet the unique poetic personality of each needs no arguing.

Eliot's Prufrock, the other monologue voices, and the whole technique of *The Waste Land* exhibit the modern chameleon poet struggling to turn to creative account his sense of fragmentation and lost identity. He speaks with many voices as a way to discover his own, a chameleon aim since Coleridge dramatized this desire with a prince searching urgently for his name. But in Prufrock's world, the only certainty is that he is not the Prince, 'nor meant to be'. The Victorian panic at the silence all round stands behind *The Waste Land*; each voice in the poem knows, sharply or vaguely, the self-same fear. The work is a grim exercise of the protean spirit, but it shows the imagination able by this means to get to grips with its situation and to master it to the extent of giving it form. In desperate circumstances which may paralyse the egotistical energies, the chameleon power offers at least a way to clarify vision. As Eliot moves away from his early nightmares, so he is increasingly drawn to the egotistical mode. The *Four Quartets* balance *The Waste Land* in this respect, recalling the polar relationships in the

long poems of Wordsworth, Byron and Tennyson. Such a complementary pattern helps to stress that the early and the late
Eliot are neither separate nor conflicting poets: there is a
positive tension between the stages of his career, as well as the
same preoccupations working themselves out. And in his particular movement from chameleon to egotistical, the process is
shown to be one from search to possession, from identity doubted
to self realized. That Eliot came increasingly to comprehend
the egotistical roots of creation is illustrated rather than refuted
by what may be termed his self-conscious concern with drama
in the post-war years, especially if we see this in conjunction
with the Romantic theory expressed in 'The Three Voices of
Poetry', that the business of character creation exposes and
exercises latent areas of the creator's own nature.[1] In the *Four
Quartets* with their egotistical poise, something of the Wordsworthian sublimity returns, but a sublimity tempered by fire and
modulated to a tone of more muted celebration. Any valid
twentieth-century conviction of a personal sovereignty, an
ordered universe, is only won from fearful acquaintance with the
'hollow behind the wood' and the waste lands of Ishmaelite
experience.

In Yeats's imagination, however, there is no purgative way
from a tormented chameleon utterance to a more serene egotistical cadence. His response to the two poles is to feel the violent
attraction of both simultaneously, and his poems reveal forcefully the self-exploratory motive which generates the power at
each pole equally. Yeats is, *in excelsis*, the egotistical chameleon:
he sophisticates the chameleon role to a conscious manipulation
of masks for his own face, not as disguises but as a means to
profound egotistical display. He pursues his identity by playing
out its potentialities, in all their contradictions, to the full. In
some ways his poems of Red Hanrahan and Michael Robartes
present the consummation of the Romantic chameleon enterprise. The goal was never otherwise than the apotheosis of the
ego, but in Yeats the apparatus designed to bring this about
reaches a high point of stylization, and the art attains the
formality of a rite. Yeats is a cardinal of the polar imagination, yet
he responds in its service with the ardour of its first neophytes.

[1] *On Poetry and Poets* (1957), p. 94.

227

Dominantly and arrogantly egotistical in some of his poems, commanding his universe with a clarion voice, he is well aware of the terrors of the self-conscious state and the ironies it brings, not least in the illusion that to play a part is to escape from such a consciousness. To call on his 'own opposite', to conjure up the anti-self is still to remain enclosed with the self, pressing on into unknown territories but not crossing frontiers. This result at once enrages and enthrals him, and his poems leap as flames out of the clash of passions. The irrevocability of the Romantic commitment to the agency of self-consciousness is acclaimed even while it is cursed in Yeats's work, and no more eloquent testimony to the great funds of creative energy the vision engenders could be given than his sustained and vital display of the protean ego in its unrestrained prowess.

4

The continued vigour of the polar energies is apparent in the ebb and flow of poetic movements, as well as in the individual imagination. It will provide a suitably inconclusive end to my study if I briefly survey the current situation with this point in mind.

There is no absolute conflict between those who advocate a quite unmasked 'confessional' poetry, and those who write in variants of the monologue form, or exploit the media of other creatures, minds, or points of view. The one is egotistical poetry, carried to a new outpost and drawing, in particular, on psychiatric experience, but still recognizable as the centripetal force imposing its will, inscribing itself upon the phenomena it attracts and incorporates into its world. In this mode as it now seems to be evolving, the sense of the fragmented self seeks new methods of expression: egotistical work is bold and creatively enterprising, not merely goaded by the terrors of its situation. Similarly, chameleon poetry is searching out more sophisticated and more subtle lines of advance. There are poems for example where a double consciousness is at work, the act of empathy being exhibited as such and the poet's own awareness coalescing with it to make the poem. Ted Hughes in *Hawk Roosting* realizes the bird in claw and feather yet imbues it with a consciousness of its nature not its own; the poem balances on the double apprehension. A twofold awareness activates Thom Gunn's 'ton-up' poems, a point which is more central to their importance than the fashionable elements. Gunn is and is not the black-jacketed boy; he shows his entry into that nature, and at the same time speaks from the perception which is born of the chameleon performance. Such a complex self-awareness in poetry includes Yeats's elaboration, but looks straight back to the Romantic experiments with encounter poems, where the sense of an experience reverberating back upon the poet as listener as well as speaker extended the poetic range of illuminated self-consciousness.

In the orthodox sphere there is much vigorous exploration afoot therefore, while in the fields of concrete poetry and computer experiment, relevant and associated researches are taking place. Here, the whole concept of subjectivity is being challenged. The creative ego, the experiencing mind, the relationship of object, emotion, the senses, and the reacting consciousness— all are under scrutiny, with no conventional assumptions left undisturbed. Yet here too, continuity and a logical furtherance in imaginative research are discernible. The inner world has been the poets' province in a ceaseless effort of trekking and charting since the Romantic initiative. That its nature should be subjected to an even more rigorous testing, perhaps involving much to shock and alarm, is no surprise. It is only the next step: having embarked on the process of self-understanding and the pursuit of identity, the imagination cannot abandon the study halfway. Poets must reach and probe to the very grounds of consciousness, and so they persist in honesty of response to the two poles. And the poles continue to exert their compulsions, whether recognizably so as the egotistical and chameleon forces familiar to us from over a century of poetic life, or whether in new versions, offering further hopes of enrichment to the self-researching imagination.

INDEX

Recipients of letters, names of editors and
similar minor references are not included.